Bristol Radical Pa

100 Fishpon

Life and Death in a Victorian Workhouse

Roger Ball, Di Parkin & Steve Mills

ISBN 978-1-911522-53-9

Bristol Radical History Group
3rd Edition 2020
1st Edition 2015
www.brh.org.uk ~ brh@brh.org.uk

Contents

List of Abbreviations

BAFHS	Bristol and Avon Family History Society
BBOS	Bristol Boarding-Out Society
BCRL	Bristol Central Reference Library
BES	Bristol Emigration Society
BRHG	Bristol Radical History Group
BRO	Bristol Record Office
BBC	British Broadcasting Corporation
BMJ	British Medical Journal
COS	Charity Organisation Society
EWMG	Eastville Workhouse Memorial Group
GA	Gloucestershire Archives
JP	Justice of the Peace
LBH	Local Board of Health
LGB	Local Government Board
MOH	Medical Officer of Health
NEL	National Emigration League
NHS	National Health Service
OLT	Outdoor Labour Test
PLAA	Poor Law Amendment Act 1834 (New Poor Law)
PLB	Poor Law Board
PLC	Poor Law Commission
TNA	The National Archive
UWE	University of the West of England
WMO	Workhouse Medical Officer

Picture Credits

Figures 1, 10, 11, 13, 20, 25, 29 33, 36, 37, 41, 49 Roger Ball
Figure 2 British Museum
Figures 3, 22, 24, 30 P. Higginbotham workhouses.org
Figures 4, 12, 14-16 Peter Box
Figure 5 Bristol Central Reference Library
Figure 7 Bristol Central Reference Library Ref. Bristol Pictorial Survey #737
Figures 8, 18 Stephen Dowle
Figure 9 BRO Ref. 42562/Ph/1/24/2
Figure 17 BRO Ref. 40945/1
Figure 19 Richard Grove
Figures 21, 28 Bristol Central Reference Library Loxton Collection
Figure 23 BRO Ref. Building plan/Volume 48/43a (1904-5)
Figure 26 http://epsomandewellhistoryexplorer.org.uk/Mittendorff2.html
Figure 31 Bristol Central Reference Library
Figure 32 BRO Ref. 40945/1
Figure 34 BRO Ref. EP/A/22/CU/3a-b
Figure 35 John Clevely
Figure 38 BRO Ref. 30105/3/3
Figure 39 Helen Wheeler
Figure 40 Pauline Hendy
Figures 42-49 EWMG
Figure 51 BRO Ref. 30105/3/1

Preface to the Third Edition

A third edition in five years of 100 Fishponds Road is a sign that the research and memorialisation of Eastville Workhouse and the pauper burial ground at Rosemary Green has remained a 'live' project.

In Chapter 5, the history of the crude disinterment of thousands of pauper graves at Rosemary Green and their reburial in unmarked common graves in Avonview Cemetery in 1972 is concluded.

A third edition has also provided the opportunity to catch up with the ongoing activities of Eastville Workhouse Memorial Group in marking the location of the workhouse and memorialising the common graves at Avonview Cemetery.

Thanks go to all those who funded, organised or participated in these successful activities.

EWMG, February 2020

Preface to the Second Edition

This second edition of *100 Fishponds Rd* came about for several reasons. A few weeks after Bristol Radical History Group (BRHG) went to press with the original version in November 2015 we discovered three important new sources of information regarding Eastville Workhouse. The first was a series of half-year books, effectively guides to the working of the institution, covering the 1870s-90s which had been re-catalogued by diligent staff at the Bristol Record Office (BRO). Secondly, searches of the Gloucestershire Archives (GA) demonstrated that there were forty or so bundles of inquest documents relating to deaths in Eastville Workhouse. Finally, a chance find pointed towards a mountain of correspondence between the Clifton/Barton Regis Poor Law Union and the Poor Law authorities in London which was held by The National Archive (TNA) at Kew. These primary sources have allowed us to significantly revise and expand this text, particularly the sections dealing with tramps, children, the mentally ill, epidemics and causes of death.

In the first edition we made one significant historical error regarding the absence of a medical officer at Eastville Workhouse (thanks to those who pointed it out!). The new sources we have discovered have allowed us to enhance the section examining provision of medical care and to analyse how doctors were treated by the Clifton/Barton Regis Board of Guardians; in itself an important part of the history of Eastville Workhouse. The TNA material, although bureaucratic and voluminous, contained some 'diamonds' in the form of letters from paupers to the Poor Law and Local Government Boards. These rare sources give us glimpses into the conditions of the Bristol poor both inside and outside Eastville Workhouse through their own eyes; a significant addition to the 'history from below' aspect of this book. Lastly, we have added an epilogue which brings up to date the story of the memorialisation of the pauper burial ground at Rosemary Green.

The extra writing that this entailed took the best part of four months and would not have been possible without the hard graft of the researchers; Maureen Ball, Di Parkin and Roger Ball at The National Archive, Trish Mensah, Di Parkin, Roger Ball, Alan Brown and Steve Mills at the Gloucester Archives and Roger Ball at the Bristol Record Office. Thanks also go to the proof readers, especially Kate Din whose help was invaluable in the final stages, and Richard Grove for designing the second edition.

This edition is dedicated to all those in Bristol Radical History and the Eastville Workhouse Memorial Groups who helped make some history.

Roger Ball, Di Parkin, Steve Mills (May 2016)

Introduction

The forgotten burials at Rosemary Green

So the baby was carried in a small deal box, under an ancient woman's shawl, to the churchyard that night, and buried by lantern-light, at the cost of a shilling and a pint of beer to the sexton, in that shabby corner of God's allotment where He lets the nettles grow, and where all unbaptized infants, notorious drunkards, suicides, and others of the conjecturally damned are laid. In spite of the untoward surroundings, however, Tess bravely made a little cross of two laths and a piece of string, and having bound it with flowers, she stuck it up at the head of the grave one evening when she could enter the churchyard without being seen, putting at the foot also a bunch of the same flowers in a little jar of water to keep them alive. What matter was it that on the outside of the jar the eye of mere observation noted the words "Keelwell's Marmalade"? The eye of maternal affection did not see them in its vision of higher things.[1]

Figure 1: Rosemary Green, the site of the Eastville Workhouse pauper burial ground in East Bristol.

1 Hardy, T. *Tess of the d'Urbervilles: A Pure Woman* (Bath: Folio Society, 1993) p. 101.

The origins of this book lie in the discovery of an anonymous burial ground next to a housing estate on Fishponds Road in Bristol. The Eastville Workhouse research project was launched in 2012, after some members of Bristol Radical History Group (BRHG) were studying a 1902 ordnance survey map of Ashley Down and Eastville.[2] They noticed that the burial ground for the Clifton/ Barton Regis Poor Law Union Workhouse at 100 Fishponds Rd, Eastville, made up part of present-day Rosemary Green, just round the corner from where they lived. After two years of research, BRHG members had gathered details of over 4,000 men, women and children from the workhouse who had been buried in unmarked graves at the site. There was no sign or marker on the spot of Rosemary Green's past use as the burial ground for the workhouse; today it is a place for dog walkers and kids playing football, making up part of the East Park housing estate.

A number of articles and letters by BRHG were published in the local and national press about the Eastville Workhouse project in the summer of 2014,[3] partly as a result of the Galway babies' scandal in June of that year,[4] which demonstrated that unmarked graveyards of 'forgotten' paupers including many babies were commonplace in the U.K. In August, Eastville Workhouse Memorial Group (EWMG) was founded after a successful public meeting with local residents. The aim of the group is to raise funds for a permanent memorial to those who lived and died in Eastville Workhouse and had been buried in nearby Rosemary Green.

Since the launch of EWMG, a number of people studying their family history have discovered from BRHG data that their ancestors lay in these unmarked graves. One of these family historians, Wendy Bull, was the subject of a BBC TV programme in January 2015,[5] which focussed on the sisters of her great grandfather who had died at a young age in Eastville

2 *Old Ordnance Survey Maps: Bristol* (Ashley Down and Eastville) 1902 Gloucestershire Sheet 72.09 (Durham, Alan Godfrey Maps).
3 See for example 'Unmarked Graves: Campaigners call for a memorial at site of baby burials' *Bristol Post* June 13-16 2014 p. 4 and 'Time to remember those buried in unmarked graves' *Bristol Post* August 26 2014 p. 7.
4 A mass unmarked grave of 800 children was discovered in a septic tank in 1975 in Tuam, County Galway, Ireland. It was claimed at the time it was a grave from the Irish 'potato famine' of 1845-1852 and was resealed. In 2012 a local historian demonstrated that the babies had died in the care of the Bon Secours nuns, a Roman Catholic organization which ran a home (effectively a workhouse) for unwed mothers (so called 'fallen women') with extraordinarily high infant mortality rates. The babies had been secretly buried from 1925-1961. An Independent Commission of investigation was set up by the Irish Government in February 2015. See https:// en.wikipedia.org/wiki/Bon_Secours_Mother_and_Baby_Home.
5 Walmsley, J. *Rosemary Green – Eastville Workhouse* BBC Inside Out West 19 January 2015 http://www.bbc.co.uk/programmes/b04ynq6r

Workhouse and were buried in Rosemary Green.[6] Members of EWMG and BRHG worked hard to prepare the burial data on the thousands of workhouse inmates to go online on the night of the broadcast. It paid off, as there were over three thousand hits over three days on the BRHG website, as members of the public downloaded the data to undertake family history research. In addition, BRHG and EWMG received numerous e-mails and messages of support and encouragement on social media for the memorial project.

However, it should be noted that the primary motive for the numerous researchers who have been involved in this project was not to appear in TV programmes, to study the history or even to write books like this. Instead, somewhat obsessively, we wanted a record in the public domain of all the men, women and children who had been buried in Rosemary Green and memorials so that they could never be forgotten again. Both of these objectives were achieved in 2015-16 with profits from this book going towards the Eastville Workhouse Memorial Project. We also hope that this book and the research it contains will go some way to highlighting the estimated one million graves of workhouse inmates that lie unmarked and largely forgotten in the U.K.[7]

Then and now

At least 1,084,684 people in the U.K. received three days food supplies from food banks in 2014/15.[8] Today, in the 21st century, the government, with its 'quantitative easing' acting in the interests of the 'haves', seems determined to pauperise the 'have nots', with cuts in welfare benefits and measures such as the 'bedroom tax'. The apparently endless austerity, principally aimed at the less well-off, comes after bailing out the bankers to the tune of £500 billion in 2008. While the rich grow richer, people in abject poverty are treated with disrespect and Tory MPs cannot understand why there is a need for food banks.

6 Albert James Wookey, Wendy's great grandfather and Alice Wookey her great great aunt, were survivors of a group of children born in Eastville Workhouse to Sarah Wookey. Three of the family were buried in Rosemary Green; Alice Wookey (d. 19-03-1879) aged 1 year, Florence Wookey (d. 24-12-1881) aged 8 years and Alice Wookey (d. 18-05-1882) aged 1 year. BRO Form T 30105/3/3 (1878-88).
7 Estimate for the post-1834 period from Peter Higginbotham, expert on workhouses in the U.K. (January 2015).
8 Source: Trussell Foodbank Statistics http://www.trusselltrust.org/stats.

In writing this book, Bristol Radical History Group wanted to take a look at the kind of society in the 19th century current and recent neo-liberal[9] governments appear to want to replicate; not from the high point of the welfare state in the 1960s-70s, but from today's increasingly harsh treatment of the unemployed, low-paid, infirm and vulnerable. We wanted to understand a period where the treatment of 'paupers' was based on similar ideological ruthlessness, where they were blamed for their own poverty and disrespected in life and in death. In the early 1980s, the birthplace of neo-liberalism, politicians such as Thatcher and her disciples often referred to a 'return to Victorian values' as if this was a progressive change; this book aims to understand what those values really meant for the urban poor of the 19th century.

This book is primarily a study of Eastville Workhouse in the Victorian period; commencing with the opening of the institution in 1847 and ending with the cessation of burials at Rosemary Green at end of the 19th century. Chapter 1 presents a contextual pre-history of 'pauper' relief up to the establishment of the modern workhouse as part of the 1834 Poor Law Amendment Act followed by an examination of the internal and external resistance to the New Poor Law and the reaction of its crusading advocates. Chapter 2 examines the nature of the new Poor Law Unions in Bristol with a particular emphasis on the Clifton Union and its new workhouse in Eastville. This is followed by a study of the management, economics and demographics of the inmates of the institution. Chapters 3 and 4 investigate everyday life and death in Eastville Workhouse respectively. This is achieved by marrying statistical and social history together to gain an informed view of life chances for the urban poor forced into workhouses in Bristol.

However, rather than just reporting on what conditions were like, intermittently in the text we also turn our focus onto understanding why workhouses were the way they were, how they changed and the unintended consequences of their creation. This approach ranges from examination of the ideological basis of the 1834 Poor Law via the financial pressures exerted by

9 Neo-liberalism is a particular form of capitalism, encouraging the so-called 'free-market', de-regulation of the financial sector, privatisation, reduction or elimination of welfare safety-nets and limiting the power of Trade Unions to protect workers' wages and conditions. In the workplace the emphasis is on freedom for the employer with flexible contracts (e.g. zero hours) leading to precarious and dangerous working environments, lower wages and the loss of benefits such as holidays and sick pay. Neo-liberal economic theorists argue that although this clearly produces more wealth in the hands of the class of business owners (the bourgeoisie), it then 'trickles down' to the rest of us. Unfortunately, as more than 30 years of neo-liberalism has shown and the economist Thomas Piketty has recently demonstrated with comprehensive statistical analysis, we now live in the most wealth divided societies since the 18th century and possibly in the history of 'human civilisation'. Piketty, T. *Capital in the Twenty-First Century* (London: Harvard University Press, 2014).

rate-payers on the workhouse system to the impact of pseudo-scientific ideas amongst the well-to-do in the late Victorian period. Despite the limitations in evidence in following the approach of 'history from below',[10] throughout this text there are glimpses of dissent and resistance to the workhouse system generated by various motivations. Outside the workhouse walls, these range from the self-seeking rate-payers of Clifton trying to protect their wealth and the reputation of their district through to whistle-blowers in the radical press and widespread anti-poor law protests and riots of the 1830s-40s. Inside the institution, resistance is marked by everyday refusals and sporadic revolts by inmates as well as fleeting, though nevertheless tantalising, evidence of more covert methods for surviving the workhouse system.

Finally and aptly in Chapter 5, we end our journey where the project began, with a history of the Eastville Workhouse burial ground at Rosemary Green and a study of the thousands of hitherto forgotten men, women and children who were interred beneath its now pleasant landscape.

A note on names and places

The institution at 100 Fishponds Rd had several different names over its 125 year history. Between its opening in 1847 and 14th March 1877 it was known as the Clifton Union Workhouse. After this date and into the 20th century it was known as the Barton Regis Union Workhouse. In 1948, when it became a dedicated home for the aged as part of the new welfare state, it was renamed '100 Fishponds Rd' in an attempt to release it from the stigma of the workhouse. To avoid confusion concerning its location the institution is generally referred to as Eastville Workhouse in this book, unless a particular document is being referenced with the name Clifton Union, Barton Regis Union or 100 Fishponds Rd. Until the 21st century the Eastville Workhouse burial ground was part of an unnamed piece of land attached to the East Park housing estate.[11] Local history group, Living Easton, named the whole site Rosemary Green in 2004[12] and this is how it is referred to throughout this text.

10 For an outline of the practice and the problems in following the 'history from below' approach see the introduction to Backwith, D., Ball R., Richardson M. and Hunt S. E. *Strikers, Hobblers, Conchies & Reds: A Radical History of Bristol, 1880-1939* (London: Breviary Stuff Publications, 2014).

11 On the original title deed it is referred to as part of a field known as the 'Upper Great Ground'. BRO Ref. St PHosp/183.

12 Two community festivals organised by Living Easton, Volunteering Bristol, Awaz Athoa and local residents were held on Rosemary Green in 2004/5. They included a fete, history walks, tree planting and the installation of carved totems on the site. The naming of the 'green' was part of the events. E-mail from J. McNeill to BRHG, 25 August 2015.

A note on Victorian terms

In this book we refer to the 'poor', 'paupers' and 'inmates' of workhouses, all of which were in general use in the Victorian period. These designations have problematic connotations, particularly in the way they are used to define an 'other'. At the time of writing four million children in Britain are considered to be in poverty. However, how many of us would openly define ourselves as being part of a 'poor' family? Similar issues relate to the terms 'imbecile', 'idiot' and 'lunatic' which were also in common usage. In the text we have explained their various meanings in the Victorian period and how they are understood today. Despite issues with all of these labels we have retained them as they appear liberally in the quoted primary sources. However, this does not mean that the authors support their usage today or their Victorian meanings.

A note on relative worth

In this text you will often see reference to sums of money whether prices, incomes or costs. Calculating their worth in today's terms is not straight forward. However the following rules should help for the period 1850-1900. In terms of purely retail prices multiply by 100, so something that cost £1 in the Victorian period would be priced about £100 today. In order to work out how much something was worth compared to the wage of an average worker multiply by 500. So paying £1 in Victorian times would feel like paying £500 today (that is, reader, unless you are very rich!).

A note on footnotes

This book is full of footnotes (nearly five hundred at the last count!). They are in the text for two reasons. First they allow readers and future historians to find the sources we have used to generate this bit of history so they can follow our path and improve or criticise our analysis (or both). Second, the footnotes contain information, explanations and sources which we think are useful and interesting background material. However, as they might distract the more impatient reader from the flow of the narrative, feel free to ignore them if you want a racier read.

1. The Poor Laws and workhouses

From the Black Death to poor relief

The present position which… the educated and well-to-do classes, occupy, is that of the Old Man of the Sea, riding on the poor man's back; only, unlike the Old Man of the Sea, we are very sorry for the poor man, very sorry; and we will do almost anything for the poor man's relief. We will not only supply him with food sufficient to keep him on his legs, but we will teach and instruct him and point out to him the beauties of the landscape; we will discourse sweet music to him and give him abundance of good advice. Yes, we will do almost anything for the poor man, anything but get off his back.[13]

Apparently, the poor 'have always been with us' and 'what to do with them' has always been a subject of cyclical debate. In feudal Britain,[14] Christian charities advocated support and help for the destitute, even if it was paternalistic and patronising. However, it would be wrong to romanticise life before capitalism; under feudalism there was still of course exploitation of the many by the landed few, poverty, enclosure, displacement and sometimes brutal campaigns against migrant paupers led by the monarchy. With the development of capitalism attitudes to the rural poor further hardened as rigid patterns of work-life discipline linked to the factory slowly overtook the rhythms of seasonal agricultural production.[15]

The critical economic theorist Karl Marx noticed that the poor served a useful function for the rich in the new capitalist economy in that they created a reserve pool of labour.[16] Consequently those in employment would always be looking over their shoulder at the misery of those who were destitute, homeless or starving. Therefore workers would accept, to a point, low wages and poor conditions in the belief that there were many desperate people ready to replace them in their given employment. This generated greater profits for the proprietors of mills, factories and mines. Harsh attitudes to the poor reinforced this relationship to the benefit of this new class of property-owners,

13 Quote attributed to Leo Tolstoy, Sinclair, U. (ed.) *The Cry for Justice: An Anthology of the Literature of Social Protest* (1915).
14 Arguably this existed from 700AD to its demise in the 1600s.
15 The seminal essay on these changes is Thompson, E. P. 'Time, work-discipline and industrial capitalism' *Past and Present* No. 38(1), 56–97 (1967). You can download it here https://libcom. org/files/timeworkandindustrialcapitalism.pdf.
16 Marx, K. *Capital Volume 1* (London: Penguin, 1990) pp. 781-94. This will give the reader an introduction to his theory.

the bourgeoisie. After the Poor Law Amendment Act of 1834, if you could not support yourself or your family, then off to the workhouse with the lot of you! But we are jumping ahead here, the laws dealing with the poor under capitalism developed through the demise of feudalism in England over several centuries.

The 'Black Death' pandemics that struck Britain in 1348-49 and 1361-62 caused misery and massive depopulation.[17] But they also had another effect; empowering the peasantry, as the shortage of labour generated higher wages which were in turn resisted by the feudal landlords. This led to the peasants' revolt of 1381 which was the beginning of the end of bonded labour in Britain. This struggle, between the aristocratic landowners and the peasants, continued until the end of 'serfdom' in the 17th century and was characterised by numerous repressive legal measures. These laws were aimed at limiting movement and tying the labouring poor to the land and thus to a landlord. Peasants would owe labour, goods and even their families to the landowner. In turn the feudal landlord would 'protect' those who worked on his land and they would often be granted a patch of land, with a small dwelling. However, after the depopulation following plague outbreaks, many peasants broke the 'feudal contract' and began to move and seek better deals for them and their kin.

In the latter part of the 15th century repressive legal measures were put in place to deal with poverty which focused on punishing the individual for acts such as vagabonding and begging. Whilst this was not directly targeting the poor, it was an attempt to stop people wandering from parish to parish. In 1495 Parliament passed the Vagabond Act. This act stated that officials arrest and hold:

> all such vagabonds, idle and suspect persons living suspiciously and then so taken to set in stocks, there to remain three nights and to have none other sustenance but bread and water; and after the said three days and three nights, to be had out and set at large and to be commanded to avoid the town.[18]

It is not particularly clear what is meant by vagabonds,[19] but we can see from the language used, that the law was concentrating on people not fully employed and without 'masters'. This category would also include minstrels, jobbers and

---

17 Half of the English population may have died as a result of these outbreaks. https://en.wikipedia.org/wiki/Black_Death_in_England.

18 http://www.kingsnorton.info/time/poor_law_workhouse_timeline.htm.

19 The dictionary definitions are a homeless wanderer or a beggar for food or money.

other travellers. During Henry VIII's reign (1509-47) there was a brutal step change in the repression with tens of thousands of executions of 'vagabonds and thieves' carried out.[20]

Parliament passed a new act in 1552. This focused on using parishioners as a source of funds to combat the increasing epidemic of poverty. This statute appointed two individuals from each parish to collect alms[21] to distribute to poor individuals inhabiting the town. These individuals were to 'gently ask' for donations for the poor. Refusal to donate to the cause would ultimately result in a meeting with the bishop who would 'induce and persuade' them. This was the start of a process to get the wealthy to pay locally to help the poor in their parish. Needless to say, this did not go down well with the Christian rich and people did not always donate as they were supposed to.

A more structured system of donations was established by an act in 1572. After determining the funds required to provide for the poor, Justices of the Peace were granted authority to determine the amount of the donation from each of the more wealthy parishioners. The act effectively turned these donations "into an imposed tax".[22] Alongside these measures for poor relief the act also:

> created a new set of punishments to inflict upon the population of vagabonds. These included being "bored through the ear" for a first offense and hanging for "persistent beggars".[23]

These brutal penalties were commonly and widely applied, with the definition of beggar and vagabond extended in order to punish: "all able bodied men 'without land or master' who would neither accept employment nor explain the source of their livelihood".[24] However, rather than the wholesale slaughter during the reign of Henry VIII, the emphasis was now turning towards forced labour as a 'solution' to the problem of vagabondage.

20 Figures of up to an incredible 72,000 executions during his reign are quoted, though apparently Henry VIII was not considered to be a particularly 'bloodthirsty' monarch!
21 Alms were given to the poor by charitable institutions, normally the church. Usually it involved giving food or clothes on specific saint's days, and was therefore erratic and not suitable for long term relief for the growing numbers of poor people and those unable to work. There were also Almshouses where charitable institutions and churches provided full board and lodgings to lucky individuals. Fowler, S. *Workhouse* (London: The National Archives, 2008) pp. 173-4. Also see Gardiner, J. and Wenborn, N. (Eds.), *The History Today Companion to British History* (London: TSP, 1995) pp. 19 and 608-9.
22 http://www.thepotteries.org/dates/poor.htm.
23 https://en.wikipedia.org/wiki/Poor_relief.
24 https://en.wikipedia.org/wiki/Poor_relief.

The first workhouses

I have heard the rogues and beggars curse the magistrate unto their faces for providing such a law to whip and brand them and not provide houses of labour for them; for surely many would go voluntarily to workhouses to work, if such houses were provided for them.[25]

In 1576 a new Act was passed with the aim of "setting the poor on work and for avoidance of idleness". According to this:

Justices of the Peace were authorized to provide any town which needed it with a stock of... materials on which paupers could be employed and to erect a house of correction in every county for the punishment of those who refused work.[26]

This was the first time Parliament had attempted to provide labour to individuals and built 'workhouses' directly for this purpose. It should also be noted that they were to operate in tandem with 'houses of correction', which were charged with disciplining the poor to eradicate their 'wayward behaviours'. A visual picture comes to mind of a John Cleese type character, berating the inmates with, "Oi, you lot, stop being poor!"

Two years later, more dramatic changes were made to the 'carrot and stick' approach for providing relief to the poor and suppressing vagabonding. An Act of 1578 transferred power from the Justices of the Peace to church officials in order to collect the new 'imposed taxes' that were established in the Act of 1572. In addition, this further Act of 1578 also extended the power of the church by stating that "... vagrants were to be summarily whipped and returned to their place of settlement by parish constables".[27]

The Elizabethan Poor Law of 1601 made each parish responsible for supporting the 'legitimately needy' in their community. Wealthier citizens of the parish were taxed to provide basic shelter, food and clothing for the poor, though they were not obliged to provide for those outside of their community. This became the generalised basis for 'poor relief' until the 1834 Poor Law Act.

In 1662 the Act of Settlement was implemented. This effectively created a 'pass' system, similar to that of the apartheid era in South Africa, whereby paupers were physically tied to their home parishes and were restricted in their

25 Stanleye (1646) quoted in Longmate, N. *The Workhouse* (London: Pimlico, 2003) p. 15.
26 http://en.wikipedia.org/wiki/Poor_Law#cite_note-Slack-5.
27 https://en.wikipedia.org/wiki/Poor_relief.

movements. The Act allowed the poor who resided in different parishes to that legally designated to be forcibly removed, generating a negative reaction from much of the population. The Poor Law Act of 1697 further formalised this 'pass' system by 'badging the poor'; that is, those receiving poor relief were required to wear, in red or blue cloth on their right shoulder, the letter P (for pauper) preceded by the initial letter of their parish.

Thus, by the end of the 17th century, a web of laws categorising, marking and controlling the poor were in place, which had developed over several hundred years. The system was made up of the following:

- The *impotent poor* (people who can't work) were to be cared for in Almshouses or Poorhouses. The law offered relief to people who were unable to work: mainly those who were 'lame, impotent, old, blind'.
- The *able-bodied* poor were to be set to work in a House of Industry with materials provided for this activity.
- The *idle poor* and *vagrants* were to be sent to a House of Correction or even prison.
- *Pauper children* would become apprentices.[28]

In the early 1700s some of the most repressive legislation in British history was introduced which asserted absolute property rights against the customary rights and practices of the mass of the population. This was the result of an alliance in 1688 (the so-called 'Glorious Revolution') between a weakened monarchy and a cabal of powerful landowners supported by emerging international merchants and traders. The new rulers began to flex their political muscle by enacting legislation such as the Riot Act (1715), the Transportation Act (1719), the Combination Act (1721) and the Black Act (1723). The number of property-related capital offences, that is crimes for which you could be executed, soared in this period whilst forced labour in the colonies became a central part of the punitive system. These Acts were aimed at restricting access to land and resources whilst suppressing popular protest and organisation amongst workers. Those who fell foul of this web of laws were subject to public hanging or, more commonly, transportation to work as forced labourers in the expanding colonial possessions of the rulers. Amongst this succession of draconian laws was the Workhouse Test Act (1723) which stipulated that in order to obtain poor relief a person had to enter a workhouse and undertake labour. As a result of its introduction between 1723 and 1750, six hundred parish workhouses were built in England and Wales.[29]

28 https://en.wikipedia.org/wiki/Poor_relief.
29 https://en.wikipedia.org/wiki/Workhouse_Test_Act.

From peasants to proletarians

These labourers, who must sell themselves piece-meal, are a commodity, like every other article of commerce, and are consequently exposed to all the vicissitudes of competition, to all the fluctuations of the market.[30]

Over the Tudor period (1485-1603), after the English Civil War (1640s) and into Georgian England (1714-1830) there were successive waves of enclosure, that is, the conversion of small landholdings and common land used by a large rural population into the private property of a much smaller class of landowners. The result of the process was the conversion of peasants into proletarians, that is, from people who had access to a means of subsistence (the land) to those with nothing to sell but their labour. Essentially, this forced much of the rural population of Britain from field to factory.

Rather than solving the problems of the rural and urban 'poor', the emerging capitalist system exacerbated them; as proletarians are vulnerable both to rises in prices of foodstuffs and unemployment. In addition, not all proletarians are able to sell their labour; the very young,[31] the old, the sick and infirm and those (usually women) bringing up children. There was little or no provision within the emerging economic system of capitalism for these groups. In fact, most of the new owning class (the bourgeoisie) believed the system functioned better for them if there was *no provision*, as they thought it would keep the new proletariat on the back foot fearing unemployment, destitution and starvation. This way, wages would be kept down and profits high. The mantra was: "best to do what you are told, work 12 hours a day, 6 days a week and keep your head down"; whilst of course making profit for the new bourgeois masters.

However, there was a problem with this plan. Despite the significant pressures on the new proletarians, collective resistance was widespread in the 18th and early 19th centuries, with food[32] and anti-enclosure 'riots', strikes, sabotage, incendiarism, machine-breaking and the formation of early Trade Unions (combinations) and eventually political organisations. This instability

30 Marx, K. and Engels, F. *The Manifesto of the Communist Party* (1848).
31 Of course the bourgeoisie weren't choosy about the age of workers; child labour was the norm in the period.
32 Proletarians attempted to control the export of food and its price through 'riots' and protests, often led by women. The seminal work on this is Thompson, E.P. 'The Moral Economy of the English Crowd in the 18th Century' *Past and Present* No. 50, 1971. You can download it here: https://libcom.org/files/MORAL%20ECONOMY%20OF%20THE%20ENGLISH%20 CROWD.pdf.

within the new capitalist system was racked up by the beacon of the French Revolution in 1789 and a series of 'free-market' famines during the period of the French Revolutionary Wars (1792-1802) which followed.[33] This led to some responses by the state to the problem of the increasingly large numbers of (angry) proletarians going hungry.

In 1795 the Speenhamland system was introduced. This policy was named after the place of a meeting of Magistrates in Berkshire during a time of distress for the poor due to inflated bread prices, their staple diet. Their plan was to tie Poor Law payments to the price of bread. Whilst the sentiments were paternalistic and well meaning, the system had a serious flaw; not least, landowners would employ people on poverty wages knowing that the Poor Law overseers would make up the difference, so that the labourers were fed. Other rate payers became resentful as they correctly felt that they were paying to subsidise the landowners' labour costs. In contrast to these worries, the precarious condition of the labourers was far more desperate; a common saying in rural England was:

[the farmers] keep us here [on the poor-rates] like potatoes in a pit, and only take us out for use when they can no longer do without us.[34]

The 1834 Poor Laws, Malthus and the 'modern' workhouse system

It is a prison, with a milder name,
Which few inhabit without dread or shame[35]

The increasing numbers of poor proletarians and thus rising costs of poor relief allied with the problems of the Speenhamland system led to a Royal Commission study of the conditions of paupers in 1832. The urgency for measures to deal with the 'problem' of the poor was heightened by the massive agricultural disturbances which swept through more than twenty counties in southern England in 1830-31. The 'Swing Riots', as they became known, had been driven by the desperate poverty of rural labourers due to underemployment brought on by increasing mechanisation of agriculture. Without land and access to common land for food and fuel, tens of thousands of hungry rural proletarians had reacted in a wave of machine breaking, incendiarism and riot, which had shaken landowners, clergy

33 Wells, R. *Wretched Faces: Famine in Wartime England 1793-1801* (London: Breviary Stuff Publications, 2011).
34 Thompson, E. P. *The Making of the English Working Class* (Harmondsworth: Penguin Books, 1986) p. 247.
35 Crabbe, quoted in Thompson, E. P. *The Making of the English Working Class* p. 43.

and the government.[36]. A significant element of the unrest were 'poor law riots' which included massed attacks on workhouses.[37] The Swing rising marked the beginning of a period of serious political unrest in Britain, with mass struggles for enfranchisement associated with violent uprisings in Methyr Tydfil, Bristol, Nottingham and Derby in 1831 and eventually the passing of the Great Reform Act in 1832. As the unrest began to subside, Longmate noted that for the landowner and bourgeoisie:

> Was this not the moment… with the Napoleonic wars safely over and the danger of revolution averted, to call a halt to the pampering of the poor, before further demands were made at the point of a pitchfork and the blazing torch?[38]

The Royal Commission's report was published in 1833-34[39] and despite its supposed empirical base it was more a product of pre-determined bourgeois ideology than a work of scientific enquiry. Central to its findings was a blistering critique of the existing system of 'poor relief', eloquently summarised by Kotouza:

> 'Old' Poor Laws were held responsible… for a demoralisation in the labouring classes that not only disturbed labour market equilibrium but also caused social unrest. The old Poor Laws were a check to industry, a reward for improvident marriages, a stimulant to population, and a blind to its effects on wages; a national institution for discountenancing the industrious and honest, and for protecting the idle, the improvident and the vicious; the destroyer of the bonds of family life; a system for preventing the accumulation of capital, for destroying that which exists, and for reducing the rate-payer to pauperism; and a premium for illegitimate children in the provision of aliment.[40]

36 The repression of the 'Swing Riots' was severe 'with nearly 2000 trials, of which 252 people were sentenced to death (19 were actually executed), 644 imprisoned and nearly 500 transported to Australia for terms of 7 to 14 years with little hope of ever returning. This was the largest group of prisoners ever transported from England for a common crime.' Ball, R. *Tolpuddle and Swing: The Flea and the Elephant* Bristol Radical Pamphleteer #12 (Bristol: BRHG 2012).
37 Recent research suggests there were nineteen 'poor law riots' during the 'Swing' unrest. Holland, M. 'The Captain Swing Project' in Holland, M (Ed.) *Swing Unmasked: the agricultural riots of 1830 to 1832 and their wider implications* (Milton Keynes: FACHRS Publications, 2005) p. 5 Table 1.1. Attacks on workhouses in Hampshire are noted by Higginbotham at *The Workhouse* http://www.workhouses.org.uk/glossary accessed 2016.
38 Longmate, N. *The Workhouse* p. 287.
39 Senior, N. W. and Chadwick, E. *Poor Law Commissioners' Report of 1834* (London: H.M. Stationery Office, 1905).
40 Kotouza, D. 'Lies and Mendacity' *Mute* Vol 2, No. 3 (2006) http://www.metamute.org/editorial/articles/lies-and-mendicity.

The key problems for the Royal Commission were how to keep the rising costs of poor relief down, whilst simultaneously increasing the control over the poor and their disciplining. The result of the enquiry led to a revision of the Elizabethan Poor Law (1601). The new piece of legislation, the Poor Law Amendment Act (PLAA) of 1834 (or New Poor Law), was a brutal piece of social and economic engineering which was to blight the lives of millions of proletarians for over a century.

The principal aim of the new PLAA was to reduce outdoor relief whilst simultaneously pushing the paupers towards indoor relief. The difference between the two was that outdoor relief (or out-relief) was a monetary or food contribution to the disadvantaged (the 'dole'), whereas indoor relief meant the individual was forced into one of the workhouses where they laboured for their food and a roof over their heads. The former was unacceptable to the new capitalist state as it was perceived to be more expensive and gave too much 'freedom' to the poor. For the ideologues of the 'free-market' who had fervently criticised the Speenhamland system, it "was calculated to lower wages, upset the working of the labour market, and demoralize those who received it".[41] However, indoor relief apparently solved the problem of cost and control, as the workhouse could recoup some of its budget through exploiting the free labour of the paupers (a 'House of Industry') and simultaneously act as an institution for disciplining the poor (a 'House of Correction'). The fusion of these two functions effectively created the Victorian workhouse system.

The new forms of poor relief enshrined in the PLAA were to be funded by a property tax levied on the residents of each parish within the Poor Law Unions. This immediately created local political pressures upon Guardians of the new Unions to reduce the costs of relief and this was combined with directives from the governing Poor Law Commission (PLC) in London to refuse outdoor relief to the able-bodied. As Hurren explains:

> Instead they had to use a workhouse test. This involved a relieving officer assessing each poor law claimant's financial circumstances on behalf of guardians. Goods had to be sold or pawned to make ends meet. Only after all material resources had been liquidated would a pauper be authorised to enter the workhouse.[42]

41 Rose, M. 'The Allowance System under the New Poor' Law *Economic History Review*. New Series, Vol. 19 No. 3 (1966) p. 607.
42 Hurren, E. T. *Protesting About Pauperism: Poverty, Politics and Poor Relief in Late Victorian England 1870-1900* (Suffolk: Royal Historical Society, 2015) p. 17.

The ideologues of the PLAA thought that the lack of access to outdoor relief allied with the new disciplinary regime of the workhouses would drive able-bodied claimants away from the relief system altogether, creating in the process new forms of 'self-reliance'. They also believed that in rural areas the new system would encourage farmers to raise wages, now that the Speenhamland system had been abolished.

However, there were more sinister pseudo-scientific forces driving the content of the PLAA, than purely economic arguments. In 1798 Thomas Malthus published *An Essay on the Principle of Population* which claimed that poverty was merely down to the supposed greater rate of population growth compared to food production. Consequently, for Malthus:

> Any assistance to the poor such… he saw as self-defeating, temporarily removing the pressure of want from the poor while leaving them free to increase their families, thus leading to greater number of people in want.[43]

This was a very attractive theory for the bourgeoisie as it helped explain poverty as something generated by the reproduction of the poor, rather than from the economic system from which they principally benefited. As Arnold notes, following through this argument led many of the powerful to conclude:

> the future health of society was being threatened by the survival of its weakest members, who were kept alive by charity and thus permitted to reproduce. Such arguments influenced the policy to discourage outdoor relief under the 1834 Poor Law Amendment Act, and contributed to the ongoing reluctance of authorities to provide adequate housing for the poor.[44]

In addition to the changes in the forms of relief, the PLAA enforced new measures relating to the family and children based on these Malthusian concepts of poverty. So, "in order to ensure the proper regulation of workhouses", there was to be strict separation of men and women, husband and wife, boy and girl. This policy was primarily focussed on preventing paupers from breeding. In addition, relief for single mothers was to be severely curtailed as it was seen as promoting "bastardy; to make want of chastity on the woman's part the

43 https://en.wikipedia.org/wiki/Poor_Law_Amendment_Act_1834#Malthusianism.
44 Arnold, N. Disease, *Class and Social Change: Tuberculosis in Folkestone and Sandgate, 1880-1930* (Cambridge: Cambridge Scholars Publishing, 2012) p. 23.

shortest road to obtaining either a husband or a competent maintenance; and to encourage extortion and perjury".[45]

These draconian changes to the already miserable relief provided by the Elizabethan Poor Law have to be understood within the context of the rampant capitalism of the period. This was neither feudal charity nor modern welfare, but a system based on pseudo-scientific principles aimed at controlling the reproduction of the poor and simultaneously creating workhouse regimes that were worse than the desperate conditions they already suffered. As E.P. Thompson noted:

> The impractical policy of systematic starvation was displaced by the policy of psychological deterrence: "labour, discipline and restraint". "Our intention," said one Assistant Commissioner, "is to make the workhouses as like prisons as possible"; and another, "our object… is to establish therein a discipline so severe and repulsive as to make them a terror to the poor and prevent them from entering". Dr Kay recorded with satisfaction his successes in Norfolk; the reduction in diet proved less effective than "minute and regular observance of routine", religious exercises, silence during meals, "prompt obedience", total separation of the sexes, separation of families (even where of the same sex), labour and total confinement.[46]

This Malthusian inspired theory anticipated that paupers would be in terror of the workhouse, driven off relief (thereby reducing costs) and into a life of "industry, frugality and prudence". E.P. Thompson passionately stated:

> The Act of 1834… was perhaps the most sustained attempt to impose an ideological dogma, in defiance of the evidence of human need, in English History.

Despite the planned deterrence of the workhouses, Thompson noted that between 1838 and 1843 the numbers of workhouse inmates nearly tripled, demonstrating "the most eloquent testimony to the depths of poverty" poor proletarians were enduring in the period.[47]

---

45 https://en.wikipedia.org/wiki/Poor_Law_Amendment_Act_1834.
46 Thompson, E.P. *The Making of the English Working Class* p. 295-6.
47 Ibid p. 296.

Popular resistance to the new 'Bastilles'

If open protest against the New Poor Law was suppressed, its covert alternative achieved some circumvention of the strict letter of the Law by Poor Law Union Boards, and this success was partially responsible of the endemic nature of incendiarism in the South East for much of the remainder of the nineteenth century.[48]

Politicians and economists in the period of the New Poor Law (and some modern historians) often cited the fact that entering the workhouse (or 'Bastilles' as they became commonly known) was voluntary and some even likened it to early welfare or charity. However, the reality was very different, with infirmity, disability, pregnancy and child birth, illness, destitution and starvation forcing vulnerable proletarians and their dependants into a life of hard labour to gain a roof over their head and some food in their bellies. Thus the workhouses became a type of punishment for the poor, with needy families split up, husband from wife and parents from children. Over three hundred and fifty new workhouses were constructed in the five years after introduction of the PLAA in 1834.[49] Needless to say, both the old and new institutions were feared and deeply unpopular with the urban and rural poor and were often targeted in protests and 'riots' from within and without.

In 1835, after the introduction of the PLAA, there were mass meetings, violent protests and attacks on workhouses in a number of counties in Southern England including serious incidents of disorder in Kent, Bedfordshire, Buckinghamshire and East Anglia plus an attempt to murder the Master of the Abingdon institution near Oxford.[50] Where local repression was fierce instances of covert protest were common including the arson of workhouse premises or the holdings of Guardians. In Midhurst in Sussex four fires destroyed properties of newly elected Guardians including the chairman of the Poor Law Union. The 'architect' of the Seven Oaks Poor Law Union in Kent, Lord Templemore, experienced two huge fires on his land on the same nights in 1835 and 1836 with damage amounting to a massive £2,600.[51] Arson campaigns against those

48 Lord Templemore to Lord Russell, 31st August 1836 PRO, HO64/6, quoted in Reed, M. and Wells, R. *Class, Conflict and Protest in the English Countryside 1700-1880* (London: Frank Cass, 1990) p. 170.
49 Longmate, N. *The Workhouse* p. 287.
50 Higginbotham, P. *The Workhouse Cookbook* (Stroud: The History Press, 2008) p. 49, https://en.wikipedia.org/wiki/Opposition_to_the_English_Poor_Laws#Resistance_to_the_New_Poor_Law_structures and Higginbotham, P. *The Poor Laws* http://www.workhouses.org.uk/poorlaws/newpoorlaw.shtml accessed 2015.
51 Rule, J. and Wells, R. *Crime Protest and Popular Politics in Southern England 1740-1850* (London: Hambledon Press, 1997) p. 107.

who supported and instigated the PLAA in rural areas were, according to many accounts, greeted by "ill-concealed pleasure...open delight...[and] a shout of exultation" by crowds of rural workers and their families who witnessed the fires. As historians Rule and Wells point out, fear and loathing of the New Poor Law and its 'Bastilles' amongst the impoverished rural proletariat had consequences:

> Terror worked both ways; protest in both its riotous and trade unionist forms left the propertied in no doubt of the depth of proletarian hostility. Once incendiarism established itself as the most durable form of resistance it exposed all concerned in Poor Law administration to potentially huge losses.[52]

In the north of England and Wales resistance to the PLAA was more overt, popular and widespread. Local Anti-Poor Law Associations sprang up and were able to mobilise large numbers of people for protests. In Wales, particularly in the central and north-western regions, resistance to the construction of workhouses was strong; by 1847 more than ten years after the PLAA, seventeen out of forty-seven unions had failed to open workhouses. Massed attacks took place on the workhouses at Llanfyllin and Narberth which were only halted by the direct intervention of the army and special constables. In Northern England, particularly the weaving districts of North-East Lancashire and West Yorkshire, in towns such as Ashton, Oldham, Rochdale, Huddersfield, Todmorden and Bradford 'riotous' crowds broke up meetings of the Poor Law Guardians and assaulted workhouses with the full support of much of the local population.[53] The aim was to halt the introduction of the PLAA and the new workhouse system; in some areas the movement was able to delay the process for several years.

By the late 1830s widespread and raucous popular opposition to the New Poor Law of 1834, which the authorities clearly feared, had translated into the radical programme of the Chartist movement. Their hatred of the PLAA and the workhouse system is summed up by this address to the London Democratic Association in 1838:

> That infamous, that vile, that atrocious ordinance (for it is no law in fact, nor should be obeyed as such), the accursed New Poor-Law Act - sprung from that parent of ten thousand crimes, the new philosophy of modern times.

52 Ibid. p. 120.
53 Thompson, E.P. *The Making of the English Working Class* p. 335, Longmate, N. *The Workhouse* pp. 77-81, Higginbotham, P. *The Workhouse Cookbook* p. 49-50, Higginbotham, P. *The Poor Laws* http://www.workhouses.org.uk/poorlaws/newpoorlaw.shtml and https://en.wikipedia.org/wiki/Opposition_to_the_English_Poor_Laws#Resistance_to_the_New_Poor_Law_structures.

A philosophy that reigns in all its hideous supremacy throughout our manufacturing and commercial systems, deforming and slaying labour's sons and daughters: seeking to seduce our young men and maidens from the land of their sires - that they may toil in the swamps of Canada, or perish in the wilds of Australia. A pretended philosophy that crushes, through the bitter privations it inflicts upon us, the energies of our manhood, making our hearths desolate, our homes wretched, inflicting upon our hearts' companions one eternal round of sorrow and sickening despair; nor is this all, when that we shall have arrived at a premature old age, our only reward for all our cares and toils is to be a horrible Bastile; where, separated from all that is near and dear to us, we may pine out the remaining period of our existence, exposed to all the brutality which demons could conceive, or worse than demons execute ; and then the pauper's funeral—consigned to the earth like dogs, or delivered over to the dissecting knife of the surgeon for the benefit of the rich! Thus does this hypocritical, Malthusian philosophy, outrage the decrees of Heaven, trample upon the best feelings of humanity, and violate all the principles of justice and morality - thus do our scoundrel tyrants pursue us from the cradle to the grave, inflicting upon us all the bitterness of poverty, and thus punish us for being poor![54]

By the early 1840s deployment of troops to put down protests against workhouses and the PLAA was fairly common, though the authorities were aware of the possible consequences. The Poor Law Commissioners stated in 1841:

The depressed condition of the manufacturing population, to which we have already adverted, and the disquietude of the public mind occasioned by the chartist riot at Newport, in Monmouthshire[55], rendered us extremely unwilling to take any step in the manufacturing districts of Lancashire which might have even a remote tendency to produce a disturbance, or which might be used by designing persons as a pretext for agitation.[56]

54 Address to the London Democratic Association 13 October 1828, quoted in Baxter, G. R. Wythen (George Robert Wythen), 1815-1854. *The book of the Bastiles; or, The history of the working of the new poor law* (London: J. Stephens 1841).
55 This refers to the armed insurrection by Chartists in Newport in 1839. See https://en.wikipedia.org/wiki/Newport_Rising
56 https://en.wikipedia.org/wiki/Opposition_to_the_English_Poor_Laws.

Figure 2: Satirical cartoon showing the horrors of the new workhouses by C. J. Grant (1833-36).

Despite the caution of the authorities, further massed attacks on workhouses occurred in Stockport during the Chartist inspired General Strike of 1842 and the following year several thousand 'Rebecca rioters' set about destroying a similar institution in Carmarthen.[57] In each case it was only the respective intervention of the Cheshire Yeomanry and Dragoon cavalry units that prevented wholesale destruction.

Internal resistance and the 1870s 'crusade'

The Fleming Circular of December 1871 stated that "neither locality, trade, seasons, weather, population" trends or a 10 per cent retail price growth during the 1860s had been the cause of higher levels of out-relief funding. Recalcitrant boards of guardians in London and the provinces were held responsible for the spiralling cost of relief.[58]

Faced with popular resistance to the new relief system some Boards of Guardians, particularly in areas of significant unrest, were loath to implement the PLAA to the letter. Instead they sought loopholes in the law in order to continue outdoor relief payments particularly to deal with fluctuations in the economy and seasonal unemployment or merely the lack of workhouse capacity. These included exploiting loose definitions in the PLAA of 'able-bodied', employing 'special circumstance' clauses which allowed payments such as medical out-relief orders and, to varying degree, they just ignored the new directives from London. It can thus be argued that, despite the wishes of the architects of the PLAA, there was some continuity between the Old and New Poor Laws in many areas of Britain at least for the first few years after the implementation.

In response to this internal resistance to the PLAA amongst some Guardians, the Poor Law Commission and its successor the Poor Law Board, introduced a series of measures to shore up the system. The first, in 1842, was the Outdoor Labour Test (OLT) which allowed Guardians to give the seasonally unemployed

---

57 The 1842 General Strike is more commonly known as the Plug Plot Riots, a reference to pulling the plug on steam boilers to bring mills to a halt. However, as with many instances of strike and protest movements in British history, these important events were reduced to 'riots' by contemporary commentators in order to belittle their political and historical significance. https://en.wikipedia.org/wiki/1842_General_Strike. The Rebecca 'riots' were a series of violent protests by tenant farmers and rural labourers against their increasing poverty caused by poor harvests, high rents, taxes and tithes and by the ravages of the free market in agricultural commodities. Toll houses and workhouses were targeted as representations of the system they despised. https://en.wikipedia.org/wiki/Rebecca_Riots.
58 Hurren, E. T. *Protesting About Pauperism* p. 23.

Figure 3: Stockport Workhouse under attack, 1842.

day-labour in the workhouse in return for a small amount of dole. Many Poor Law Unions were in the middle of building new workhouses in this period and used this extremely cheap source of labour to save on construction costs. It was somewhat ironic that in many areas of the country the poor built their own 'Bastilles'. The OLT had been generally applied to men, so in response, the Poor Law Commissioners issued another directive in 1844, the Outdoor Relief Prohibitory Order which:

> stipulated that out-relief regulations were to be tightened in rural areas. Its primary objective was to ensure that all able-bodied applicants and their dependents had to enter the workhouse or support themselves independently.[59]

However, once again, some Poor Law Unions circumvented this instruction, which led to a further clarification in 1852; the Outdoor Relief Regulation Order. This attempted to solve the problems of out-relief in relation to the sick, aged and widows. It was met by significant protests from Boards of Guardians who resented that their discretionary powers were being restricted and was re-drafted later that year.

59 Ibid. p. 19.

All this bureaucratic blundering about was a reflection of several problems with the PLAA. The ideologues behind the policy had not taken into account the actual 'human' effect of what they proposed; whether exacerbating the misery of the already desperately poor, the consequent widespread public unrest and, faced with this, the resistance of some Guardians to its implementation. In addition, the PLAA in its original form did not clearly discriminate between the various categories of poor people, such as the seasonally unemployed or under-employed able-bodied, the sick, those with children or the elderly; leaving both confusion and loopholes that could be exploited by recalcitrant Guardians. However, these issues did not lead to the repeal of the New Poor Law; in fact quite the opposite.

Prior to 1865, each individual parish was responsible for paying for the relief of its poorer inhabitants. This had led to wealthy rate-payers undertaking a series of devious schemes to avoid paying tax including encouraging paupers from their parishes to migrate. It also put an unfair burden on small householders in districts where there were concentrations of severe poverty. As a result, the Union Chargeability Act was introduced which determined taxation on the basis of a fixed rateable value according to the size of a property and thus effectively:

revised rateable assessments by making property rather than poverty... the basis of parish contributions to the common expenses of the union.[60]

The new law not only increased the pool of money in the Poor Law Union funds but also made all parishes responsible for every pauper in the Union. This in turn encouraged wealthier parishes to scrutinise Union relief expenditure in detail as they resented having to pay their now larger share of the bill. It was in this agreeable climate that a *crusade* against outdoor relief was launched from central government.

In 1871 there was a concerted attempt to revive the tenets of the New Poor Law led by "a powerful lobby of senior politicians, civil servants, leading economists and influential philanthropists".[61] Their aim was to reduce local government expenditure, primarily welfare spending, with the main target of the 'cuts' being outdoor relief. This plan was to be introduced and controlled by the Poor Law authorities in London, which had just been reorganised into the more powerful Local Government Board (LGB). The LGB was actively supported in its crusade by the Charity Organisation Society (COS),

60 Ibid. p. 22.
61 Ibid. p. 1.

a private body formed by wealthy anti-welfare activists in 1869.[62] COS members believed outdoor relief destroyed the self-reliance of the poor and "exacerbated pauperism by encouraging the work-shy, idle and profligate". The COS helped promote the idea of the 'deserving and undeserving' poor, marrying 'laissez-faire' economic theory with Social Darwinism.[63] The membership of the COS:

> has been likened to a 'new urban squirearchy' of middle-class professionals who strongly emphasised 'leadership and deference'. They envisaged their role was to separate the 'respectable poor' from the undeserving. This would ensure genuine claimants would be supported and the work-shy would be disciplined in workhouses.[64]

The LGB engaged the COS at a national level to draft directives for the crusade and locally as administrative partners with Boards of Guardians. The COS's local role was to act as investigators and gate-keepers for the allocation of welfare. In another sense they acted as political commissars, monitoring paupers and assessing the actions of guardians from their ideological standpoint. The first signs of COS influence in national Poor Law policy appeared in the 1871 Fleming Directive, as Hurren explains:

> Amongst the eleven new recommendations, civil servants stated that no outdoor relief was to be granted to any able-bodied applicant, male or female – even if he or she had children. If a husband deserted his wife, she would not be granted outdoor relief until a period of twelve months had elapsed. The same rule applied to able-bodied widows with children. The financial situation of each pauper had to be investigated... If they had previously claimed regular outdoor relief, guardians should treat their claim unfavourably because generosity had been unsuccessful. Anyone granted outdoor relief would only receive assistance for a maximum of three months.[65]

---

62 Interestingly the COS was originally named 'The Society for Organising Relief and Repressing Mendicity'. Ibid. p. 60.
63 Hurren notes: "COS literature explained that guardians were following a maxim of natural selection when they characterised paupers into 'deserving and undeserving' classes. Poor relief should not be given to a pauper residuum. Those who displayed incurable hereditary characteristics, like laziness, idleness or drunkenness should be ignored. Likewise, ratepayers must disregard the demands of illegitimate children and their profligate mothers" Ibid. p. 63.
64 Ibid. p. 21.
65 Ibid. p. 62.

The withdrawal of outdoor relief for mothers with young children would force them into the workhouse or alternatively they would be encouraged to:

hand over the care of their children to workhouse personnel who would arrange to board them out and educate them, giving women freedom to seek employment.[66]

Older, unemployable men were considered by the COS *crusaders* to be a drain on the community and their out-relief funding was also to be withdrawn, a policy that would condemn many to end their lives in a hated Bastille.

The stage was now set for an assault upon poor relief, with a vanguard of forty-one Poor Law Unions leading the charge:

Customary welfare payments outside the workhouse were withdrawn in these unions. The children of elderly paupers faced maintenance prosecutions; private charity replaced public welfare-to-work schemes; and regulations were tightened to discourage outdoor medical claimants… Recent research indicates that the policy caused deep impoverishment, notably in rural England, which was at the same time experiencing an unprecedented recession.[67]

The influence of the COS and this vanguard upon the rest of the Poor Law Unions across Britain was considerable with the majority, to varying degree, falling into line behind the new policies. This crusade, initiated in the early 1870s, to target the poor for 'cuts' without reference to the realities of poverty and economic cycles on a human or systemic basis was to last more than twenty years.

However, there was resistance from both within Poor Law Unions and without. Some Guardians opposed the COS/LGB crusade in board meetings whilst others even went public with their criticisms; one leading Guardian, who wrote a critical pamphlet on the impact of cuts to out-relief, claimed:

Hundreds of thousands of our aged poor and infirm are in the most miserable conditions; that the small allowance which we make to them is not sufficient to sustain nature, and that the horses, nay the very dogs of our aristocracy are better stabled, kennelled, and fed than our deserving poor are housed, clothed and fed.[68]

66 Hurren, E. T. *Protesting About Pauperism* p. 23.
67 Hurren, E. and King, S. "Begging for a Burial': Form, Function and Conflict in Nineteenth-Century Pauper Burial' in *Social History*, Vol. 30, No. 3 (Aug., 2005) p. 333.
68 Quoted from Hurren, E. T. *Protesting About Pauperism* pp. 64-5.

In some areas struggles to elect *anti-crusading* Guardians arose, which led to the formation of political pressure groups concerned with the nature of the Poor Laws and control of Poor Law Unions. These were often headed by radicals, socialists and trade unionists and became important arenas for debate over current and future forms of welfare. The *anti-crusaders*, that these pressure groups helped elect, created splits over policy within Poor Law Unions, challenged the withdrawal of various forms of out-relief and implemented improvements to conditions in workhouses. Increasing enfranchisement, particularly through the Third Reform Act of 1884 and crucially the Local Government Act of 1894, hastened this process of democratisation of the Poor Laws and eventually led to the demise of the COS/LGB initiative that had blighted a generation.[69]

Having surveyed the history of the Poor Laws up to the beginning of the 20th century, in the next chapter we turn our attention to the Poor Law Unions in Victorian Bristol, the origins of Eastville Workhouse, its management and a study of its inmates.

69 Ibid. Chap. 9.

2. Eastville Workhouse

Poor Law Unions in The Bristol Area

As we have seen workhouses were not created by the 1834 Poor Law Amendment Act, more than two thousand were already in existence, but their numbers and physical size were significantly expanded in combination with a programme of rationalisation and standardisation. Central to this process was the reorganisation of existing and the formation of new Poor Law Unions. After April 1836, Bristol and its environs were served by three such organisations (as shown in Figure 4), all of which operated workhouses:

¶ **Bristol Corporation of the Poor** had been in existence since 1696 and catered for the central wards of the city covering 755 acres of the ancient city parishes.[70] The workhouse at St Peter's hospital was at the rear of St Peter's church in Castle Park until it was destroyed by bombing in 1940. In 1837 the Corporation of the Poor opened a second workhouse located in the old French prison at Stapleton.[71]

¶ **Bedminster Poor Law Union** was formed in April 1836 and covered parishes in south of the city and Somerset.[72] The Union built a new workhouse in 1837-38 at Flax Bourton to accommodate 300 inmates and costing £6,600.[73] According to the 1831 census the population in its catchment area was 29,399.

---

70 The parishes were All Saints, Castle Precincts, Christ Church, St Augustine the less, St Ewen, St James, St John the Baptist, St Leonard, St Mary-le-Port, St Mary Redcliffe, St Michael the Archangel on the Mount Without, St Nicholas, St Paul, St Peter, St Philip & Jacob (in-parish), St Stephen, St Thomas, St Werburgh and Temple. BRO *The Poor Law in Bristol* (Bristol: BRO, Dec 2013) p. 24.

71 Higginbotham, P. *The Workhouse* http://www.workhouses.org.uk/Bristol/ accessed 2015.

72 The parishes were Abbot's Leigh, Backwell, Barrow Gurney, Bedminster, Brockley, Chelvey, Clapton in Gordano, Easton in Gordano or St George's, Clevedon, Dundry, Flax Bourton, Kenn, Kingston Seymour, Long Ashton, Nailsea, Portbury, Portishead, Tickenham, Walton in Gordano, Weston in Gordano, Winford, Wraxall and Yatton. BRO *The Poor Law in Bristol* p. 24.

73 Higginbotham, P. *The Workhouse* http://www.workhouses.org.uk/Bedminster/ accessed 2015. Bristol Radical History Group have published the following concerning this workhouse; Caldicott, R. *Bedminster Union Workhouse and Victorian Social Attitudes on Epilepsy: A Case study of the Life and Death of Hannah Wiltshire* Bristol Radical Pamphleteer #35 (Bristol: BRHG, 2016).

¶ **Clifton Poor Law Union** was also formed in April 1836 and covered the parishes which lay outside the city centre to the west, north and east in Gloucestershire,[74] which had a combined population of 51,345 according to the 1831 census.[75]

Clifton Poor Law Union

On its formation the Clifton Poor Law Union was operating three old parish workhouses, each supposedly catering for different groups of paupers:

¶ The former St George's poorhouse in Hudds Vale Road was used for children.[76]
¶ Able-bodied paupers were accommodated in the Pennywell Road workhouse, Easton in the parish of St Philip and Jacob (Without).[77]
¶ The Clifton poorhouse, for the aged and the sick, was located on the southern end of Church Lane in Clifton Wood, on the hillside just above the Mardyke public house.[78]

However, the Clifton Board of Guardians eventually proposed to build a new large combined workhouse at Eastville. Large notes that there were number of reasons for this:

Firstly the number of paupers was increasing to such an extent as to overwhelm the existing poorhouses. In the first year of the Union it had catered for 406 indoor poor but from 1842-44 the number had been steady at just over 800. Secondly, the Pennywell Road establishment, the Guardians admitted, was a disgrace... [with reports showing] that "the insane, sick and able-bodied were all in the same ward", that it was severely overcrowded, had no infirmary ward and no room exclusively for tramps. One of the Guardians spoke of

74 The parishes were Clifton, Compton Greenfield, Filton, Henbury, Horfield, Stapleton, St George, Stoke Gifford, Westbury-on-Trym, Winterbourne and the out parishes of St James & St Paul and St Philip & St Jacob. BRO *The Poor Law* in Bristol p. 24. Note: The parish of Shirehampton became part of the Barton Regis Poor Law Union in March 1885 and Compton Greenfield ceased to be a parish for Poor Law purposes on that date.
75 Higginbotham, P. *The Workhouse* http://www.workhouses.org.uk/Clifton/ accessed 2015.
76 The original building survives and can be viewed at the end of Hudds Vale Rd (BS5 7HE).
77 The original buildings at 28 Pennywell Rd were demolished in 1925.
78 The original building on the corner of Old School lane and Church Lane has since been demolished, only a section of wall and a window apparently remain (BS8 4TY).

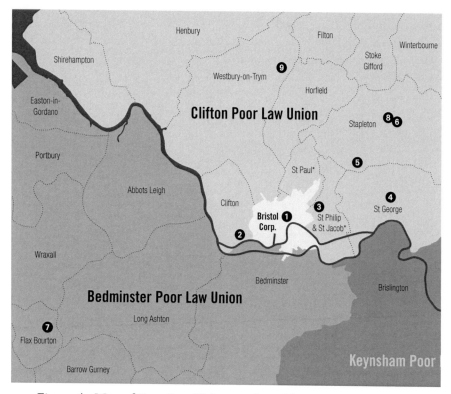

Figure 4: Map of Poor Law Unions and workhouses in Bristol from 1836 to 1898.

'Bristol Corp.' refers to the Poor Law Union known as the
Bristol Corporation of the Poor.

*These are the 'out-parishes' of St Paul and St Philip and St Jacob as against
the 'in-parishes' which were smaller and lay within the boundary
of the Bristol Corporation of the Poor.

1. St Peter's Hospital workhouse 1699-1842 (Bristol Corporation of the Poor)
2. Clifton Poorhouse 1837-1847 (Clifton Union)
3. Pennywell Road workhouse ?-1847 (Clifton Union)
4. St George workhouse 1801-1847 (Clifton Union)
5. Eastville Workhouse 1847-1948

(Clifton/Barton Regis Union)
6. Stapleton workhouse 1837-1948 (Bristol Corporation of the Poor)
7. Bedminster workhouse 1838-1929 (Bedminster Union)
8. Bristol Lunatic Asylum 1860-1992
9. Southmead workhouse 1902-1930 (Barton Regis Union)

having found a woman there with a bastard lying dead and "itched paupers" [paupers with scabies, lice or infectious skin diseases] in no way separated from other inmates.[79]

The state of the Pennywell Rd workhouse and the treatment of inmates were notorious in Bristol. As early as 1835 a visiting Assistant Poor Law Commissioner had been so shocked by the conditions he had demanded immediate action from local magistrates.[80] More than ten years later Mary Attwood complained to the bench:

> She had been in the Pennywell-road-workhouse… but last Sunday morning she found that her two children were nearly dead and her feelings as a mother would not allow her to stay in the house any longer. When her children had been taken into the poorhouse they were as fine healthy children as ever were seen, but now, although they had been in there only three weeks, they were mere skeletons: you could reckon every bone in their bodies, and they were so ill that she did not think they could ever recover[81]

Despite the appalling conditions in the existing Clifton Union workhouses it was not concern for the paupers amongst the Guardians that was the principal reason for building a new combined institution. As Large explains:

> Lastly, and perhaps decisively, the chairman of the Guardians… observed that managing the poor in one general Union workhouse would be cheaper than in three existing houses. The cost in one institution would be £2,148-19s-9d per year while the present cost in three houses would be £2,682-19s-3d.

Instead, the drive to reduce the costs of poor relief made this 'economy of scale' crucial in the decision. A saving of over £500 per year was a considerable sum in the 1840s and certainly should have been attractive for the ratepayers.[82] However, there was considerable opposition amongst the clergy and 'well-to-do' of Clifton. Despite the Guardians explaining that in the long-run increases

79 Large, D. *Bristol and the New Poor Law* (Bristol: Historical Association, 1995) p. 7.
80 Charles Mott's account can be read at Higginbotham, P. *The Workhouse* http://www.workhouses.org.uk/Clifton/ accessed 2015.
81 *Bristol Mercury* 28 November 1846.
82 Depending on the criterion for relative worth, this equates to a saving of somewhere between £50,000 and £1.8 Million per year. See http://www.measuringworth.com/ukcompare/relativevalue.php.

to the poor relief fraction of the rates would be minimal, in a crowded public meeting in 1844 a resolution was passed "urging the abandonment of the scheme for a new workhouse" and to petition the Poor Law Commission to separate Clifton parish from its poorer neighbours.[83] Large comments that:

> The truth was, as a number of speakers made clear, Clifton ratepayers did not see why they should have any responsibility for the poor of St Philip and Jacob and their wretched workhouse.[84]

Despite this vociferous (and unchristian) opposition from the wealthy of Clifton, the project went ahead. However, this was not the end of moves by Cliftonites to separate themselves from the less well-off parishes in their Poor Law Union.

As we have seen the creation of the Clifton Union married the wealthy parishes of Clifton and Westbury-on-Trym in the west of the city with the rapidly growing populations of the much poorer parishes such as St Philip and Jacob in the east. There was also a secondary effect of this amalgamation which concerned health statistics, the first signs of which appeared in 1849 in the wake of one of the most serious cholera outbreaks in Bristol. Confusion had apparently arisen because the epidemic was being associated with the district of Clifton rather than the wider Clifton Poor Law Union. As one belligerent journalist pointed out:

> Of all places, perhaps, in the country, Clifton is one where people may consider themselves safest from cholera or other epidemic visitation… the disease almost always makes its attack in small miserable courts, out of back-streets, and that the places of public resort and traffic are as safe from the liability of being infected from these as *if they were in a different country*, and in point of fact these wretched places are far removed from the principal thoroughfares of the city.[85]

This statement exposes a feeling amongst the wealthy in Clifton of 'two countries'; their affluent neighbourhoods in the west of the city and those of the 'social residuum' in the inner-city slums. It also hints at a characteristic Victorian trait of the upper and middle-classes who regarded the poor working class as an 'other' and associated them with filth, degeneracy and disease. The problem of this 'other' was to continue in the 1850s when quarterly reports on

83 The disparity in wealth between Clifton and its poorer neighbours can be judged by the fact that more than 50% of Clifton's tenements were valued at £20 or over, whereas in the parish of St Philip and Jacob with almost double the number, less than 5% fulfilled this criterion. Large, D. *Bristol and the New Poor Law* n. 7 p. 30.
84 Ibid. p. 7.
85 *Bristol Times & Bath Advocate* 14 July 1849. Our emphasis.

mortality in each Poor Law Union were issued by the Registrar General and the summaries were published in *The Times*. Once again the root of the issue for Clifton residents lay in the association of their 'Clifton' with the much larger Clifton Poor Law Union. The Clifton of:

> crescents, terraces and broad avenues running along or just below an elevated ridge of mountain limestone, and abutting on breezy downs', filled with houses belonging to 'persons in possession of the comforts and luxuries of life, and the means of preserving health...and... a thorough system of public sewage.

was being statistically combined with:

> a very destitute district in the parish, and also with a poor-law district... densely crowded with the poorest of houses and inmates (a large proportion not to be surpassed in their destitution by the tenants of the closest and dirtiest quarters of an over-peopled commercial city or sea port).

Consequently a cursory reading of mortality statistics published in *The Times* led many outsiders to believe that "Clifton" was "one of the most mortal of watering places" with a death rate around 50% higher than rival resorts for the Victorian rich such as the Isle of Wight, Torquay or Cheltenham.[86] This would not do. However, rather than trying to directly improve the conditions and thus life-spans of their numerous poorer neighbours in order to bring the overall mortality figures down, the wealthy rate-payers chose instead to campaign for the name of the 'Clifton' Poor Law Union to be altered. This was in order to separate them from this 'other':

> Repeated remonstrances having been made on the injustice of the arrangement, the Local Government Board at length ordered that, from the 14th March, 1877, the name of the Union should be changed to Barton Regis.

Cliftonites could now rest easy as the subsequent mortality statistics for their Clifton, having ditched their annoyingly poor and sickly neighbours in 1877, demonstrated "the parish to be one of the most salubrious in the kingdom".[87]

---

86 Symonds, J.A. Sanitary Statistics of Clifton in Taylor, T.D. (ed.) *The British Association for the Advancement of Science, Bath 1864: Authorised reprint of the reports in the special daily editions of the "Bath Chronicle"* (London: Bath Chronicle, 1864) pp. 128-9.
87 Latimer, J. *The Annals of Bristol in the Nineteenth Century* (Bristol: W & F Morgan, 1887) pp. 493-4.

Design and construction

After the stormy meetings of angry rate-payers in the autumn of 1844 Clifton Poor Law Guardians were careful not to publicise full details of their arrangements for financing the planned new workhouse. Faced with opposition, they had argued in public that the Union would only have to finance £4,000 out of a capital cost of £16,000 and that after offsetting the savings of having a single institution this would reduce the extra burden on the rates to three eighths of a penny in the pound. However, this was being 'liberal' with the truth; in fact, they had quietly agreed to borrow £20,000 from the Poor Law Commission and within a year of the opening of the institution another £5,000.[88]

In the summer of 1845 the Clifton Guardians paid £3,500 for a group of fields on a hill several miles from the city centre, not far from the village of 'Lower Easton', situated between the road to the Ridgeway and Fishponds and Coombe brook.[89] Construction of the new workhouse was completed in 1847 at 100 Fishponds Road, in what was to become the district of Eastville, in east Bristol (see Figure 5).

Eastville Workhouse was a massive cluster of buildings covering almost the entire area between modern day Fishponds Rd, Robertson Rd and Greenbank View, an expanse of 73,600 m^2 or 7.36 hectares[90] (see Figure 6 and Figure 7). The new structures were based on designs by Bristol-based architect Samuel T Welch who conceived a number of similar institutions in Somerset and followed the general lay-outs of workhouses post-1835. Surrounded by high walls on all sides, the complex was designed both to isolate inmates from the 'outside world' and to segregate them by gender and then by age, infirmity and disability on the inside.[91]

The three storey main building was fronted by an entrance block to the south-west topped by a clock-tower. To the rear, a walled central spine running the length of the building divided the male and female sides, each of which had enclosed airing courtyards separating the able-bodied, aged, sick, 'imbeciles' and 'insane'. The majority of the dormitories (which mirrored the strict segregation) were located on the first and second floors. The spine was dominated by the chapel, centrally located on the first floor (see Figure 8), which was adjoined on

88 Large, D. *Bristol and the New Poor Law* pp. 7-8.
89 The conveyed properties were Upper Great Ground, Lower Great Ground, the Bottom, Ellisham, Little Linterns and the Rudgeway. BRO Ref. St PHosp/185, St PHosp/183 and St PHosp/184.
90 Plans of Eastville Workhouse state its area as 18.202 acres. BRO 45110/1/3.
91 The earliest 'block' drawings of the site of Eastville Workhouse date from 1847. BRO St PHosp/194.

Figure 5: Eastville Workhouse viewed from the junction of Argyle St and Fishponds Rd (c. 1960s).

either side by two octagonal shaped towers which acted as central observation points with panoramic views over the six main airing yards. This particular design feature was related to the panoptic influenced layouts of 19th century prisons.[92]

National management of Poor Law Unions

In 1847, the year that Eastville Workhouse opened for business, the Poor Law Commission which governed the administration of the 1834 Poor Law Amendment Act was abolished. This unusual action had been spurred by a growing litany of scandals in workhouses ranging from the brutal separation of parents from children or husband from wife, overcrowding, cruel punishments, starvation diets, neglect leading to epidemics and

92 A *panopticon* is a building, such as a prison, hospital, library, or the like, so arranged that all parts of the interior or exterior are visible from a single point; the idea being that a single person can observe the inmates of an institution without the inmates being able to tell whether or not they are being watched. The panopticon was a design created by the British philosopher Jeremy Bentham (1748-1832) and had a significant influence upon the layout of Victorian prisons and workhouses. Its use is discussed in detail in Foucault, M. *Discipline and Punish: The Birth of the Prison* (Harmondsworth: Penguin Books, 1991) Part 3, Chap. 3.

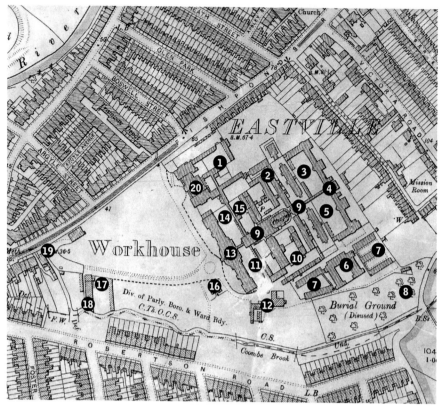

Figure 6: Layout of Eastville Workhouse from County Series - Epoch 2 1902-04
Ordnance Survey Map.

1. Female 'insane' airing yard
2. Able-bodied women's airing yard
3. Male 'insane' airing yard
4. 'Lunatic' wards (constructed 1867)
5. 'Imbecile' boy's airing yard
6. Infirmary (constructed 1880)
7. Wooden pavilion sick wards (constructed 1886)
8. Burial ground (1851-1895, now Rosemary Green)
9. Panoptic towers on either side of the chapel
10. Able-bodied men's airing yard
11. Aged men's airing yard

12. Laundry, boilers and piggery
13. Male and female receiving wards
14. Aged and sick women's airing yard
15. Aged women's airing yard
16. Master and Matron's House (constructed 1892)
17. Stone-breaking yards (constructed 1868)
18. Casual wards (constructed 1873)
19. Workhouse entrance at 100 Fishponds Rd
20. Nursery and wards for women with children

Figure 7: Eastville Workhouse from the air (c. 1967).

Figure 8: Central spine of Eastville Workhouse showing chapel, viewed from able-bodied men's yard (c. 1972).

even murders, all of which bore some relation to the harsh regime of the institution engineered by the Poor Law Commissioners.[93] The relative autonomy of the Commission from Parliamentary control combined with infighting amongst its officers had generated significant criticism from within central government and the final straw was the Andover workhouse scandal of 1845. This was an unholy marriage of a brutal penal regime with sexual assaults by workhouse officers, starvation and inmates resorting to eating rotting bones.

After 1847 all the local Boards of Guardians reported to a new central government authority, the Poor Law Board.[94] This was led by a President (typically a powerful establishment figure) and comprised the following 'worthies': the Lord President of the Council, Lord Privy Seal, Chancellor of the Exchequer and Secretary of State of the Home Department. By the 1870s even the Secretaries of State for India and the War and Colonial Departments had been added to the Board.[95] However, what relevant knowledge these dignitaries had of poverty and workhouses is somewhat of a mystery! This new body had the power to put Parliamentary Acts into operation, formulate workhouse regulations and procedures, collect statistics and produce reports for Parliament. From the very inception of the 1834 Poor Law Act, the aim of national government was to reduce parish autonomy with respect to poor relief, instead centralising management in London and to push through the new 'workhouse' system. The Poor Law Commissioners had lacked the legislative powers to achieve this; in contrast the new Poor Law Board was given greater freedom to standardise 'outdoor' and 'indoor' systems of relief. In Bristol there were considerable battles between the Corporation of the Poor and the new authority in London especially concerning auditing of Union accounts, the provision of paid medical and relieving officers and standardisation of workhouse diets. However, by the mid-1850s Poor Law Board had gained the upper hand and was issuing orders and circulars which all three Bristol Poor Law Unions were implementing.[96]

Central to the whole philosophy of the 1834 PLAA was to demonstrate that the new system reduced costs. Higginbotham notes that from the outset the bureaucratic mentality was tuned to monitoring these savings:

93 Higginbotham, P. *The Workhouse Cookbook* p. 49-50
94 The new Poor Law Board was later renamed the Local Government Board in 1871 and finally became the Ministry of Health in 1919. Higginbotham, P. *The Workhouse* http://www. workhouses.org.uk/admin/index.shtml#plb accessed 2015.
95 *Clifton Poor Law Union - Statement of Accounts 1872-75* BRO Ref. 22936/129.
96 Large, D. *Bristol and the New Poor Law* pp. 11-12.

One of the main responsibilities of the Commissioners was to produce an annual report summarizing their activities and the progress of Act's operation. The report also included a wealth of statistics which aimed to demonstrate significant reductions in the overall costs of poor relief resulting from the new system.[97]

Thus, despite the upheavals in managerial organisation, the modus operandi throughout the Victorian period remained broadly the same; rather than reform of a creaking feudal system of 'poor relief' and heading towards early welfare provision, instead the primary aim was to reduce the financial burden of the burgeoning poor upon the better-off in society.

Local management

Workhouses were run by a 'Master' who reported to the management bodies of the Poor Law Unions, known after 1834, as Boards of Guardians. In the Eastville Workhouse, after the Master came the officers and staff; a Matron, an assistant Matron, a school master and school mistress, an infant school master and a boys' industrial trainer. In addition there were a clerk and a porter, a superintendent for women's indoor labour, a superintendent of vagrants and outside labour and a female vagrant attendant. There were six 'lunatic' nurses, one infant nurse and four other nurses. Finally there was an engineer, a tailor and a shoemaker. All other trades and labour required were fulfilled by the pauper inmates themselves. Outside of wages[98] the Master was provided with a four-bedroom house in the grounds (see Figure 6) and the paid staff with 'rations, lodging and washing'.

In the Victorian period Boards of Poor Law Guardians, to which the Master reported, were generally comprised of local elites and the middle-classes. Guardians came from two sources, by annual ballot and drawn from unelected ex officio magistrates who typically took the senior positions on the board. For example, when Eastville Workhouse opened in 1847 the Chairman of the Clifton Union was the Rev. Willliam Mirehouse, a magistrate, curate, rector and large landowner.[99] The balance between the elected and unelected Guardians for a selection of years is shown at the base of Table 1.

97 Higginbotham, P. *The Workhouse* http://www.workhouses.org.uk/admin/index.shtml#plb accessed 2015.
98 Salaries for the Master and Matron of a Workhouse were very lucrative. In 1902, just after our period, they were respectively £423 and £381 a year (typically they were husband and wife). The estimates of relative income worth in 2015 range from £40,000 to £400,000 and £37,000 to £360,000 respectively. http://www.measuringworth.com/ukcompare/relativevalue.php.
99 Large, D. *Bristol and the New Poor Law* p. 24.

Figure 9: Barton Regis Board of Guardians with women members in front of Eastville Workhouse (c. 1880s).

The elected Guardians were derived from the various parishes which made up the Poor Law Union with the franchise the same as that for electing MPs. From 1832 only men who owned a house with an annual value of £10 could vote; in 1867 the franchise was extended and by 1884 a majority of men were able to vote for Parliament, the local council and for Poor Law Guardians. Election as a Guardian was seen as an important local role and political parties debated the choice of candidates including the local Liberal Association and even working men's organisations such as the Bristol Radical Operatives Association.[100] Table 1 gives the numbers, trades and professions of the elected Guardians for a selection of years from the mid-1850s to the late 1880s.[101] A cursory examination of this data demonstrates that the most common occupation (if you can call it that) of the elected Guardians was 'gentleman' (or 'gentlewoman' after 1882).[102] Despite the advancing franchise, the majority of the rest of the

100 *Bristol Mercury* 9 November 1894.
101 Data is derived from TNA Ref. MH 12/4007 (1855), *Clifton Poor Law Union - Statement of Accounts 1872-75* BRO Ref. 22936/129 and *Barton Regis Poor Law Union - Statements of Accounts 1881-1889* BRO Ref. 22936/130. It should be noted that the numbers of unelected Guardians are merely those listed in the Half-year accounts for Clifton/Barton Regis Poor Law Union; the document also states "And all other (if any) of Her Majesties Justices of the Peace residing within the Union and acting for the City of Bristol, or the Division of Lawford's Gate."
102 It appears that the 'occupations' of 'widow' and 'spinster' assigned to two of the successful female candidates in the elections of 1882 had mutated into 'gentlewoman' by 1884.

Guardians were businessmen, with a smattering of farmers, military officers and clergy. Higginbotham states:

> Although Guardians were forbidden from directly supplying goods to the Union, Guardians with local business interests could use their Board membership to develop their business, political and social contacts.[103]

So rather than just a nominal role in local governance, being on the Board of Guardians could be a lucrative position for local entrepreneurs.

At first it was required that Guardians had to be members of the Church of England, but according to Johnson in Bristol from the reign of George IV (1820-30) onward, religious 'dissenters' were allowed into the fold.[104] He noted in the 1820s that a great part of the Guardians were 'dissenters' because they were not eligible to serve in any offices belonging to the Church. The religious schisms and discrimination continued into the latter part of the century; in July 1862 the Guardians of the Clifton Union submitted a petition to the Poor Law Board in London protesting at the possible introduction of minimal facilities for Roman Catholic worship and schooling in the workhouse and consequent payments to priests.[105] It is unclear whether it was the extra cost involved or merely bigotry that drove their protest. In 1881 a similar circular was issued by the Protestant Alliance complaining of attempts by Roman Catholics to be elected to the Board of Guardians.

After the Municipal Franchise Act of 1869, despite the fact that women were not allowed to vote in Parliamentary polls, they were able to stand for election for Boards of Guardians provided they met the property requirement. The first woman Poor Law Guardian was successfully elected in London 1875 and women began to enter the Barton Regis Board of Guardians in the 1880s. The first female candidate in the Bristol area was a Miss Ball who stood in the Westbury on Trym parish in 1881 but was defeated. However, opposition was brewing to the intervention of women in this sphere of local government. As Martin explains:

103 Higginbotham, P. *The Workhouse* http://www.workhouses.org.uk/admin/index.shtml#plb accessed 2015.
104 Johnson, J. *Transactions of the Corporation of the Poor, in the City of Bristol, During a Period of 126 Years* (Bristol: P. Rose, 1826). A 'dissenter' 'refers particularly to a member of a religious body who has, for one reason or another, separated from the Established Church or any other kind of Protestant who refuses to recognise the supremacy of the Established Church in areas where the established Church is or was Anglican' https://en.wikipedia.org/wiki/Dissenter.
105 TNA Ref. MH 12/4010 19 July 1862.

Occupation	Year of election to Board of Guardians						
	1855	1872	1874	1881	1882	1884	1889
Gentleman	11	9	8	15	12	7	8
Gentlewoman	-	-	-	-	2	4	4
Widow	-	-	-	-	1	-	-
Spinster	-	-	-	-	1	-	-
Grocer	2	-	-	2	1	3	1
Builder	-	2	2	2	-	2	2
Farmer	4	5	6	4	4	5	4
Baker and corn factor	1	-	-	1	1	1	1
Boot maker	-	2	2	-	-	-	-
Brewer	-	-	-	-	1	1	-
Brick maker	1	-	-	-	1	1	-
Nurseryman	1	1	2	-	-	-	1
Hairdresser	-	-	-	1	1	-	-
Coach builder	-	1	1	1	1	1	1
Merchant	1	3	3	1	1	1	1
Maltster	3	-	-	1	1	-	-
Cotton manufacturer	-	-	-	1	1	-	-
Accountant	1	-	-	1	-	-	-
Clergy	3	1	2	-	-	1	2
Yeoman	1	2	-	-	1	-	-
Surgeon	-	-	1	-	-	-	1
Haulier	-	-	1	-	-	-	-
Cattle dealer	-	1	1	-	-	-	1
Wool stapler	-	1	1	1	1	-	-
Victualler	-	2	1	-	-	-	-
Master painter	-	-	1	-	-	-	-

Occupation	Year of election to Board of Guardians						
	1855	1872	1874	1881	1882	1884	1889
Military Officer	-	-	-	-	-	2	3
Civil Engineer	-	-	-	1	1	1	1
Chemical manufacturer	-	-	-	-	-	-	1
Ironmonger	-	-	-	-	-	1	1
Contractor	-	-	-	-	-	-	1
Draper	-	1	1	-	-	-	-
Cabinet maker	-	1	-	-	-	-	-
Music seller	-	1	-	-	-	-	-
Provision curer	-	1	1	-	-	-	-
Bookseller	-	-	-	-	1	-	-
Laundry proprietor	-	-	-	1	1	1	-
Barge owner	-	-	-	-	-	1	-
Total elected Guardians	29	34	33	33	34	33	34
Unelected Guardians	-	40	40	55	56	53	50

Table 1: Occupations of those elected to Clifton/Barton Regis Board of Guardians for selected years 1855-1889.

The following year a leaflet was published in Clifton entitled 'Why women should not be elected as Guardians'. One of the arguments against women Guardians was the problem of discussing 'cases of vice' in the presence of ladies. The double standard with regard to middle and working class women was criticised in the Englishwoman's Review which claimed that the only indecency was that of female applicants for relief being required to discuss their personal circumstances and their sexual history in front of men.[106]

In spite of this laughably hypocritical opposition and the reservations of some members of the Barton Regis Board, Susannah Prentice, Alice Winkworth, Catherine Woollam and Mary Clifford were elected as Guardians in April 1882,

106 Martin, M. 'Guardians of the Poor: A Philanthropic Female Elite in Bristol' in *Regional Historian* Summer 2002, Issue 9, p. 7.

with the latter three 'gentlewomen' topping the polls.[107] However, resistance from male members of the board to these female interlopers was to continue despite their popularity with the enfranchised.

Prior to the successful elections of 1882 the role of women (such as Mary Clifford) in monitoring conditions in Eastville Workhouse had been confined to informal visits, which it appears were a source of annoyance to the Guardians. In 1885 they laid down stringent rules on who could call at the institution, limiting the duration of their stay and access to wards. It seems this was a reaction to informal monitoring as they stated that now women had become Guardians "there would not have been much necessity for lady visitors" and they truculently added that now they had formalised such visits, "they could not be charged with neglecting the inmates of the house".[108] However, by 1894 the Guardians meeting concluded that the involvement of women led to an improvement in the nursing conditions[109] and by 1896 six out of the thirty-eight Guardians at the meeting of the Barton Regis Board were female.[110] This change was reflected in the other two Bristol Poor Law Unions which by the mid-1890s had female members making up a total of twelve women Guardians in the Bristol area.[111]

These successful female candidates of 1882, who were re-elected on numerous occasions over the succeeding decades,[112] were part of a philanthropic female elite comprising middle and upper class, often single women, who were "already involved in some form of activism, whether it be related to philanthropy, temperance, social purity, suffrage reform or, campaigns for higher education for women and girls".[113] These dedicated reformers brought a particular brand of benevolence to the workhouse which was clearly related to their gender

107 *Bristol Mercury* 13 and 22 April 1882.
108 *Bristol Mercury* 24 October 1885.
109 *Bristol Mercury* 8 October 1894
110 *Bristol Mercury* 9 May 1896. According to Longmate 'In the West of England, never the most progressive of areas, there were by 1900 fifty women Guardians, out of a total of 2,000' Longmate, N. *The Workhouse* p. 267.
111 Martin, M. 'Guardians of the Poor: A Philanthropic Female Elite in Bristol' p. 8.
112 Martin notes; "The Bristol women elected as Guardians in 1882 proved to be particularly popular with the voters. Mary Clifford served for 25 years, Alice Winkworth served for 37 years and Catherine Woollam served for 27 years, until her death in 1909". Martin, M. 'Guardians of the Poor: A Philanthropic Female Elite in Bristol' p. 8.
113 Martin notes: "Middle class single women enjoyed political rights that were denied to the majority of their married sisters and they were in a relatively privileged position until the property qualification for the municipal franchise was abolished in 1894, making it easier for married women to stand for office and vote in local elections." Martin, M. 'Single Women and Philanthropy: A Case Study of Women's Associational Life in Bristol, 1880-1914', *Women's History Review*, 17, 3, 2008, pp. 395-417.

and class position and has been described as a "civilising mission to the poor". For example, in a case-study of Mary Clifford, an influential and renowned Christian philanthropist and one of the Barton Regis Guardians mentioned above, Martin outlines her and her colleagues' politics concerning "relief of the poor":

> She remained concerned to improve the welfare of elderly inmates in the workhouse and thought charitable assistance could be better organised to help the *more deserving aged*, however, *she disagreed with the move to introduce old age pensions*. She was keen to see children removed from the workhouse, *or from family homes she considered unsuitable*, and she promoted fostering and *child emigration as the means to remove children from moral danger and neglect*. Similarly, she was concerned about the plight of unmarried mothers and of *women who were considered to be mentally defective*… Generally Mary and the other women Guardians elected in Bristol in the nineteenth century favoured the *strict administration of Poor Relief* and supported moves towards better classification in the workhouse and further investment in additional institutions, such as hospitals and children's homes.[114]

These paternalistic views about the 'poor' were clearly trapped within a framework of middle and upper-class Victorian values. Although the actions of these 'reforming ladies' softened some of the harsher aspects of Eastville Workhouse (at least for the 'deserving'), it would take working class pressure and socialist vision to begin the process of abolition of the workhouse and creating the welfare state. Twenty-five years after the appointment of the first female Guardians in Bristol, working class socialist, Jane Tillett,[115] was elected in 1907.

Costs and numbers

A central tenet of the New Poor Law was the collection of statistics concerning the operation of the recently formed Poor Law Unions. Delivery to the Poor Law Commissioners of detailed accounting of the numbers of people receiving indoor and outdoor relief and consequent costs was a strict requirement each half-year. This bureaucratic approach allows study of the usage of Eastville

114 Martin, M. 'Guardians of the Poor: A Philanthropic Female Elite in Bristol' p. 10. Our emphasis.
115 Jane Tillett was the wife of Ben Tillett, an Easton born Bristolian who had been an important leader of the Dockers Union in the strike waves of 1889-93 and founder of the Transport and General Workers Union. See McNeil, J. *Ben Tillett* (Bristol: Bristol Radical Pamphleteer #20, 2012).

Workhouse and the relative expenditure on indoor and outdoor relief during the Victorian era.

Figure 10 presents the average number of inmates in the Eastville institution excluding casual wards over the period 1857 to 1898 with an overlaid linear trendline.[116] It is immediately obvious from the trendline that the average number of inmates was increasing in the second half of the 19th century. Comparison with population statistics for Bristol and environs demonstrates that, over the same period, numbers in the Eastville Workhouse were growing at a faster rate than the increase in population of the city.[117] This in turn suggests that additional factors were inflating the numbers of people forced into indoor relief. Within the overall increase in workhouse numbers there are a series of fluctuations that are compared in Figure 10 with the economic recessions of the era shown in Table 2.[118] Figure 10 indicates positive correlation between cyclical economic recessions and the numbers of inmates in the Eastville Workhouse. This feature, although perhaps unsurprising, provides evidence for the economic precariousness of sections of the working classes in Bristol rather than for the stubbornly recalcitrant 'professional paupers' alluded to by many Victorian champions of the New Poor Law.

One of the primary aims of the New Poor Law was to drive the cost of outdoor relief down. Appendix 2 Table 11 gives the yearly costs of indoor and outdoor relief for the Clifton/Barton Regis Poor Law Union and numbers of recipients over a forty year period. This data is plotted in Figure 11. It is clear that between 1858 and 1897 the ratio between the two kinds of relief remained fairly constant, with the cost of the workhouse being approximately one third of the total expenditure on relief. However, there is one anomaly which relates to the 'crusade' against welfare spending, particularly outdoor relief, launched by the Local Government Board in 1871 and discussed in Chapter 1.

116 The average inmate numbers are based upon the arithmetic mean of the January and July half year figures and are given in Table 10 in Appendix 2. The data is derived from Table 14 in Archer, I., Jordan, S., Ramsey, K., Wardley, P. and Woollard, M. 'Poor Law Statistics, 1835-1948' in Wardley P. (ed.) *Bristol Historical Resource* (Bristol: UWE, 2000).

117 This comparison was achieved by plotting total population statistics from census information, creating a linear trend line and comparing the gradient with that for the Eastville Workhouse inmate numbers. Population data was taken from: http://www.visionofbritain.org.uk/unit/10056676/cube/TOT_POP.

118 Table 2 is derived from https://en.wikipedia.org/wiki/List_of_recessions_in_the_United_Kingdom and e-mail to R. Ball from M. Richardson (24 August 2015). *In the 1850s-60s it is estimated that one in five British people were dependent on the textile industry, ten percent of British capital was invested in it and Britain produced 98% of the world exports of cotton cloth. BBC4 Documentary *Clydebuilt: The Ships That Made The Commonwealth* Episode 3 of 4: Robert E Lee (2015).

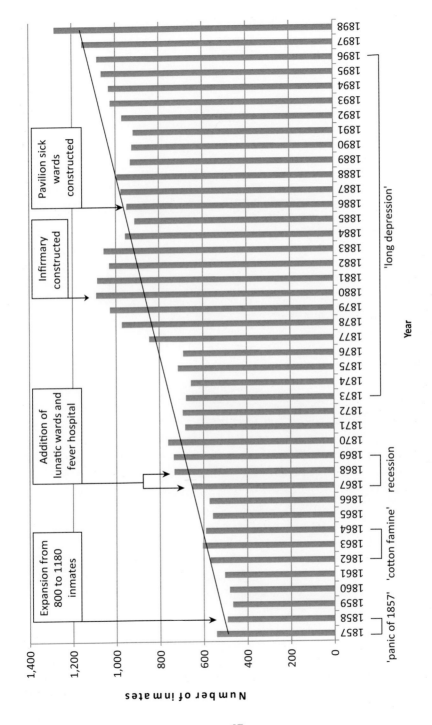

Figure 10: Average inmate numbers in Eastville Workhouse excluding casual wards (1857-98).

Period	Duration	Recession	Notes
1857-58	~1 year	Panic of 1857	Originated in the U.S. as a banking crisis; regarded as the first truly global economic recession.
1862-64	~2 years	Cotton Famine	Crisis in U.K. textile industries generated by huge increase in price of U.S. produced cotton due to civil war blockades and speculation. Over 1,500 East Bristol cotton workers thrown out of employment.*
1867-69	~2 years		Impact on exports resulting from U.S. recession after civil war.
1873-96	~20 years	Long Depression	Longest economic contraction in modern history; triggered by Austrian/U.S. banking crises in 1873. Britain hardest hit in Europe, particularly agricultural workers. Winter 1878-9 in Bristol saw extreme hardship, especially for quay labourers, farm and construction workers.

Table 2: Economic recessions affecting Bristol and Britain (1850-1900).

The effects of this national policy are apparent in the Clifton Union statistics shown in Figure 11. Over a five year period from 1870-75, the fraction of the total bill made up by outdoor relief falls from around 70% to about 60%. In addition, overall costs of relief reduce for a few years before racing up as the brutal effects of the 'long depression' begin to be felt towards the end of the 1870s. Another objective of the theorists of the New Poor Law was to make the cost of the workhouse inmate to the Union lower than if they were receiving outdoor relief. According to Appendix 2 Table 11, this was never achieved in the Victorian period, with the average cost of an inmate being between two and three times higher than the outdoor recipient throughout.

Outside of directives from the Poor Law authorities in London the constant drive to reduce costs of indoor and outdoor poor relief was an ongoing issue for Boards of Guardians; the Clifton/Barton Regis Union was no exception. Detailed accounts of expenditure for the Eastville Workhouse were vital tools for micro-managing cost and comparisons with statistics from other such institutions and Unions were common. In 1884 a parliamentary paper reported data on pauper numbers and the costs of poor relief for a range of metropolitan

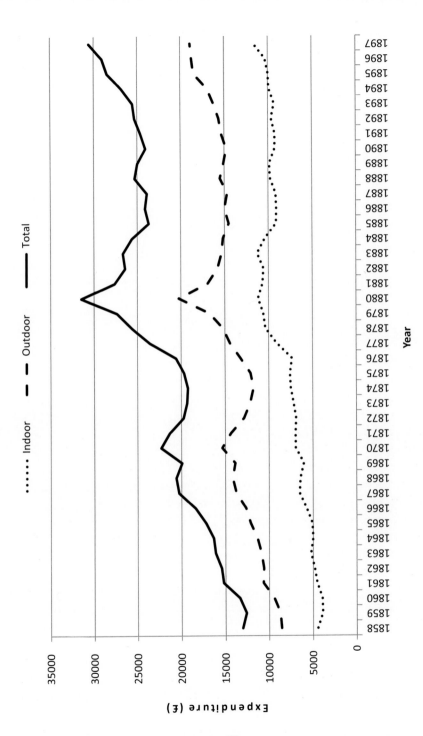

Figure 11: Expenditure on relief for the Clifton/Barton Regis Poor Law Union (1858-97).

Union	Population	Total Paupers	Ratio of Paupers to population (%)	Total costs of relief (£)	Cost per head of population (s/d)
Leeds	190,847	5,072	2.7%	£26,832	2s 9d
Stoke/Trent	104,313	3,506	3.4%	£16,385	3s 1d
Barton Regis	**166,136**	**5,425**	**3.3%**	**£26,761**	**3s 2d**
Sheffield	183,135	7,180	4.0%	£39,080	4s 4d
Birmingham	246,353	8,134	3.3%	£41,234	3s 4d
Manchester	148,794	4,845	3.3%	£33,604	4s 6d
Bristol	**57,479**	**3,549**	**6.2%**	**£21,702**	**7s 6d**

Table 3: Pauper numbers and costs of poor relief for a sample of metropolitan Poor Law Unions (1881 census).

Poor Law Unions based upon 1881 census returns.[119] This allows a comparison between Barton Regis and other Unions. A sample of this report is presented in Table 3.

The Barton Regis Poor Law Union is in the middle group in terms of the costs of maintaining paupers per head of population and has an average percentage of the population categorised as paupers; whereas the central wards of Bristol had one of the highest ratios of paupers and consequently the largest cost per head of population. Differences in the demographics of the poor and subsequent costs between Poor Law Unions would be the source of endless quarrels between rate-payers, politicians and neighbouring Boards of Guardians, as each accused the other of being 'soft on the paupers'. This objective and bureaucratic approach to management of Poor Law Unions, where cost was a paramount consideration, relegated the actual welfare of the paupers to a secondary concern; after all, making conditions in the workhouse too agreeable for the paupers would have been counter-productive.

The attention to cost-saving and financial detail is demonstrated by a meeting of the Barton Regis Board in September 1881. The Guardians discussed the yearly accounts and revealed with consternation that they had spent £113 on bread in a year compared with £75 at other workhouses. The anxious Guardians also noted that they gave children five pints of milk a week, compared with three pints at other institutions in the Bristol area. They

119 *Return of paupers (England)*, Parliamentary paper, June 16 1884.

also established that they used 26,650 hundred weights (1332 tonnes) of coal and coke, considerably more than other workhouses. Consequently "It was suggested it might be well to contract the size of open grates at backs and sides, while retaining the same size at the front" to enable less coal to be burnt.[120]

Demographics

So what do we know about the inmates of Eastville Workhouse in the 19th century? It is fortuitous that census data for the establishment are available and allow us to analyse a 'snapshot' of the residents. Taking the 1881 returns, which are helpfully documented online,[121] it is possible to study the gender, age, marital status, occupation, birthplace and disabilities of the 1,064 inmates.

Figure 12 shows the distribution by age[122] of the Eastville Workhouse inmates of 1881, of whom 56% were male. A majority (57%) of the workhouse residents were minors (<15 years) or elderly (>65 years), demonstrating the prevalence in the institution of vulnerable groups physically and mentally less able to sustain themselves in the outside world. In addition to and within these two groups lay a series of further categories relating to physical and mental disability. These were the so-called 'lunatics', 'imbeciles' and 'idiots' who made up 15% of the workhouse population according to the 1881 census.[123]

A more detailed breakdown of inmates by age and gender is shown in Figure 13. Of particular note are the large proportion of male children (<10 years) and male seniors (60-70 years). Despite the majority of inmates being male (56%), females dominate in the child bearing age range of 20-40 years suggesting that many mothers with children were present. This is supported by the fact that 77 boys and 45 girls under the age of 16 are listed as being sons or daughters of inmates in the 1881 census. The remaining majority of 217 inmates under the age of 16 are listed without this reference and thus assumed to be deserted by their parents or orphaned.

This set of statistics beg the question; if the aim of the New Poor Law was to consciously make the workhouse experience as harsh as possible in order to

120 *Bristol Mercury* September 17 1881.
121 See Higginbotham, P. *The Workhouse* http://www.workhouses.org.uk/Clifton/Clifton1881.shtml#Inmates accessed 2015.
122 The age divisions in the figure are based upon those defined in the *Consolidated General Order* (1847) Art. 98 e.g. adults as being of 15 years or over. The definition of seniors (aged adults) as being 65 years of age or older is included to provide an estimate of infirm adults. In practice in the workhouse adults would become infirm when they were unable to work.
123 Victorian and more modern definitions of these groups are given in Table 5.

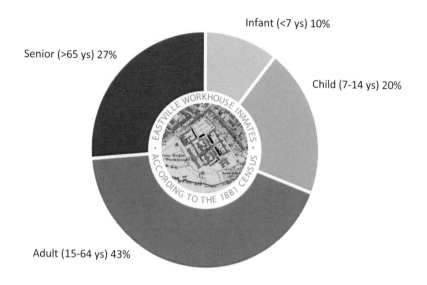

Infant (<7 ys) 10%

Senior (>65 ys) 27%

Child (7-14 ys) 20%

Adult (15-64 ys) 43%

Figure 12: Ages of Eastville Workhouse inmates (1881 census).

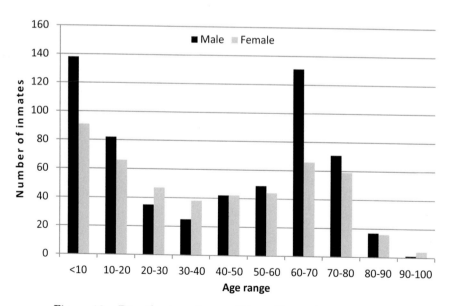

Figure 13: Distribution of ages of Eastville Workhouse inmates
(1881 census).

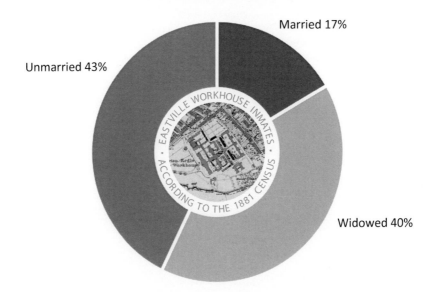

Married 17%

Unmarried 43%

Widowed 40%

Figure 14: Marital status of Eastville Workhouse inmates >14 years of age (1881 census).

force the poor into productive work, what about those groups who were not able to be fully productive in the 'outside world'? It seems that in the 1880s most of those in the institution were classified in these semi- or unproductive groups. Of these, only the young were likely to escape the punitive regime after reaching adulthood, though probably spending much of their childhood in the institution. For most of the remainder the workhouse was doubtless a life sentence, with the only reprieve being the county asylum or the burial ground.

Figure 14 shows the marital status of the 738 Eastville Workhouse inmates who were over 14 years of age[124] according to the 1881 census. The large number of widowed inmates (297), of which about a third were under 65 years of age is a reflection of the high mortality rate amongst the Bristol poor but it may also represent the financial impact of losing a partner, especially if there were children in the family. This burden would normally be assumed to fall more heavily upon women. This is supported by the statistics which show

124 Until the Age of Marriage Act of 1929 (which increased it to 16 years), marriageable age was covered by Common and Canon law which stated that a person who had attained the legal age of puberty could contract a valid marriage. The legal age of puberty was fourteen years for males and twelve years for females. However it was unusual for marriages to be undertaken at these ages, so for sake of simplicity 14 years has been chosen as a threshold in this analysis.

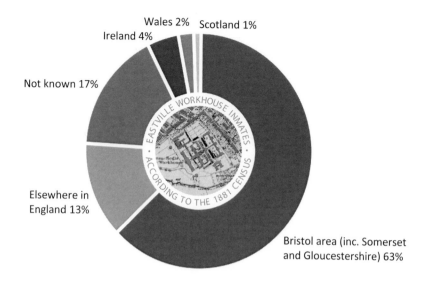

Wales 2%   Scotland 1%

Ireland 4%

Not known 17%

Elsewhere in
England 13%

Bristol area (inc. Somerset
and Gloucestershire) 63%

**Figure 15:   Birthplace of Eastville Workhouse inmates
(1881 census).**

that a significant majority (61%) of the widowed under the age of 65 in the
workhouse were female.

In addition, the large number of adults (>14 years of age) who were
unmarried (314) is interesting. Of these 84% were of 21 years or greater,
thereby discounting the potential effect of a large proportion of unmarried
teenagers. In fact, overall marriage rates were falling in the latter part of the
19th century, only beginning to rise again in the 1930s.[125] So these figures are
not that surprising especially amongst the urban poor whose severe economic
instability would have made home-making and marriage difficult. Of course,
for many in the 'respectable' classes of the Victorian period this would have
been typically interpreted as another sign of the 'moral degeneracy' of the poor.

Figure 15 gives a breakdown of the birthplace of inmates in Eastville
Workhouse. As might be expected nearly two-thirds of those recorded in the
1881 census are from the city of Bristol or the surrounding counties of Somerset
and Gloucestershire. There are small, but significant groups of Scottish, Welsh

125 Wilson, B. and Smallwood S., *Understanding recent trends in marriage* (Family Demography
Unit, Office for National Statistics, 2007). This is also borne out by statistics for Bristol which
show the number of marriages falling between 1877 and 1897 despite an 18% increase in the
population over the same period. BCRL *Bristol Medical Officer of Health Annual Reports 1898-
1901* p. 89.

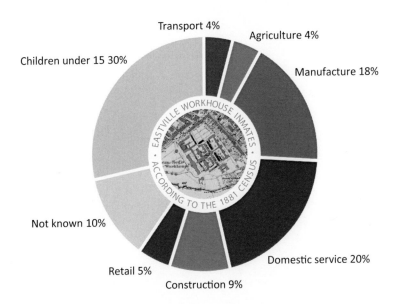

Figure 16: Occupations of Eastville Workhouse inmates (1881 census).

and particularly Irish born inmates and a larger group from locations scattered across England. The 17% labelled as 'not known' are mostly less than 14 years of age, suggesting that they were orphans, or marked as 'lunatics', 'imbeciles' and 'idiots'. There are surprisingly very few inmates born in mainland Europe or further afield, with two from Germany, one from the Netherlands and another from Malta. It is clear that this was, in general, an institution made up of people from Bristol or its immediate environs.

Figure 16 gives categories of occupations of the 1881 inmates and Table 4 gives examples of the various occupations within these categories. Despite the category of 'not known' there are very few inmates with no specified occupation. The majority of the 'not knowns' are listed as 'lunatics', 'imbeciles' or 'idiots'. The three dominant categories in order of importance; domestic service, manufacture and construction, making up nearly half the sample and the majority of the working age occupations, give us a clear indication of the trends in the Victorian economy, at least as far as the working classes were concerned. When the New Poor Law was introduced in the 1830s, we might have expected the most numerous workhouse occupants to be farm labourers who were being driven into desperate poverty by under-employment due to the increasing mechanization of agriculture. By the 1880s, agricultural workers only make up 4% of the sample, showing that the process of displacement

Occupational category	Examples of occupations
Transport	Boatman, Bargeman, Cabman, Engine driver, Haulier, Quay Labourer, Seaman, Warehouseman, Waterman
Agriculture	Labourer, Cattle drover, Farm servant, Fisherman, Market Gardener, Stableman
Manufacture	Blacksmith, Boilermaker, Bootmaker, Brass maker, Brick maker, Candlemaker, Chemical worker, Clockmaker, Coachmaker, Cooper, Cordwainer, Cotton weaver, Currier, Cutler, Dressmaker, Engine fitter, Flax spinner, Gas fitter, Hatter, Iron worker, Lacemaker, Oil factory worker, Machinist, Miner, Nailmaker, Penmaker, Pipemaker, Printer, Potter, Ropemaker, Sawyer, Seamstress, Shipwright, Shoemaker, Stay maker, Tailor, Tinman, Watchmaker, Wheelwright
Domestic Service	Charwoman, Coachman, Cook, Gardener, Groom, Housekeeper, Ironer, Laundress, Nurse, Servant, Needlewoman, Ostler, Washerwoman
Construction	Bricklayer, Carpenter, Labourer, Mason, Navvy, Painter, Plasterer, Wellsinker
Retail	Baker, Butcher, Confectioner, Fish hawker, Fishmonger, Grocer, Hawker, Publican

Table 4: Examples of occupations within Figure 16 categories.

of rural proletarians to urban manufacturing, domestic service and through 'assisted emigration' to countries such as Canada and Australasia was well advanced.

It is of interest that by the 1880s the most precarious workers as far as incarceration in the workhouse was concerned were those engaged in domestic service, the majority of whom were female. This was due to a number of reasons. Typically domestic servants were 'in-house', that is, they were accommodated in their employers residence. In some senses this was a benefit whilst they were in work, as they did not have to find and sustain rented accommodation elsewhere. However, if they became pregnant, sick or elderly then they would be 'released' by their employers. This often left them destitute, homeless and could lead them directly or indirectly to the workhouse.

Finally, there is one aspect of the statistics which does scotch some mythology about the workhouse. Victorian novels sometimes allude to the once respectable upper or middle-class person who has fallen on hard-times because of dastardly plots, bad fortune or merely that they are heart-broken. As a result they have taken to drink and ended up on the tramp or in the workhouse. These (horror?) stories usually rely on the fear of the 'other', in this case the paupers, in order to provide entertainment for the well-to-do reader. However, a detailed search of the occupations of those in the Eastville Workhouse in 1881 yields few occupations from the Victorian elite or the middle-class. The best we can do is a Commission Agent (basically a salesman), a Tea Dealer Master, a Teacher and a Publican; hardly the fallen Lords and Ladies of the novels. The workhouse was clearly the province of the precarious sections of the working classes.

Expansion, the welfare state and demolition

After the expansion of Eastville Workhouse to take 1180 inmates in 1858 a number of further extensions were reluctantly approved by the Board of Guardians, usually because of persistent pressure from central government. These included the addition of:

- two dedicated 'lunatic' wards in 1867
- a fever hospital and stone-breaking yards in 1868
- a 'casual' ward for tramps in 1873
- an infirmary providing lying-in provision for the sick in 1880
- five wooden pavilion sick wards in 1886
- a four bedroomed house for the Master and Matron in 1892[126]

By the mid-1880s the capacity of the Workhouse had increased to almost 1400 persons (excluding the casual wards). In the late 1890s this was limited by the Local Government Board to 1161 people in the workhouse itself and 216 in the infirmary.[127]

On 14th March 1877 the Clifton Poor Law Union was renamed Barton Regis, and despite years of resistance to a merger by the Guardians, it was eventually absorbed into a single Bristol Poor Law Union. This occurred in two phases; the first by Act of Parliament in 1898 saw the Corporation of the Poor absorb major parts of the Barton Regis, Bedminster and Keynsham Poor Law Unions. Eastville Workhouse thus came under the control of the new single city Union. As a result, the much diminished Barton Regis Union was forced to

126 Higginbotham, P. *The Workhouse* http://www.workhouses.org.uk/Clifton/ accessed 2015 and TNA Refs. MH 12/4013, MH 12/4037.
127 *Barton Regis Poor Law Union – Statements of Accounts 1881-1889* BRO Ref. 22936/130 and *Barton Regis Poor Law Union Annual Book 1897* BRO Ref. 10900.

construct a new workhouse at Southmead.[128] In 1904 the Barton Regis Union was abolished and its remaining parishes distributed between the Bristol City and Chipping Sodbury Poor Law Unions. The new Southmead Workhouse was passed over to the former.[129]

The Local Government Act of 1929 abolished Poor Law Unions and passed their responsibilities over to Local Authorities who were encouraged to convert workhouses into infirmaries. Consequently, in the 1930s Eastville Workhouse became a home for the aged. In 1948 the National Health Service was formed and the National Assistance Act implemented which finally abolished the Poor Law system and created the modern welfare state. These policy changes led to extensive changes to the interior of the Eastville institution with the aim of improving conditions for its elderly and infirm residents.[130] The old people's home at '100 Fishponds Rd' (as it had been renamed)[131] was progressively wound down through the 1960s and in 1972 the workhouse buildings were demolished to make way for the development of the East Park housing estate (see Figure 18).

The demolition of the huge complex of buildings that made up Eastville Workhouse was systematic and almost comprehensive. Significant parts of the landscape were remodelled for a new system of roads within the estate making it difficult to imagine the original layout.

The only physical legacies of the original workhouse that remains are some of the walls surrounding the site, notably on Fishponds Rd (see Figure 19). As shown in Figure 20, the main gateway pillars situated on Fishponds Rd are still intact, including the iconic '100' nameplates. The walls and entrance features are listed with Historic England and thus are likely to survive for some years at least.[132]

The site of the workhouse burial ground is completely unmarked and now forms part of Rosemary Green.

---

128 Several major buildings of the original Southmead Workhouse are still intact. They are now named Beaufort House and make up part of Southmead Hospital. They can be viewed from Southmead Way, the original entrance and road to the workhouse, just off Southmead Rd, Bristol, BS10 5LZ.

129 BRO *The Poor Law in Bristol* p. 1 and Higginbotham, P. *The Workhouse* http://www.workhouses.org.uk/Bristol/ accessed 2015.

130 Visual details of these improvements are given in BRO Ref. 40945/1.

131 One correspondent (formerly a registrar of births, deaths and marriages) claimed that around 1912 "all Boards of Guardians were instructed to give an alternative name to Poor Law Institutions under their care...to avoid stigma when births or deaths were registered that had taken place in such buildings" *Western Daily Press* 14 July 1948.

132 The listing can be viewed at http://list.historicengland.org.uk/resultsingle.aspx?uid=1202221.

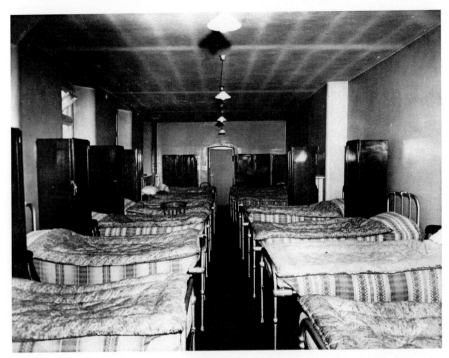

Figure 17: Typical dormitory in 100 Fishponds Rd prior to the 'welfare state' improvements (c. 1948).

Figure 18: Demolition of Eastville Workhouse in March 1972.

Figure 19: The surviving perimeter wall of the Eastville Workhouse on Fishponds Rd (c. 2015).

Figure 20: Surviving main entrance to Eastville Workhouse at 100 Fishponds Rd (c. 2016).

3. Life in Eastville Workhouse

The… workhouse system was less interested in alleviating suffering then in promoting behavioural change… Poverty is seen as a badge of moral turpitude. The task of the workhouse was to rehabilitate the afflicted by further afflicting them… making poverty so unendurable its victims would embrace the virtues of the saved: industry, selflessness and personal discipline.[133]

This chapter considers the conditions that forced people into the workhouse, and the experience of everyday life in the Eastville institution at 100 Fishponds Rd in the Victorian period.

Entering the Workhouse

In its majestic equality, the law forbids rich and poor alike to sleep under bridges, beg in the streets and steal loaves of bread.[134]

Higginbotham notes that entry into the Victorian workhouse was, on the face of it, a voluntary process:

People were not 'thrown' or 'sent' into the workhouse, rather they resigned themselves to it, albeit often as a last resort when all other options had been exhausted.[135]

However, unlike feudal and pre-feudal societies, coercion by economic circumstance was and remains the dominant power-relation of the capitalist social order. There are no laws that state you cannot own a skyscraper or live off the wealth created by those you employ. Neither was there any legislation in the Victorian period that directly forced the poor into the workhouse. Taking this blinkered legal perspective allowed commentators, both then and now, to claim they lived in a 'free society'. However, as is fairly obvious, those living in capitalist societies cannot really exercise power over their everyday lives and futures unless they have access to significant amounts of land, property and/or capital. Without these assets, you have to sell your own labour or be dependent on others that do. Consequently you are subject to the power of employers and economic forces far beyond your immediate control. It was these *non-legal* forces

133 Kelly J. *The Graves Are Walking: The History of the Great Irish Famine* (London: Faber & Faber, 2013).
134 Quoted from the French novelist Anatole France in his novel *The Red Lily* (1894).
135 Higginbotham, P. *The Workhouse Cookbook* p. 41.

that drove millions of British subjects faced with destitution, homelessness and even starvation, into the workhouse during the Victorian period.

The usual process for entering a workhouse involved a meeting with a relieving officer from the local Poor Law Union. This officer decided whether the applicant or family were to be given outdoor relief (a small 'dole' payment in money or food) or whether they would be offered indoor relief - the workhouse. Those families who were denied out-relief, or who could not survive on the pitiful payments, were often faced with desperate circumstances such as going freezing or hungry or being evicted from their homes. The following extracts from letters sent to the Poor Law Board (PLB) in London provide some glimpses of the coercive forces that drove people through the gates of Eastville Workhouse.

The first is an appeal to the PLB from Ann Daniel, the wife of a miner who lived in St George (probably written on her behalf due to illiteracy). The letter explains her economic circumstances and the contradiction of being told to 'support herself' by the Clifton Union relieving officers:

Feb 25 1856

Most Worthy gentlemen of the Board...your humble petitioner is by name Ann Daniel Wife of Thomas Daniel. Now left widow with two small children and that the said Thomas Daniel was by occupation a colier but ten weeks last Friday him and another had an accident at the pit which killed one dead but the said Thomas Daniel was taken to the Infirmary and died a month to the day he was taken in and more I am left with 2 children like 2 babeys one 3 years and the other 2 years old and being but little for me to do not enough to get my own living I was compelled to ply for relief and from the time of his death up till last Monday they allowed me 2s and one loaf of bread but last Monday they took of 1s and says they cant allow me but 1s and a loaf and I must support myself and the others While at the same time if I goes out to get anything I am obliged to pay 6d per day to have my children looked to for the day and oftentimes I don't get 6d Therefore gentlemen how am I to support myself and one child and not only that but a shilling and a loaf is not enough for the one child...it is not enough for house rent and fuel I am willing to try my best to live but I cannot do anything with that as there is nothing to be done to get a living...[136]

The following correspondence to the PLB was from an elderly couple from Hotwells looking after their granddaughter:

136 TNA Ref. MH 12/4007.

February 29th 1862

Gentlemen,

Please excuse the liberty of me sending to you but me and my wife is both greatly afflicted and alone 60 years of age and I want to ask you Gentlemen if you will be kind enough to intercede in my case and try to get us a little allowance out of the union. We have had a little pay for about 12 months and i have been in the [work]house. But the pay is stopped on account of a child, a grandchild of ours that we have had since she was 1 month old and now she is 9 years nearly we took the child to dry nurse it and now we have her but we should not like to part with her in our old years for she is the only comfort we have if you will be kind enough to look into our case I should be very thankful for your kindness to allow us a little out of the house for we are both destitute since the pay has been stopped and have nothing...[137]

And from a hungry elderly man from Kingswood Hill in the parish of St George:

July 11th 1862

Gentlemen,

I am sorry to have to lay my case before you. I am an old man, now of 76 years of age and through old age and infirmity I am unable to do any work. I have made application to the Board of Guardians for relief and they have allowed me 2s shillings per week to support me, out of that I have to pay 1s per week for my lodging and then I have 1s per week to live on after. Gentlemen I have no wife nor any friends. If you could allow me any more I shold feel obliged to you as I am now wanting the necessaries of life. Gentlemen I should have said that I have applied for more relicf repeatedly; and the officers have refused relief to me. I dont desire to burden you with my tale of woe; but often times I have to lay down at night and rise in the morning without anything to eat. If you could relief me a little (that would be a great deal to me). I should feel much obliged to you.[138]

137 TNA Ref. MH 12/4010.
138 TNA Ref. MH 12/4010.

The following report by two Medical Officers from the Clifton Union in 1867 concerned the case of William Fox, a ten year old boy with congenital physical and mental disabilities:

It appears that the idiot was some time ago at the Bristol Borough Asylum from whence he was transferred to the Clifton Workhouse, and from there he was removed by his mother who alleged that he had been illtreated. Being in very poor circumstances she applied to the Guardians for outdoor relief, but in consequence of reports they received of the miserable condition in which the idiot was kept, they refused to grant it unless the boy was sent back to the workhouse. This the mother has hitherto refused to accede to...

The Medical Officers visited the child and his mother in a "miserable court in one of the lowest quarters of the town" and described the conditions they were living in:

The house consists of two rooms and is in a state of indescribable dirt and dilapidation. Except one chair without a bottom, and a block for chopping wood, it does not contain a single article of furniture. Mrs Fox who seemed to fear that we had come to take away her child, refused to let us see him, but we followed her up the stairs to the upper room and there found the poor boy rolled up amongst some filthy, nearly black rags...The mother obtains a precarious living by chopping old wood for firing, her weekly earnings rarely exceeding 3/- [3s] and its seems wonderful how she can possibly live on this sum...[139]

The next communication is from the Clerk of Eastville Workhouse to the PLB describing the circumstances of the Cordy family also from St George:

10th October 1870

I beg to inform you the following case has just occurred. James Cordy is a labourer residing in the parish of St. George in this Union, he has a wife & 8 children all under 16 years of age, the man is in regular employ earning 13/- [13s] per week, the wife earns nothing. They have rent of 2/- [2s] per week to pay. The man is able-bodied with the

139 TNA Ref. MH 12/4013 24 June 1867.

exception that he is ruptured [Hernia] and has to wear a Truss. Fever has attacked the family who are in a dreadfully destitute state…They were brought to the Workhouse almost naked having only a few rags & those extremely filthy about them.[140]

Finally, this letter is from a single-parent living in Easton, Charles Vale, who was laid off by his employer four months previously:

Dec 4th 1874

To the Poor Law Board

Gentlemen,

I am being a deaf and dumb man aged 43 masons labourer and my wife died last Feb. and left me one little daughter. I have taken the liberty to address this note to you, Gentlemen, & ask you for to give me every assistance in my behalf, if you, Gentlemen, will kindly inquire with the Clifton Union Guardians for me about getting to relieve me out instead of a Workhouse Order, Sir, Gentlemen, I have applied the Guardians three times until again last Friday for relief but they have refused to assist me and ordered me for a Workhouse, then I would not go, because I don't like to break up my home for my poor daughter's sake. I have not got a friend in the world to help me. I am so tired of the Workhouse but rather work to get my own bread honestly…[141]

These letters demonstrate the effects of unemployment, family bereavement, disability, epidemics, child-care and old-age on the ability to earn money through waged work. The pleas to the Poor Law Board for granting or increasing the pitiful outdoor relief were in all these cases ignored. As these applicants had no wealth, land or property to fall back on, the workhouse or vagrancy were the only options open to them. For the aged, sick, disabled, pregnant or those with young children, the former was often the only realistic choice. Having accepted indoor relief, an applicant would be given an admission order by the relieving officer and would then, with their family, make their way to the workhouse.

140 TNA Ref. MH 12/4015.
141 Vale provided an accompanying letter from his recent employer substantiating his claims. TNA Ref. MH 12/4018.

Admission

On admission to Eastville Workhouse, through the main gate at 100 Fishponds Rd (see Figure 20) guarded by a porter, paupers would 'make the long walk' through the grounds to the main building to enter the receiving wards on the ground floor. Here they were separated into male and female sections and were assessed by a relieving officer who recorded their personal details in an admissions register. At this point they were searched for prohibited items (such as alcohol), stripped and their own clothing and possessions taken from them. Children had their hair cut, and all entrants were bathed and given a workhouse uniform.

The uniform performed several functions. Sometimes entrants to the workhouse were literally in rags or without shoes, or carrying parasites in their clothing such as lice or fleas; so providing clean clothes was a medical necessity. The uniform also designated the difference between workhouse staff and inmates, as well as allowing for categorisation of different classes of paupers within the institution. In some cases this categorisation was not just based on gender or age, as Higginbotham explains:

> At Bristol, in the 1830s, for example, prostitutes wore a yellow dress, and unmarried pregnant women a red one.[142]

By the 1840s this practice was frowned upon by the Poor Law authorities in London and it is unclear if such practices were carried out in Eastville Workhouse, though they did continue in some Poor Law Unions. The last function of the uniform was prohibitive. Inmates could, on giving three hours' notice and having gained permission from the Master, obtain their clothes and discharge themselves from the workhouse. However, if they left the institution without permission in the workhouse uniform they would be charged with theft which could lead to a prison sentence with hard labour.

After being kitted out, the new inmates were examined by the workhouse Medical Officer and divided into the following groups:

Class 1. Men infirm through age or any other cause.
Class 2. Able-bodied men, and youths above the age of fifteen years.
Class 3. Boys above the age of seven years and under that of fifteen.
Class 4. Women infirm through age or any other cause.
Class 5. Able-bodied women, and girls above the age of fifteen years.

142 Higginbotham, P. *The Workhouse* http://www.workhouses.org.uk/life/uniform.shtml accessed May 2016.

Class 6. Girls above the age of seven years and under that of fifteen.

Class 7. Children under seven years of age.[143]

Once assigned a classification, the paupers were sent off to the designated ward and airing yard where they were to remain "without communication with those of any other class". The strict gender division, as we have seen in Chapter 2, was physically enforced by the bifurcated design of workhouses in the period. Eastville Workhouse was no exception, with a high wall running through the centre of the institution, splitting it into male and female compounds. This division was primarily driven by the religious and social mores of the Victorian elite. It also served explicitly to prohibit heterosexual activity between inmates predicated on the dominant idea amongst this elite that 'the poor reproduced the poor'.

Interestingly, it appears some inmates developed a method of overcoming this enforced separation by exploiting a loophole in the admissions procedure. In a letter to the Poor Law Board in 1869 the Clifton Guardians stated:

> ...some of the able-bodied paupers in the [Eastville] Workhouse are in the habit of taking their discharge and returning to the [work]house again the same day. This in some cases happens four or five times a week; the male and female paupers go out the same day, it is believed they go out for immoral purposes.[144]

Work and the working day

Unpaid manual labour of various forms was central to the workhouse experience, not only to operate the institution and help offset its costs for the rate-payers but also to supposedly 'reform' the paupers, whether adults or children. In the Eastville institution (as with all workhouses) the obligatory work included domestic labour[145] (undertaken mainly by women and girls) such as laundry, cooking and cleaning as well as sewing, spinning and net-making. Men also undertook tasks for maintaining the institution such as painting, carpentry, shoemaking, tailoring, mat making and wood chopping. Eastville

143 *Consolidated General Order* (1847) Art. 98.

144 The Guardians proposed to the PLB that the workhouse Master should be able to detain these miscreants. TNA Ref. MH 12/4014 1 October 1869.

145 And, reader, if you think domestic work was easier than other forms of labour then I would suggest you read the following account: Higgs, M. *Glimpses into the Abyss* (London: P.S. King & Son, 1906) which can be downloaded for free here: http://www.gutenberg.org/ebooks/40122.

Figure 21: Front of Eastville Workhouse showing horticultural gardens by Samuel Loxton (1857-1922).

Workhouse also developed horticultural gardens for growing vegetables in the grounds which were cultivated by inmates (see Figure 21).[146]

One task in which both sexes and all age groups were engaged was oakum picking. This dirty and painful work involved teasing out fibres from old hemp ropes; the resulting threads were then sold to the navy or shipbuilders, mixed with tar and used to seal the lining of wooden ships.[147] The hardest physical work was stone breaking; literally hammering large rocks into chippings for road building (see Figure 22). Men who resided in the workhouse had to break 30 cwt (approximately 1.5 metric tonnes) a day.[148] On the Eastville Workhouse site the stone breaking yards were situated close to the main entrance on Fishponds Rd (the site of the old Eastville Health Centre, see Figure 6).

From spring to autumn the working day, standardised by the Poor Law Board, lasted ten hours (7-12 am and 1-6 pm) and over the autumn and winter nine hours (8-12 am and 1-6 pm). This labour was carried out six days a week throughout the year, with the only 'holidays' being Good Friday and Christmas Day.[149] There was no 'retirement' from this labour due to age; the elderly were literally worked until they became infirm and could work no more.

146 *Clifton Poor Law Union Statement of Accounts, 1874* BCRL Ref. PR2 Pamphlet Box: Societies IV B2401 p. 42.
147 This is probably the origin of the expression 'money for old rope'.
148 *Bristol Mercury* 24 February 1883.
149 *Clifton Poor Law Union Statement of Accounts, 1874* BCRL Ref. PR2 Pamphlet Box: Societies IV B2401 p. 32 and Higginbotham, P. *The Workhouse Cookbook* p. 43.

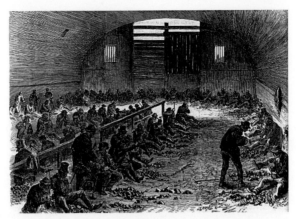

Figure 22: A typical stone breaking yard.

One particular case in Eastville Workhouse in 1860 clearly demonstrates this state of affairs. A ninety-year-old inmate was brought before the Clifton Board of Guardians complaining that the Master of the workhouse had tried to force him to labour in the market gardens. After declining to work for a week, the Master: "seeing that the pauper's refusal to work was having a bad influence on the rest of the inmates, employed two men to carry him into the garden, but when taken there he refused to do anything." The unnamed elderly man claimed that the Master had declared that he would starve him and another eighty-year-old inmate into obedience despite what the Guardians or anyone else thought (or words to that effect). One of the Guardians objected, saying he: "thought it was time an old man as the pauper should leave off swearing. The pauper replied that it was enough to make any man swear". The Guardians of course came down in support of the Master of Eastville Workhouse but suggested that perhaps he should not order ninety-year-old men to work.[150]

Diet and economics

As we have seen the governing philosophy of the New Poor Law aimed at making daily life in the workhouse worse than the experience of poverty outside its walls. This also applied to the food and drink given to the institutions inmates. In 1835 the Poor Law Commissioners stated categorically that the workhouse diet should not be "superior or equal to the ordinary mode of subsistence of the labouring classes of the neighbourhood".[151] Within this

150 *Western Daily Press* 17 November 1860.
151 Higginbotham, P. *The Workhouse Cookbook* p. 51.

statement lies an apparent contradiction if we assume the primary objective of the workhouse was to engage labour in order to produce commodities for sale.

As any slave-master knows, you need to feed and house your labourers adequately; else they are weak and produce less or prone to sickness and thus often unfit for productive work. In profit terms it is better for slave-masters to concentrate on the rate of production of their chosen commodity rather than costs of food or housing for the upkeep of slaves. In any case, slave-masters own their slaves as property and thus have a direct interest in their physical well-being. So slaves get housed, fed and watered. In contrast, for the bourgeois factory owner, there is no need to worry about these costs as through the wage-relation they are the responsibility of the proletarian. If the worker loses productivity because of illness or bad health due to malnutrition or bad housing conditions, then the factory owner just fires them and hires a fitter specimen. More important than the fixed costs (factory, heating, materials) is to keep the variable cost (the wage) down and concentrate on increasing productivity by whatever means possible.

The relation of Poor Law Guardians to the pauper inmate was somewhat different to either of these systems with labour being of lesser importance than the fixed costs of keeping a pauper in the workhouse. This was because pauper labour, although tough and menial, did not produce significant economic value and was often merely aimed at reproduction of the institution. For example, the available accounts for the Clifton/Barton Regis Poor Law Union from 1872-1889 show that the total income to the Eastville Workhouse from sales of commodities produced by the inmates ranged between a paltry 2% and 7% of the total cost of 'In-Maintenance', effectively the bill for running the institution.[152] In addition, many paupers were chronically unproductive (infirm, elderly, mentally ill or young children) and therefore produced costs rather than reducing them through labour. So, in the workhouse the drive to keep expenditure down was of far greater importance than, say, increasing rates of production of farm produce, picked oakum, mats, nets or aggregate for roads. The workhouse was not a plantation or a factory competing with other such entities for sales of commodities, its economy was more akin to a prison. The combination of punishment with the primary objective of keeping fixed costs at a minimum was to impact directly on the living conditions and the quantity, diversity and quality of the diet offered to paupers.

152 The actual figures per half-year were (Income/Cost); 1872 (£111/£3139), 1873 (£58/£3217), 1874 (£232/£3467), 1881 (£368/£5058), 1882 (£176/£5359), 1884 (£286/£4942) and 1889 (£262/£4371). *Clifton Poor Law Union - Statement of Accounts 1872-75* BRO Ref. 22936/129, *Barton Regis Poor Law Union – Statements of Accounts 1881-1889* BRO Ref. 22936/130.

From the very initiation of the new workhouse system pauper diets were strictly regulated. In 1835, the Poor Law Commissioners published six 'dietaries' which were aimed at dealing with regional variations in habit and accessible produce. The key components of these diets were bread and oats. In Eastville Workhouse throughout the Victorian period the evidence suggests that a slightly reduced version of Dietary Table No. 5 for able bodied paupers was in use.[153] Breakfast, at 7.30 am in winter and 6.30 am in summer (following prayers), generally consisted of a few slices of bread and a bowl of gruel, a weak and runny porridge made from oats and water. Dinner, the main meal of the day was at 12 noon. For able-bodied males (women received smaller portions in some cases) the unchanging routine was as follows:

¶ Monday and Thursday: 4oz (110g) of meat and 12oz (340g) of potatoes or 10oz (280g) of boiled rice.
¶ Tuesday and Friday: a bowl of split pea soup with a few slices of bread.
¶ Wednesday and Sunday: 14oz (400g) of suet pudding (with vegetable broth, gravy, treacle or 'sauce').
¶ Saturday: bread and 1½oz (40g) cheese.

Supper at 6pm consisted of bread and 1½oz (40g) of cheese three times a week and potatoes for the remainder. Other than a small ration of tea and butter for the elderly (over 60 years of age), infirm and imbeciles and milk for children, there were no 'luxuries' in this diet. Comparisons with recommended dietary intake for the modern era show that the typical workhouse diet of the mid-19th century for the able-bodied fell considerably below the minimum requirements for a healthy life. Crucially the energy intake is about 75% of that needed and there are clearly serious deficiencies in minerals and vitamins.[154] This diminutive diet also has to be put in context with hard-labour and sometimes freezing living conditions in the winter; it is no surprise that able-bodied workhouse inmates were far from 'healthy' and thus prone to disease

153 No. 5 Dietary Table is given in Higginbotham, P. *The Workhouse Cookbook* p. 55. The Eastville Workhouse diet cards for the 1870s are given in *Clifton Poor Law Union - Statement of Accounts 1872-75* BRO Ref. 22936/129 and they appear to be unchanged in 1897 for the able-bodied apart from a tiny ration of butter (1/2 oz.) on Sundays for breakfast. *Barton Regis Poor Law Union Annual Book 1897* BRO Ref. 10900.
154 Higginbotham, P. *The Workhouse Cookbook* p. 56-7. It is useful to note for comparative purposes that rations during World War II were (with the exception of cheese) larger, more nutritious and far more varied than workhouse diets, including milk, eggs, butter, tea, lard, preserves, sweets, sugar and margarine. Fruit, vegetables and bread were not rationed though obviously certain items were in short supply. See https://en.wikipedia.org/wiki/Rationing_in_the_United_Kingdom#World_War_II.

and infection. It was often pointed out by critics of the New Poor Law that workhouse diets were of lesser quantity and lower quality than Victorian prison diets, lending more weight to the perception that paupers were being 'punished' for being poor.[155]

Paupers were not silent about deficiencies in the diet; in a letter to the Poor Law Board (PLB) in London a group of men working in the stone yard complained about their food and conditions:

October 5th 1868

To the right honourable the Earl of Devon.

My Lord,

I have to write to your board on the behalf of the able-bodied men in Clifton Union who are working in the stone yard (I myself being one). We at present during this coming winter have no fire to warm ourselves by and are compelled to drink cold water with our bread & cheese at supper. We considering this proceeding most cruel, have written to you asking you kindly to grant us an allowance of gruel, broth, or tea according to what you think will be most fit and I am sure we able-bodied men will join with thanks to you. Some of us are not fit to work in the stone yard, one has piles and is suffering from weakness, [others] troubled with rheumatics in their limbs. The doctor is very negligent. I was in the sick ward for three weeks and after I got roused....I was sent down to the stone yard the first morning. The doctor kept me on No.1 House diet all the time and treats the others very carelessly. Hoping you will see into this and make it right for the stonebreakers of Clifton Union Workhouse.

My Lord, your very humble servants the undersigned,

Charles Edkins, John Wills, Charles Pugsley, Edward Gill.

The Clifton Guardians responded to the PLB by denying any increase in the diet and dodging the question of the freezing conditions in the stone yards.[156]

155 Hurren, E. T. *Protesting About Pauperism* p. 66.
156 TNA Ref. MH 12/4013 10 October & 28 October 1868. Four months after the request was denied by the Guardians one of the signatories, Charles Pugsley, was amongst a group of men involved in a disturbance at Eastville Workhouse. Pugsley received an eight month prison sentence for assaulting the Master of the workhouse. See page 124.

The issued dietary tables were only the 'official' recommendation, in practice these meagre diets could be tampered with by a number of semi-legal and illegal means. There were a number of scandals in workhouses during the Victorian period where diets were reduced by overseers through theft or corruption. Adulteration of food was common in Britain before the 1880s and it was usually the poor who suffered most from its effects. As the workhouse tenders generally went to the cheapest suppliers, the inmates of these institutions were very vulnerable to such practices. The scale of the problem was exposed by an investigation by the medical journal *The Lancet* in the 1850s which demonstrated that all forty-nine random samples of workhouse bread they analysed had been adulterated.[157] There is some evidence of the adulteration of food supplied to Eastville Workhouse which is discussed amongst the Guardians. This included the common practice of watering down milk and the supply of 'bad potatoes'.[158]

Even when suppliers appeared to be being paid at reasonable rates, this did not necessarily mean the quality of food was better; it could just be a sign of corruption. In a comparison between costs of workhouses in the Bristol and Barton Regis Poor Law Unions in 1881 one Guardian:

> referred to the various articles of food consumed in both Unions, and quoted prices to show that in nearly every case a higher price was given at Barton Regis than at Bristol.[159]

This curious discrepancy could be down to inadequate or adulterated food being supplied to the Bristol Union workhouse or alternatively financial corruption such as price-fixing or nepotism by the Barton Regis Union Board of Guardians. It could also signal that the plundering of workhouse food-stocks by officials, which it was claimed was rife in these institutions in the period, was being covered up.

Official changes to the workhouse diet, or suspicion amongst inmates of 'short diets' could cause serious unrest. This is no surprise, as with soldiers, sailors and prisoners in general, where a disciplinarian regime and hard labour is interspersed with long periods of boredom, food becomes central to daily-life. When it is reduced or tampered with there is understandably a vociferous response which is usually a reaction to the overall conditions rather than just a food protest. In the Stapleton Workhouse in April 1857, the Bristol Poor Law Guardians attempted to reduce and revise the existing diet to be in line with

157 Higginbotham, P. *The Workhouse Cookbook* p. 86.
158 Western Daily Press 17 August 1877 and TNA Ref. MH 12/4037 15 January 1892.
159 *Western Daily Press* 17 September 1881.

nearby Unions (such as Clifton) in order to satisfy the Poor Law Commissioners and, of course, to save money:

> One of the alterations effected has been a substitution for the provisions heretofore served out for dinner on Sundays, of a pound of boiled rice sweetened with sugar. This change would appear to have given great umbrage to some of the female paupers. On the meal being served out they expressed great dissatisfaction, numbers of them refusing to partake of it. In the afternoon, when in chapel, they commenced a great uproar, and interrupted the service by observing they wanted some food to put in their bellies: and subsequently their dissatisfaction took a more decided form, and they not only assumed a menacing attitude towards the officers, but smashed in a number of the windows….some twenty of the malcontents were arrested and conveyed before the district magistrate… who committed nine of the principal offenders to the House of Correction.[160]

The lack of variety and minimal quantity of food for workhouse inmates also led to an internal 'black-market'. Bread was often traded for tobacco and overseers attempted to clamp down on the practice of saving and hiding food with searches and confiscations. Covert resistance to the privations of the workhouse sometimes extended to passing food and other items from the workhouse to those on the outside. In 1846, Jane Weaver and Elizabeth Hobbs, an inmate of the Pennywell Rd workhouse with two 'illegitimate' children, were charged:

> the latter with stealing, and the former with receiving, a quantity of meat, potatoes, and bread, the property of the Guardians of the Clifton Union [and] part of the rations served out to the paupers…Mr Simmonds, who lives opposite the workhouse, stated that he saw four bundles thrown over the wall, and Weaver, who was waiting on the outside, picked them up.

According to the workhouse master "it had become a *regular system* for the paupers to get rid of their food in the way described" and that "bed clothes and other things were given away in the same manner". He also alluded to a practice whereby "one party got into the [work] house and supported the rest out of it".[161] Whether such systems for supporting families outside the institution by

160 *Bristol Mercury* 4 April 1857.
161 *Bristol Mercury* 4 July 1846. Our emphasis.

collaboration with inmates on the inside were widespread is unclear, but this fascinating piece of evidence suggests that similar covert practices would have been present in Eastville Workhouse which opened a year after this incident.

The sparing and monotonous diets created by the Poor Law Commissioners in the 1830s remained, despite local variations, pretty much in place until the latter part of the 19th century. However, pressure from reformers and Poor Law Union medical officers, particularly concerning children's diets allied with cheaper imports from the USA and Australia helped increase the quantity and quality of food at the pauper table. Some of these effects are noticeable in dietary tables for Eastville Workhouse published in 1897 which show small concessions to the aged, infirm and 'imbeciles' such as rations of cake on Sunday and Thursday and bacon on Fridays.[162] The meagre children's diets were supplemented by small rations of jam, cake, cocoa and fruit pudding once or twice a week. However, these minor improvements did not extend to the able-bodied whose fare remained as bleak and under nourishing as it had been earlier in the century.

Tramps, 'mouchers' and 'spikes'

[Tramps and Beggars] take care you don't go to Clifton, or else…you will be sure to find yourself 'safe in the arms of a policeman'; and, through his affectionate care of you, you will be right royally lodged, fed, and cared for with the most tender solicitude for a week or two, in a beautiful castellated mansion, by the most gentle of officials, and not even at your own expense.[163]

Going 'on the tramp' to find work was customary practice in the 18th and 19th Centuries particularly for apprentice or 'journeymen' artisans; in fact early Trade Unions often helped their members find employment in this way. However, the burgeoning industrial revolution spatially concentrated labour in manufacturing centres and progressively displaced rural workers. These pressures, allied with cyclical economic slumps, substantially increased the number of proletarians on the move. As Chesney explains:

162 Elderly males (over 62 years old) and imbeciles were allowed, at the discretion of the workhouse Master, a tobacco ration of 1oz. (28g) per week. Elderly women were offered ¼oz. (7g) of snuff. Tobacco and snuff rations for the able-bodied were only to be distributed to pauper inmates whom the Master regarded as undertaking "work of disagreeable character". The tobacco ration was therefore a useful bargaining counter for the Master; what we might call a 'perk' or even a 'bribe'. *Barton Regis Poor Law Union Annual Book 1897* BRO Ref. 10900.
163 "Tramps and Beggars" referring sarcastically to Eastville Workhouse in *The Bristol Magpie* 31 October 1885.

The end of a large job might release hundreds of navvies: in a district of big arable farms the harvest would attract scores of migrant field workers. At such times large gangs of labourers, which might include some women and children, would drift through an area, coalescing and dispersing as they went. When a regional industry suffered prolonged depression, considerable parties might set off on the trek together, drawn by reports of a demand for labour somewhere else.[164]

To hasten this process, one of the objectives of the New Poor Law of 1834 was to allow freer movement of labour in order to facilitate the redistribution of workers to new industrial centres. Consequently, in 1837, a new Poor Law regulation was introduced which required food and a night's shelter to be given to any destitute person in case of 'sudden or urgent necessity' in return for their performing a task of work. These shelters were usually adjoined to workhouses and called tramp wards, casual wards or, more colloquially, 'spikes'.[165] They were designed to provide the most basic level of accommodation, inferior to that in the main workhouse buildings. There was at all times a distinction made between regular workhouse inmates and 'tramps' who were passing through. The latter would often stay a short while in the 'tramp or casual' ward before being given a ticket by the tramp relieving officer for another workhouse.

Throughout the Victorian period there was an obsession amongst Poor Law authorities, Boards of Guardians and the press with the problem of vagrancy, particularly the concept of the 'professional tramp' and the connected fear of dangerous gangs of 'sturdy beggars' roaming the countryside. The former was related to the idea of the 'deserving and undeserving' poor, whereby a distinction was to be made between people on the roads who had been forced 'onto the tramp' in order to find work, and those who were considered 'criminal vagrants', who had no intention of 'honest toil' and instead cynically intended to exploit the Poor Law system. The latter 'folk devil' merely represented the organisation of these supposed miscreants and confounds our contemporary idea of 'tramps' as noted by Chesney in his study of the Victorian underworld:

The itinerants who most consistently gave trouble both to local authorities and to country people in general were what may be called the regular *mouchers*. Sometimes alone or with a single female companion, sometimes in quite formidable parties, padding along the

164 Chesney, K. *The Victorian Underworld: A fascinating recreation* (Harmondsworth: Penguin, 1991) pp. 61-2.
165 See Higginbotham, P. *The Workhouse* http://www.workhouses.org.uk/vagrants/index.shtml accessed 2015.

dusty verges of the summer roads, they were a common and universally unwelcome sight…ragged and usually filthy, the moucher did not necessarily present the physically collapsed appearance that a later age came to associate with tramps. Indeed the number of young, sturdy men, confirmed in a life of wandering idleness and fully prepared to resist attempts at coercion, was in official eyes a most disturbing feature of the vagrancy problem.[166]

These particular groups of travellers were often referred to as 'vermin' or 'predatory animals' in the press; and were regarded by many 'respectable' Victorians as the product of either 'hereditary pauperism', weak-willed Poor Law Unions or even naïve members of the public. An editorial in the *Western Daily Press* in 1871 stated:

> did the British public make more resolute inquiry into the genuineness of plausible tales of distress, the principal feeders of criminal vagrancy would be cut off, and the inducements to continue such irregular careers done away. People with benevolent hearts, who will not use their reasoning faculties, are as truthfully a cause of crime as carrion by the wayside in summer is the breeding-spot of swarms of offensive insects.[167]

It was partially in response to these fears and pressure from the Local Government Board that in 1872 the Guardians of the Clifton Union sanctioned the construction of a new, expanded 'casual ward' adjacent to the stone breaking yards, close to the entrance to Eastville Workhouse (see Figure 6). The building, erected using pauper labour, was based on a new design known as the 'cellular system'.[168] This was specifically aimed at disciplining and controlling itinerants. It consisted of thirty-six separate cells (or 'spikes'); nineteen for men or women, five for women with children and twelve labour cells (see Figure 23).[169] In the

166 Chesney, K. *The Victorian Underworld* p. 65. Evidence for the 'sturdy beggar' as a Victorian folk devil is discussed by David Jones in *Crime, Protest, Community, and Police in Nineteenth-Century Britain* (London: Routledge & Kegan Paul, 1982) Chap. 7.
167 *Western Daily Press* 21 July 1871.
168 The cost of the new casual wards was cheap at £350, mainly due to the use of pauper labour for the construction. *Bristol Mercury* 20 April 1872.
169 The original casual ward accommodated 22 men and 14 women (with or without children). This was a similar number to the new casual ward which was opened in 1873. *Clifton Poor Law Union - Statement of Accounts 1872-75* BRO Ref. 22936/129. In 1905 the casual ward was extended (see Figure 23) but still retained the cells for women and children. This suggests that destitute women with young children were on the 'tramp' in the 20th century. BRO Building plan/Volume 48/43a (1904-5).

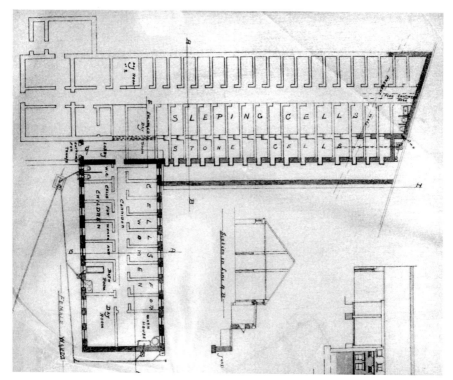

Figure 23: Detail of the casual wards in Eastville Workhouse in 1905, showing labour ('stone') cells and those for women and children.

block there were also two bathrooms, one fumigating room, a drying room and a residence for the Superintendent and his wife. Admiring Guardians from the Bedminster Union commented after a visit to the facilities at Eastville that:

> the arrangements enforce cleanliness, and prevent the communication and herding together of the tramps which is found to be one of the attractions of the ordinary system....The Chairman remarked that the committee were convinced that the system was a very valuable one, by which the means of communication between the tramps were destroyed[170]

For the Guardians it was not only important to inhibit the congregation of tramps and communication between them, but also to keep them isolated

170 *Western Daily Press* 29 November 1882.

from the rest of the workhouse inmates. The original casual ward had adjoined the workhouse, the new building was situated several hundred metres from the main complex. As a workhouse master writing to the Bristol Mercury explained:

> To allow the professional tramp to mix with the ordinary pauper in dayrooms of the workhouse would give rise to endless mischief. It would engender a spirit of resistance to law and order and of discontent, and would propagate disease, and otherwise lead to trouble and expense.[171]

Admittance for tramps to the casual wards was allowed between 6pm and 9pm in winter and 8pm and 10pm in summer. Males were placed in labour cells with 10ft (3.0m) by 4ft (1.2m) sleeping chambers, with a metal bed without a mattress and a small adjoining work section called the 'stone cell'. This compartment had a moveable grill which would be swung open and rocks placed inside the cell (see Figure 24). With the grill closed again, the vagrant would then break up the rocks and feed the fragments out through the holes into the yard. Male tramps were required to break three hundred-weight of stone (150

Figure 24: Stone cell and grill.

kg)[172] and the women to work for three hours picking oakum or cleaning the wards. If they had completed their work they could leave at 11am that morning. Men were given 16 oz. of bread (about 450g, a small loaf), women 12 oz. (about 340g); they also were given two pints of gruel.[173]

Once in the 'spike', failure or refusal to complete the assigned work in the given time could be severely punished:

---

171 Letter to the editor. *Bristol Mercury* 15 February 1883.
172 This was upped to four hundred-weight (200 kg) in the 1880s in order to "discourage vagrants from coming to the wards so frequently". *Barton Regis Poor Law Union – Statements of Accounts 1881-1889* BRO Ref. 22936/130 and *Western Daily Press* 5 December 1885.
173 *Clifton Poor Law Union - Statement of Accounts 1872-75* BRO Ref. 22936/129, *Barton Regis Poor Law Union – Statements of Accounts 1881-1889* BRO Ref. 22936/130.

Thomas Reed, a vagrant, charged with refusing to work while staying in Clifton Workhouse, was sentenced to ten days' imprisonment.[174]

William Evans a tramp, was charged with refusing to do the task of work allotted to him that morning at the Barton Regis Workhouse. The labour master, who pressed the charge, stated that when he told defendant to go on with his work he said he would rather go to gaol. He pleaded guilty, and the bench sent him to the city gaol for 21 days with hard labour.[175]

William Jones, a carpenter, was charged with refusing to work at the Barton Regis Union Workhouse, Eastville. The prisoner was admitted into the tramp ward on Saturday, and on Monday morning he was ordered to break the regulation quantity of stones. After performing a very small portion of his task, he refused to do any more, alleging he was not used to that kind of labour. In reply to the bench, Jones said he belonged to London, and was on [the] tramp seeking employment. He was willing to do any work set him except stone breaking, but he was not used to that labour. He was sentenced to seven days imprisonment.[176]

Tramps developed a number of tactics to deal with their predicament if they were forced to use the 'spikes'. These ranged from communicating information about the most benign casual wards to visit in a region, through to using the workhouse as a resource for clothes and food. For example, in 'doing a tear-up' vagrants in the casual wards would rip up their own clothes (usually filthy rags) in order to obtain a better set from the Poor Law Union.[177] Workhouse officers often responded to these behaviours by humiliating the offenders (or 'tear-ups', as they were known) by forcing them to wear sacks or stripping them naked in the 'spikes'.[178] Under the more draconian Poor Law regime of the 1870s and 80s

174 *Bristol Mercury* 17 April 1869.
175 *Western Daily Press* 21 December 1877.
176 *Bristol Mercury* 23 February 1886.
177 Rose, L. *'Rogues and Vagabonds': Vagrant Underworld in Britain 1815-1985* (London: Routledge, 2016) p. 215.
178 In 1881 the Bedminster Workhouse Guardians responded to 'tear-ups' by reverting back to a system that had been introduced in the 1697 Poor Law Act, that of 'badging the poor' (see Chapter 1) and which had been finally discontinued in an Act of 1810. The Guardians of the Bedminster Poor Law Union approved the use of purposefully 'obnoxious' workhouse uniforms branded in large letters with the name of the Union for vagrants who had torn their clothes and were awaiting punishment for the offence. However, of the first six men who had been forced to wear the 'branded suits', one had torn out the brand and three others had ripped the clothes into shreds. *Bristol Mercury* 19 October 1881.

it became more common to put 'tear ups' before the magistrates. In this period there are numerous cases of vagrants being sent from Eastville Workhouse to the Lawfords Gate petty sessions to face criminal charges over damaging their own clothes. The resulting prison sentences, usually with hard labour, typically ranged from 14 days to one month.[179]

As far as the Clifton Poor Law Guardians were concerned, the object of the new casual wards with their prison-style cells and draconian work regime was to deter the so-called class of 'professional tramps' and thus reduce the numbers using the facility. How successful the Guardians were with their plan can be gauged by the overall numbers of vagrants passing through the casual wards. Figures available for Eastville Workhouse for the years 1872 to 1888 are shown in Figure 25.[180]

Despite the intentions of the Guardians, for the first few years the introduction of the new 'cellular system' casual wards in 1873 made little difference to the numbers of vagrants using the workhouse facilities. Instead what is striking is the rapid increase in the numbers of people 'on the tramp' between 1877 and 1882. This period corresponds to the increasing effect of the 'long depression' on the working classes, with under and unemployment, consequent homelessness and the need to go on the road to find work elsewhere. One Guardian of the Bedminster Union had the revelation in 1882 that the 'cellular system' at Eastville Workhouse:

> had not the deterrent effect; and although it was adopted…the numbers [of tramps] continued to increase as well as in their own [Union]. It did not reduce the numbers, but the *increase commenced with the bad times*, so that he did not think there was such an increase of professional tramps as some supposed[181]

As discussed in Chapter 1, running in parallel to this economic crisis was the programme of the anti-welfare crusaders in the Local Government Board which from 1871 cut out-relief to the able-bodied and other groups, whilst

179 See for examples *Western Daily Press* 14 January 1870, 14 March 1871, 14 July 1871, 28 November 1871 and 20 December 1881.
180 Figure 25 was constructed from half-year data from the following sources: *Clifton Poor Law Union - Statement of Accounts 1872-75* BRO Ref. 22936/129, *Barton Regis Poor Law Union – Statements of Accounts 1881-1889* BRO Ref. 22936/130, *Western Daily Press* 10 August 1876, 18 December 1878 and 17 June 1879. Data was not available for the years 1880 and 1885-7. The 1881 figure is determined from doubling the first quarter figures from *Bristol Mercury* 28 May 1883.
181 The 'bad times' referred to the economic depression. Our emphasis. *Western Daily Press* 29 November 1882.

toughening up the workhouse regimes. The confluence of these two forces, economic and political, on the precarious sections of the working class certainly had a major influence on the numbers of those 'on the tramp' in the 1870s and 80s.

The statistics for vagrants plying the 'spikes' in this period for all of the Poor Law Unions in the Bristol area are astounding. In 1881 the Bedminster Union accommodated 5,634 tramps in its workhouse in Flax Bourton (a twenty-fold increase from 1875).[182] Extrapolating from the half-year figures for 1882 in Figure 25, Eastville Workhouse accommodated close to four thousand (a four-fold increase from 1873). It should be noted that studying those accommodated in casual wards in workhouses gives only a partial view of the situation; it was estimated by a contemporary commentator that the real number of vagrants either sleeping rough or lodging in doss-houses was four or five times this figure.[183] Either way, the desperation of the period is palpable with thousands of men and hundreds of women and children 'on the tramp' in Bristol and its environs.

Unlike the Guardian quoted above who at least recognised the relationship between destitution and economic recession, most Poor Law Unions remained trapped in the ideological position that much of vagrancy was the result of either hereditary pauperism or a cynical choice made by the recalcitrant 'lazy'. For example an editorial in the *Bristol Mercury* in 1883 was explicit in its advocacy of the former:

No one, we should say, need be informed that there are hundreds of families in this country in which the pauper spirit is hereditary, having been handed down from father to son though more than one generation. Persons of this class possess no feelings of independence, and have, consequently no stimulus to self-exertion, but are contented to live at the expense of the self-reliant, toiling classes around them. It cannot be for the interests of society to encourage this state of things, and such it has been abundantly proved is the effect of a lose distribution of out-door relief.[184]

It was from these narrow perspectives that the Local Government Board and Poor Law Unions sought ways of dealing with the problem of the homeless masses that were on the march in the 1870s and 80s. Contemporary proposals

---

182 *Western Daily Press* 29 November 1882 and *Bristol Mercury* 31 January 1883.
183 Borrer, J. H. *Vagrancy: In Special Relation to the Berkshire System. A paper read at the West Midland Poor Law Conference* (London, Knight & Co, 1882) p. 9.
184 *Bristol Mercury* 28 May 1883.

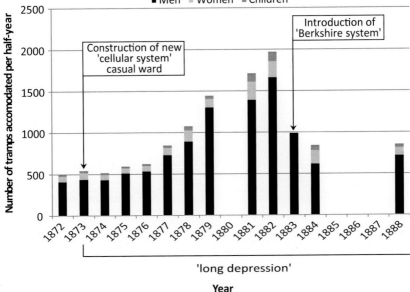

Figure 25: Numbers accommodated in the casual wards at Eastville Workhouse per half-year (1872-88).

for government policy to deal with vagrancy included setting up labour camps, conscripting vagrants into the armed forces, increasing prison sentences, and even punishing members of the public who gave food or money to beggars, or magistrates who were too soft on those who transgressed the vagrancy laws.[185]

The policy that the Guardians of Eastville Workhouse and many other Poor Law Unions chose to introduce was known as the 'Berkshire System' which had been first implemented in that county in 1871 with the explicit aim of the suppression of vagrancy.[186] The main advantage many Poor Law Unions saw in this approach was that it could be undertaken within the existing legal framework and thus instigated almost immediately. Essentially, the 'Berkshire system' aimed at policing the movement and distribution of food to vagrants. This was to be achieved by introducing a 'pass system' based on identifiable personal ration tickets and force-marching those 'on the tramp' to the newly created relief offices at police stations in order to obtain a small ration of bread. At the same time the direct supply of food or money from the public was to be cut off and the laws against vagrancy and begging

185 Borrer, J. H. *Vagrancy: In Special Relation to the Berkshire System* pp. 10-11.
186 Ribton-Turner, C. J. *A History of Vagrants and Vagrancy and Beggars and Begging* (London: Chapman and Hall, 1887) p. 319.

harshly enforced. The fundamentals of this system were described by one of its proponents in 1882:

1. When entering the first union in the county, the vagrant, on applying for an admission order to the workhouse, receives from the police a ticket which records his description, the place he comes from, and his final destination. The next union he is ordered to go on to is endorsed on his ticket, and so on throughout the county.

2. Relief offices are named, at police stations between the unions, where a vagrant can obtain a ration of food on producing his ticket, provided he is on the route there specified. The relief stations are so arranged that a vagrant must have done a fair morning's walk before he can get the food.

3. The cost of the food, and every other expense connected with the system, is met by private subscription.

4. The unions are urged to give an uniform task of work as far as possible, to all vagrants who make use of the casual wards.

5. The police apprehend all persons found begging, or otherwise infringing the Vagrant Acts.

6. On conviction, an uniform sentence of not less than fourteen days is given, or of not less than a month if the vagrant has been impudent, or has used threats.

7. Placards showing the relief stations are hung up in all casual wards.

8. The public are invited by circulars, etc., to co-operate with the Committee, and to refrain from giving either money or food to vagrants.[187]

Supporters of this policy also recommended the use of the 'cellular system' with regards to the design and operation of casual wards which made it doubly attractive to the Barton Regis Board of Guardians who, as we have seen, had already implemented such facilities at Eastville Workhouse. In April 1882 the 'Berkshire System' was adopted by the Guardians and within a year they were crowing about its impact in reducing the numbers of vagrants using the 'spikes'

187 Borrer, J. H. *Vagrancy: In Special Relation to the Berkshire System* p. 4.

at Eastville Workhouse by 50 per cent (see Figure 25). As to where these people had disappeared to was of little concern to the Guardians whose excitement about the cost savings to the rate-payers was only tempered by their reluctance to make personal donations to help fund the scheme (see point 3. above).[188] For many 'on the tramp' within the boundaries of the Barton Regis Union, whether men, women or children, avoiding the new regime of forced labour, forced marches and strict enforcement of vagrancy legislation, entailed leaving the district and heading for easier climes. The alternative was either to knuckle under or enter into the increasingly clandestine life of the beggar in order to survive. Either way, a result of the 'Berkshire System' was to make an already miserable life on the road, even more difficult.

Treatment of children

> I used to see my mother, but only in the distance. We used to be on the other side of the railing, we could see them come out, shout to them. They used to wave back but… they weren't allowed to go across and talk to you.[189]

Children were separated from their mothers in the workhouse. In 1888 the Clifton Board of Guardians discussed a letter from Dr Bernard, the Eastville Workhouse medical officer at that time stating that children "should be removed from their mothers, as soon as they were weaned and no later than one year of age". The ratio of carers for children was proposed to be 1:5 in the day and 1:10 at night. In addition the Board decided that the mothers should be permitted to see their children occasionally, perhaps once a day and that infants under two should be placed in the nursery, but could sleep with their mothers in their beds at night, from 6.30 pm. Motherless children were to sleep in cots.[190]

The New Poor Law required workhouses to provide schooling for boys and girls:

> The boys and girls who are inmates of the workhouse shall for three of the working hours at least every day be respectively instructed in reading, writing, arithmetic and the principles of the Christian religion and such other instruction shall be imparted to them as fit them for service and train them to habits of usefulness, industry and virtue.[191]

188 *Western Daily Press* 1 April 1882 and 26 May 1883.
189 Memories of a man born in the workhouse. Longmate, N. *The Workhouse* p. xi.
190 *Bristol Mercury* 28 January 1888.
191 *Reports from Commissioners: Poor Laws Vol XIX Eighth Annual Report of the Poor Law Commissioners Session 3rd February -18th August 1842* (London: HMSO, 1842) p. 50.

However, for several years there was considerable debate amongst Poor Law Unions as to whether this schooling should be subject to the eligibility clause; that is, it should be a lesser standard of schooling than that provided to the lowest classes outside the workhouse. By the time Eastville Workhouse had opened in 1847 it had been conceded that giving pauper children basic reading and writing skills would ultimately help keep them from claiming poor relief. More than fifty years later the *Poor Law Handbook* stated:

> The care and training of children are matters which should receive the anxious attention of Guardians. Pauperism is in the blood, and there is no more effectual means of checking its hereditary nature than by doing all in our power to bring up our pauper children in such a manner as to make them God-fearing, useful and healthy members of society.[192]

Workhouse schooling was of variable quality depending on the number and skill of the teachers that the Guardians were willing to employ, which of course was contingent on how much they were willing to spend. In the 1870s there were four teachers employed in Eastville Workhouse: a Schoolmaster, a Schoolmistress, an Infant-mistress and a Boys Industrial Trainer. Their combined annual salaries in 1875 were £135. Less than a decade later, in 1884, the Guardians had increased this to six teachers, with the addition of an Assistant Schoolmaster and a Girls Industrial Trainer and an overall salary bill of £213.[193] The snapshot of the Eastville Workhouse population presented in the 1881 census (see Chapter 2) demonstrates that there were 214 children in the age group for schooling (7-14 years).[194] With two dedicated classroom teachers in the 1870s and three in the mid-1880s, class sizes on paper were huge, apparently varying between seventy and hundred plus pupils. These figures suggest that the classroom experience may not have been the dominant 'educational' activity. Frost points out that as the century progressed:

---

192 *Poor Law Handbook* of the *Poor Law Officers' Journal* (1901). Quoted in Higginbotham, P. *The Workhouse*. http://www.workhouses.org.uk/education/accessed 2 May 2016.
193 The annual salaries for teaching staff at Eastville Workhouse in 1875 were given as Schoolmaster £50, Schoolmistress £35, Infant-mistress £25 and Boys Industrial Trainer £25. In 1884 they were Schoolmaster £50, Schoolmistress £53, Infant-mistress £30, Assistant Schoolmaster £35, Boys Industrial Trainer £25 and Girls Industrial Trainer £20. *Clifton Poor Law Union - Statement of Accounts 1872-75* Ref. 22936/129 and *Barton Regis Poor Law Union – Statements of Accounts 1881-1889* Ref. 22936/130.
194 See Higginbotham, P. *The Workhouse* http://www.workhouses.org.uk/Clifton/Clifton1881.shtml#Inmates accessed 2015.

the [workhouse] school day lengthened over time too, though this was somewhat illusory. Half the hours spent on education were actually industrial training. Boys learned some sort of trade or worked at agriculture while the girls did laundry, cooked, cleaned, or worked in a dairy. Poor law officials insisted that children had to have employable skills, which left less time for academic study.[195]

There is evidence of this 'industrial training' regime in a report written in 1896 by the Master of Eastville Workhouse to the central Poor Law Commissioners. This describes the labour undertaken by fourteen girls aged between eleven and fourteen in a typical week. From Monday to Saturday they were expected to work from 9am to 12 noon in the morning and from 2pm to 5pm in the afternoon. In addition to this, all girls "who were able" had to work before school from 7am to 8.30am and "after school in the afternoon". Thus, for a girl from the age of eleven, the working week was more than forty-five hours. The types of work included cooking, scrubbing, sweeping, dusting and cleaning bedrooms, officers' rooms and kitchens.[196] Clearly classroom-time was a somewhat secondary activity for boys and girls of this age group in Eastville Workhouse. On passing fourteen years of age, boys and girls became 'adults' and took on normal workhouse labour, something they had clearly been prepared for in their younger years.

The harsh working conditions for youngsters in the workhouse did not go unnoticed or uncontested. The following anonymous letter sent to the Poor Law Board (PLB) in London by an ex-inmate, provides a fascinating insight into both the backgrounds of some workhouse children, and their treatment in the Eastville Workhouse:

27 January1874

To the mister gentalmen of the Govment Poor Board, London

Mister gentalmen,

i beg pardon i am only a poor woman i have had children of my owne and i cant bear the poor children to be put on the people the union are very hard the gardians come there once a week and have a good feaste wat do them kare about the way the poor children are served now i must aske you Mister gentalmen to looke into it and have it put

195 Frost, G. S. *Victorian Childhoods* (London: Praeger, 2009) p. 127.
196 TNA Ref. MH 12/4041 2 May 1896.

all rite i will tell you too poor boys were keped loked up a bit a go for a weeke in bed for no harm and now a poor boy that ill for several years with a bad heade is put out in the cold craking stones all day is father is in jale and the father of one poor boy lossed is site and the father of the other poor boy is in americul the poor mothers are all dead oh i wold not rite you i nowes one of the poor boys is mother was a grate frend of mind

i was in the Clifton union once but hope i shall never go thare gain O its sad doings thare please mister gentalmen to look to the poor children and don't let them be put on the master hes very hard he dont care[197]

Children were frequently 'boarded-out' from the workhouse. This was the practice of placing children in the long-term care of foster parents. Boarding-out was an attractive proposition for the fiscally driven Poor Law Unions as it was a cheaper option than accommodation in the workhouse. This was particularly true for orphaned or deserted children who were likely to spend much of their childhood in such institutions. In the 1870s foster families received a weekly allowance of four shillings for each child staying with them and a set of clothes. The half year accounts for the Eastville Workhouse in 1874 describe the clothing to be provided for boys and girls who were boarded-out:

Boys: 2 caps, 2 suits of clothes, 3 shirts, 3 pairs of stockings, 2 pairs of boots, 3 neckerchiefs, 3 pocket handkerchiefs, 1 pair of braces, 1 brush, 1 comb, 1 Bible, 1 Prayer Book and a clothes box.

Girls: 1 brown hat, 1 sun bonnet, 3 pinafores, 3 frocks, 3 shifts, 3 pocket handkerchiefs, 3 pairs of stockings, 3 skirts, 3 flannels, 2 pairs of boots, 2 jackets, 1 brush, 1 Prayer Book and a clothes box.[198]

In Eastville Workhouse children were boarded-out or adopted where the parents had deserted them, were in prison, or where their continued role as

197 The PLB declined to forward the letter to the Clifton Union as it was anonymous, but suggested that they take a look at the condition of the boys on their next visit. Of course, such visits were planned in advance giving ample time for the Guardians and Workhouse Master to prepare. As to the "feastes" of the Guardians referred to in the letter, the PLB official noted that "it is within my own knowledge that they [the Guardians] pay for it themselves". TNA Ref. MH 12/4018 27 January 1874.
198 *Clifton Poor Law Union Statement of Accounts, 1874* BCRL Ref. PR2 Pamphlet Box: Societies IV B2401 p. 36.

parents would (in the Guardians' view) be "prejudicial to the wellbeing of the children". In the half-yearly accounts for the 1874 twenty-five children were noted as being boarded-out from the institution. Their ages are unknown but the evidence shows the preferred age-range as being between two and nine years.

Research indicates that children often preferred fostering to being in the workhouse, though this was of course dependent upon the home environment into which they entered. Prior to the 1870s there had been considerable fear amongst the Poor Law authorities in London that the weekly allowance paid to families would be an incentive to exploit the system for profit, leading to the abuse and neglect of children.[199] However, in 1870 the Poor Law Board issued a formal framework for fostering in the form of the Boarding-Out Order. The order laid down the ground-rules including limits on age (2-10 years), weekly maintenance fees (4s) and location of suitable homes. In addition it specified that:

> A Boarding-Out Committee be formed in each union to supervise the boarding-out arrangements - Committees were to have at least three members at least one of which was to be female.[200]

Prior to the election of female guardians to the Clifton Union Board in the early 1880s, this body offered one of the only opportunities for women to take on a formal role within the management of the Poor Law Union. Applications for the role of Honorary Secretary to the Boarding-Out Committee required female candidates to provide evidence of their social status by reference to their husband's or father's occupations, which effectively restricted the role to the well-to-do 'lady'. If accepted on to the committee these gentlewomen were expected to find suitable homes for workhouse children and to act as home-visitors and inspectors once a child had been fostered. Despite the restrictions regarding social class, the intervention of women in the boarding-out process and the regulations provided by the 1870 Order, helped improve conditions for foster children, as is demonstrated by an examination of the reports to the Committee.

For example, in 1892 the home-visitors reported on six children fostered out to three families saying that the houses seemed very clean and that they had "a good room and bed to themselves" with a good stock of clothes. However

199 Higginbotham, P. *The Children's Home* website http://www.childrenshomes.org.uk/boardingout/ accessed 25 April 2016.
200 Higginbotham, P. *The Workhouse* http://www.workhouses.org.uk/boardingout accessed 2015.

another child, Alice, was fostered with a Mrs Harding and her widowed father. Alice "who looked older than nine" shared a room with old Mr Harding with only a thin curtain between them; there was no blanket on the bed, only some old clothes. According to the inspectors the "home was very unsatisfactory" and consequently Alice was removed by the Boarding-Out Committee from the care of the Hardings.

Jessie was a child whose first foster parents were convicted of ill-treating her so she was placed with a new family. The inspectors reported that the "foster father works in a brush factory and the wife puts in bristles at home. Jessie was not clean, nor was her bed and stock of clothing satisfactory". However, the inspectors did not propose to move her "as another removal would be damaging to the child, but recommend that the home is carefully watched".[201]

Alongside official bodies such as the Poor Law Union Boarding-Out Committees, other private organisations had sprung up to deal with the problem of the numerous orphaned or deserted pauper children in workhouses. The Bristol and Clifton Society in Aid of Boarding-Out Union Orphans and Deserted Children (or in short the Bristol Boarding-Out Society) had been operating for several decades. It was led in the 1890s by JP Francis Tothill, and had thirty other female committee members as well as three female philanthropic vice presidents, Florence Davenport-Hill, Agnes Beddoe and a Miss Littlejohn.[202] Organisations such as this were created and had flourished in the climate of austerity and moral self-help of the 1870s where 'charities' were encouraged to take on responsibilities of the local and national state. By the 1890s the Bristol Boarding-Out Society (BBOS) had built close ties with the Clifton/Barton Regis Board of Guardians and begun to operate as a proxy team of inspectors. Their mission, laid out in their handy pocket-book, was to choose and supervise suitable homes for workhouse children with the following criteria for guidance:

1. Moral character of both foster parents

2. The number of bedrooms (so that children of opposite sexes do not have to share)

3. The income of the household

4. The age and health of the foster parents.[203]

201 TNA Ref. MH 12/4037 16 February 1892.
202 TNA Ref. MH 12/4037.
203 It is unclear if this list is in order of importance. TNA Ref. MH 12/4037.

Members of the Society regularly inspected homes examining the temperance of the parents, the cleanliness and the amount of clothing provided for the children. Although the regulation of boarding-out and the intervention of women in the process, improved the situation for children who left the workhouse in this manner, the unequal relationship of power that existed between the inspectors, their charges and the families who fostered them, was tangible. Higginbotham notes that:

> Although occasional cases of ill-treatment emerged, these were far outweighed by stories of children filled with dread at the possibility of being taken away from their foster homes.[204]

The well-to-do inspectors often made their recommendations to the Boarding-Out Committee based on elitist concepts of acceptable daily living conditions, moral behaviour and lifestyle. Owing to their obsession with working-class self-reliance and fiscal conservatism, which was whole-heatedly supported by the Board of Guardians, difficult economic circumstances of a foster family did not lead to monetary help from the Union, rather it could lead to the removal of the fostered child. The financial sums involved could be trifling - in one case the Committee refused to pay a halfpenny a week to allow a boarded-out boy to attend school. It seems this ideological imperative was very strong and this is reflected in the following report by the BBOS inspectors to the Barton Regis Boarding-Out Committee.

> Charles Richards and another boy were boarded out with Mr and Mrs Niblett, Lower Stone a couple with one girl of their own. The foster-father works at a steam laundry. Charles Richards looked fairly well, but he had a bad cold on his chest. He had been very mischievous and the (local) farmer complained of his tricks, such as letting cattle and horses out of the fields. The other boy had a bad head. There were only two bedrooms and the boys shared with the Niblett's girl. I think they should be removed as soon as a more suitable place can be found.[205]

The Committee also reported on what happened to children after they left the workhouse; a girl Clara Bennett, aged 15, had gone into service "but she has gone wrong and lost her character" [a euphemism for getting pregnant]. They felt she should not come back into the workhouse, but paid £10 a year for her to

204 Higginbotham, P. *The Children's Home* website http://www.childrenshomes.org.uk/boardingout/ accessed 25 April 2016.
205 TNA Ref. MH 12/4037.

be in the Hope House Temporary Rescue Home in Bath.[206] This was a cheaper option for the Guardians than returning Bennett to Eastville Workhouse and reflected their increasing reliance on charitable initiatives to reduce their costs. One such charity, the Society for Friendless Girls, complained in a letter to the Barton Regis Board of Guardians:

> Our shelter has received a great many girls/adults from Barton Regis Union and put them into service. They generally have to remain in the [workhouse] for two or three weeks while an outfit is being made, or places found and sometimes a girl needs a little testing before going to a place. As our funds are very limited it would be a great assistance if the Guardians can give us some help in the form of an annual subscription. We have taken 13 girls from Barton Regis.[207]

Collaboration between private charitable organisations and the Barton Regis Poor Law Guardians was realised in another scheme for reducing the costs of keeping children in the workhouse. This strategy was effectively an extension of the practice of boarding-out and involved many of the same philanthropists. This was arranging for "deserted or orphaned" children to be sent to labour in colonies of the British Empire.[208] As workhouses received more and more of these youngsters, and it became increasingly clear that 'suitable'

206 TNA Ref. MH 12/4037 19 May 1892.

207 TNA Ref. MH 12/4037 19 January 1892.

208 Assisted emigration to Canada and other colonies had been part of government policy from the 1840s as the effects of enclosure and mechanisation under capitalism produced massive rural under and unemployment and subsequent desperate poverty. Rather than reverse the brutal rationalisation of agriculture and rural depopulation by land reform as radical Chartists had suggested or provide a state welfare system, the bourgeoisie responded with organised displacement of 'surplus' population to British colonies where menial labour was required. On Malthusian grounds organisations such as the National Emigration League (NEL) blamed population growth rather than the effects of the economic system for the increasing poverty. 'Gentlemen' from the NEL lobbied government to provide funds to assist the emigration of paupers, which after 1847 became the norm. Close collaboration between government emigration departments and Poor Law authorities to determine suitable candidates was therefore required, and in a Malthusian manner they decided that children and young pauper women "properly qualified in respect of health and age and of unexceptional character" would be their primary targets for emigration to the colonies. It is estimated that over 100,000 child immigrants left Britain between 1869 and 1939. See Vitucci, M.N. 'Emigration and the British Left, 1850-1870' in *Class, Culture and Community: New Perspectives in Nineteenth and Twentieth Century British Labour History* Eds. Baldwin, A., Ellis, C., Etheridge, S., Laybourn, K., and Pye, N. (Newcastle: Cambridge Scholars Publishing, 2012); http://www.exodus2013. co.uk/tag/national-emigration-league/; https://personal.uwaterloo.ca/marj/genealogy/reports/emigrationsoc.html; http://emigrated.bafhs.org.uk/.

foster parents were in short supply, 'assisted emigration' became an attractive proposition. Poor Law Boards were the legal guardians of abandoned children in the workhouse, so they were in a good position to instigate and organise the emigration process.

In 1882 a loose group of wealthy individuals headed by Agnes Beddoe founded the Bristol Emigration Society (BES). Beddoe had been influenced by the reformer Mary Carpenter who believed that emigration was in the best interests of pauper children.[209] Two important zealots in the leadership of the BES were Mark Whitwill and Mary Clifford. Whitwill was an ex-officio Guardian of Barton Regis Poor Law Union and:

> a non-conformist ship owner, a ship and insurance broker, a shipping agent, a justice of the peace (JP) and a manager of the Park Row and Clifton industrial schools for boys as well as the Carlton House industrial school for girls. In addition he was chairman of the Bristol School Board, a Bristol city councillor and a supporter of the women's suffrage movement.[210]

Clifford, a deeply Christian philanthropist whom we met in Chapter 2, was elected to the Board of Guardians of Barton Regis Union in 1882 and shared Whitwill's keen interest in child emigration. In February 1883 Whitwill and Clifford began their 'mission' to extend the new BES project into Eastville Workhouse where they were both now (conveniently) on the Board. Central to their arguments for adoption of the emigration scheme was that the fee to transport a pauper child to Canada was about £5, "equal to their cost in the [work] house for about 20 weeks". Having dangled this financial 'carrot' in front of the Guardians, that emigration would save the rate-payers the cost of keeping these unfortunates in the workhouse, Clifford and Whitwill were disappointed to meet opposition from some of the Board. Clifford stated that she had already selected ten boys, five of whom had been deserted and five of whom were orphans that "were anxious to go [to Canada]". The Clerk then pointed out that "the mother of one of the boys referred to by Miss Clifford had protested against her child being sent abroad" and that the cost of 54 girls, 100 boys and 34 women and children sent by the Bristol Guardians to Canada from 1870 and 1874 was nearly £11 5s per individual, more than twice the figure cited by Clifford. One Guardian quoted from reports of Government inspectors arguing that "the emigration of pauper children to Canada was a

209 http://britishhomechild.com/resources/sending-agencies-organizations/551-2/.
210 Parker, R. *Uprooted: The Shipment of Poor Children to Canada, 1867-1917* (Bristol: Policy Press, 2010) p. 121.

complete failure" and another asked for assurance that "a proper system of supervision was maintained over children emigrated". Clifford and Whitwill narrowly lost the subsequent vote.[211]

Undeterred, the following month Clifford returned to the boardroom at Eastville Workhouse with a revised proposal, this time offering enhanced financial incentives, and guarantees over the welfare of the emigrants. Whitwill stated in a letter to the Board that:

> I am so convinced that it would be for the welfare of the lads that they should commence life as bread winners in the Dominion of Canada rather than this country, that if the board will consent to give the usual outfit and to pay £3 ocean fare, I will undertake to bear whatever cost beyond this may be necessary to send them to farms in New Brunswick; and I will further undertake to have homes ready for them by the time they arrive out.

He went on passionately (and revealingly) to state that:

> For about one quarter of a year's maintenance they would be enabled to send these boys to a new country, where they would have a career open to them more promising than they could hope for in this country. By emigrating these boys they would be striking a blow at the hereditary system of pauperism which was the dark side of English poverty.

Despite the protests of a recalcitrant minority of the Board who claimed that the emigration system to Canada amounted to little more than 'semi-slavery', Whitwill's improved financial offer, along with the assurances over care and custody, won the argument. The resolution was passed and the BES scheme was launched in Eastville Workhouse with the formation amongst the Guardians of an 'emigration committee'.[212] However, the rosy picture painted by Clifford and Whitwill of the BES scheme to the Board of Guardians, was far from reality.

A central problem with the emigration scheme in Bristol was the definition of 'orphan' and what actually constituted 'desertion' by the parent(s). There were a number of cases where apparently orphaned children from Eastville Workhouse were lined up for emigration by the committee and yet turned out to have parents who declined to give consent for their children to leave the

211 *Bristol Mercury* 24 February 1883.
212 *Western Daily Press* 17 March 1883.

country.[213] This was not necessarily a bureaucratic error, rather a reflection of the moralistic views of members of the BES and Barton Regis Union emigration committee. It appears that if members of these bodies decided that the parents were 'immoral', then the child was considered to be effectively *orphaned*.[214]

Consider the example of George and Emily Derrett, children from Eastville Workhouse, who in 1895 were listed on the emigration forms as 'orphans' and were planned to be shipped to Canada for the sum of £12 each. However a letter in August of that year from Miss Woollam, a Barton Regis Guardian of long-standing, stated that the children's:

> mother is a coarse ignorant woman. Whenever she goes out from the workhouse she returns the worse for drink.[215]

It is hard to imagine that with the family in the workhouse together, there could be any confusion about whether the two children were actually 'orphans'. It would likewise be difficult to argue that despite the activities of their mother, they had been 'deserted'.

The dictatorial policy regarding 'orphans' and their parents was further reinforced by Mary Clifford who sat on the new Barton Regis Union emigration committee. Clifford aimed to 'protect' child inmates of the workhouse from the "baleful influence" of their families by removing them to work on farms in Canada. She was obsessive in her approach to the operation as explained by one commentator:

> [Clifford] was quite ruthless about denying parental rights. She went to immense trouble to ensure that the parents should have no clues as to their children's whereabouts.[216]

The problem was that the BES often had no idea where their young charges ended up either. The organisation, which, over a twenty year period, transported more than a thousand children (9-14 years of age) to New Brunswick, Quebec, Winnipeg and Nova Scotia in Canada, was a shambles both at home and

213 See for example TNA Ref. MH 12/4025 (1882).

214 Higginbotham notes that a similarly loose interpretation of 'orphan' was undertaken by the famous philanthropist Dr Barnardo the founder of numerous children's homes. Higginbotham, P. *The Children's Home* website http://www.childrenshomes.org.uk/DB/boardingout.shtml accessed 25 April 2016.

215 TNA Ref. MH 12/4040 28 August 1895. The mother of the children signed the consent forms a few weeks later.

216 Hollis quoted in Parker, R. *Uprooted: The Shipment of Poor Children to Canada* p. 121.

overseas.[217] The huge demand for free child labour on Canadian farms allowed organisations like the BES to sign private agreements with unregulated immigration agents who put the children out to work.[218] The shortcomings of this scheme were numerous:

> The Society required no formal agreement between itself and host farmers nor was there any record of where the children had been placed. Without a written contract spelling out the obligation of the farmers, great reliance was placed on verbal agreements to house, clothe and feed the children. Noticeably absent from the arrangement was any undertaking to educate or pay the children. Farmers routinely loaned the children to other farmers without maintaining any record of their change in situation. Follow-up inspections by the Society were rare, if any. In some cases, the children were sent unescorted and with no provisions made for their upkeep upon arrival. Understandably, several children believed they were masters of their own destiny and simply wandered off to make their way in the world.[219]

A large number of children from Eastville Workhouse underwent this displacement; however for some, escape from the workhouse environment through this dramatic journey across the oceans was a blessing in disguise. In 1883, when the first 'shipment' of children were put on a boat to New Brunswick, Canada from Avonmouth, the Chairman of the Board of Guardians went to see them off.[220] Almost a year later the Guardians reported receiving

217 In 1906 the BES "ceased operations in much the same way it had conducted itself from the outset; abandoning any further responsibility for the welfare of the children it had sent overseas" http://britishhomechild.com/resources/sending-agencies-organizations/551-2/.

218 An 1897 report on the living conditions of twelve youngsters (11-15 years of age) from Eastville Workhouse who had been placed in Canada showed that almost all of them worked on farms and none of them received a wage for their labour, only board and clothes. It was claimed, however, that they attended day school and church. TNA Ref. MH 12/4042 (1897)

219 *British Home Child Group International* http://britishhomechild.com/resources/sending-agencies-organizations/551-2/. This position is backed up by correspondence between Whitwill and his Canadian contact H.B. Richardson in 1881. Richardson complained that "Mr Whitwell had asked if Canadians could arrange for someone to travel from Quebec to St John's with a party of young people he proposed sending to Canada. I gather that my doing so in this instance is likely to be used as an argument in favour of the emigration of these young people….If the young people you propose sending are from a workhouse or industrial school, it would be necessary for you to know something of the people with whom they are to be placed, also to have a reliable person to visit them from time to time. I regret that I cannot take any responsibility, beyond arranging for their comfort and safety on the journey" TNA Ref. MH 12/4024 8 July 1881.

220 *Bristol Mercury* 30 June 1883.

a letter from one of the boys who had emigrated saying he was well pleased with his house and would not like to be back in Barton Regis workhouse.[221] In 1888 a statement was read to the Guardians from a Government agent in New Brunswick praising the excellent behaviour of the boys who had been sent there.[222] These 'official' reports are unsurprisingly positive considering the close links between the BES and Eastville Workhouse brokered through Whitwill, Clifford and others of their ilk. Nonetheless, the realities of BES operations in Canada suggest that for the majority of transported children the experience must have been extremely traumatic and the life that awaited them even tougher than that they had left behind. However, as far as the Guardians were concerned, each child emigrant was a cost saving.

Another option for Boards of Guardians to relieve themselves of the responsibility of workhouse children was the Naval Training Ship. This scheme originated in the 18th century as a method for both removing young boys from workhouses and providing recruits for the Royal Navy. By the mid-1800s the scheme was being promoted by both public and private bodies, and by the end of the century there were about thirty such ships moored around Britain. Life on board for the young 'recruits' was tough, as Higginbotham describes:

> Boys typically joined the ships at the age of eleven or twelve and stayed until they were fifteen or sixteen. Discipline aboard the ships was strict and the birch often used to enforce it. Food was limited in quantity and variety — biscuit, potatoes, and meat were the staples, with occasional green vegetables. Many of the new boys could not swim and needed to be taught — unfortunately some drowned before they mastered the skill! Sleeping accommodation was usually in hammocks which could be comfortable in the summer but icy-cold in winter.[223]

In the Bristol area the Training Ship *Formidable*, loaned by the Admiralty, was moored at Portishead and from 1869 provided 350 places for boys aged 11-15 years (see Figure 27). A number of children were sent from Eastville Workhouse to *Formidable* to be trained for a 'sailor's life'. They were each provided with a medical certificate stating that they were suitable and a payment of 7 shillings per week was made by the Poor Law Union to the National Nautical School, a private organisation set up by Bristol businessmen and magistrates to oversee

221 *Bristol Mercury* 11 April 1884.
222 *Bristol Mercury* 10 May 1888.
223 Higginbotham, P. *The Children's Homes* website http://www.childrenshomes.org.uk/TS/ accessed 02 May 2016. .

Figure 26: Satirical cartoon by George Cruikshank on the issue of child emigration to Canada (1869).

The captions read:

From the man on the left with the broom -
There are many plans suggested for providing for the neglected children of drunken parents, but none such a sureform(?) measure as this, for by this plan we provide for them at once and get rid of the dear little ones altogether.

From the woman with the broom -
This is a delightful task and we shall never want a supply of these neglected children whilst the pious and respectable Distillers and Brewers carry on their trade and we shall always find plenty of the little dears about the Gin Palaces and the Beer Shops.

From the man in the centre with the shovel -
According to the teachings of Jesus all these little gutter girls are our sisters and therefore I feel it my duty as a Christian Minister to assist in this good work.

From an unseen cart driver -
I am greatly obliged to you Christian ladies and gentlemen for your help and as soon as you have filled the cart I'll drive off to pitch the little dears aboard of a ship to take them thousands of miles away from their native land, so that they may never see any of their relations again.

And from children in the cart -
Mother! Mother! I want my Mother!
Oh! Mother, Mother.
I want my Father

Figure 27: The training ship for boys, HMS Formidable, moored at Portishead.

the scheme.[224] The only hesitancy Boards of Guardians had with sending their charges to Training Ships was the cost, which could be higher than keeping the boys in the workhouse or Industrial Schools. There is some evidence that the Barton Regis Board of Guardians were sending "bad boys" to *Formidable*, suggesting a punitive strategy for removing misbehaving inmates of Eastville Workhouse.[225]

Poor Law Guardians endeavoured to find employment for children from their workhouses in Bristol; each one placed in a job reduced the cost to the ratepayer. Prior to the opening of Eastville institution the Clifton Poor Law Union had brokered several deals with major manufacturing enterprises to take pauper children into employment. For example, the massive Great Western Cotton Factory (see Figure 28), which opened in Barton Hill in 1838, was situated in the centre of one of the most populous areas of the Clifton Poor Law Union, the out-parish of St Philip and Jacob. By 1840 the factory had 923 employees, the vast majority of whom were very low-paid, child labourers: 609 girls and 115 boys aged between 13 and 14.[226] After 1833, the employment

224 TNA Ref. MH 12/4042 5 June 1897 and https://en.wikipedia.org/wiki/National_Nautical_School.

225 TNA Ref. MH 12/4042 5 June 1897 and Higginbotham, P. *The Children's Homes* website http://www.childrenshomes.org.uk/TS/ accessed 02 May 2016.

226 The Great Western Cotton Factory was financed from the 'dirty money' obtained as compensation for the abolition of slavery. Atterton, G. *Cotton Threads: The History of the Great Western Cotton Factory* (Bristol: Barton Hill History Group, 2015) pp. 3-6 and Richardson, M. *The Maltreated and Malcontents: Working in the Great Western Cotton Works 1838-1914* Bristol Radical Pamphleteer #37 (Bristol: BRHG, 2016) pp. 18-21.

Figure 28: The Great Western Cotton Works by Samuel Loxton (1857-1922).

of child labour in textile factories (except silk) was subject to regulation, as Richardson notes:

> The 1833 Factory Act stipulated that no children were to work in textile mills under the age of nine. Children, aged between nine and thirteen, were limited to working nine hours per day or forty-eight hours per week… Early reports by factory inspectors, however, indicated that some employers were circumventing the law…Moreover, the omission of setting up the machinery to enforce this Act amounted 'to nothing more than a barren declaration of principles' making it easy for textile employers to disregard legislation if they so wished.[227]

To satisfy the demand for low-waged child labour in the Great Western Cotton Factory, the Clifton Guardians 'put-out' child paupers from their workhouses. This was despite the reservations of some Guardians that "the establishment was too large to admit of there being proper control over the morals and conduct of those employed". However, the practice was partly

227 Richardson, M. *The Maltreated and Malcontents* p. 16.

curtailed by Poor Law Commissioners in 1839, not because child labour was illegal or because of issues concerning 'morals and conduct' but instead the 1834 PLAA stated "persons receiving relief shall not enter into competition with persons supporting themselves by their own labour".[228] Ironically, this clause was in place, not to safeguard children (or adults for that matter) from exploitation, but merely to protect employers from unfair competition.

Poor Law Guardians thus had to ensure that if they put 'their' children out to work, they had to prove that the employer was taking full responsibility for them rather than taking advantage of the fact that some part of their living expenses were covered by poor relief. Consequently, living-in apprenticeships and permanent employment were favoured for pauper children in the workhouse. A good example of this practice was uncovered by Brian Blessed in the TV programme *Who Do you Think you are* when he established that an ancestor had been apprenticed as a shoemaker, from a workhouse, at the age of 11, in the early nineteenth century.[229]

Another occupation which fitted these requirements was domestic service, where the employer provided food and lodging as part of the contract. Boys and Girls as young seven from the workhouse could be taken on as servants and employers wanting to take minors on in this role had to make a formal application to the Board of Guardians with the written backing of "some respectable ratepayer of the Union". There were some terms fixed to this employment which give us an idea of working conditions for these children:

- The Wages of such Boy or Girl is not to be less than one shilling per week.
- If the Boy or Girl is to be employed at a Trade, the time for work must not exceed 10½ hours per day, exclusive of meals.
- The Boy or Girl must attend a place of worship on Sundays.
- The Guardians do not, under any circumstance, allow a Boy or Girl to be transferred from one place to another without their written consent.

After a successful probationary month, the Guardians would provide the new servants an outfit of clothes and personal items similar to that for children who were boarded out. The relative concern the Guardians had for the child is revealed by the following warning to potential employers:

228 Richardson, M. *The Maltreated and Malcontents* p. 17. However, this apparently did not stop the Bristol Corporation of the Poor from sending groups of girls and boys to work in the Cotton Factory; as late as 1845 this was the practice in the Stapleton workhouse. In order to protect the 'morals' of the young teenagers they were billeted in a house with a nurse from the institution and taken to church twice every Sunday. *Bristol Mercury* 13 December 1845.
229 BBC TV Programme *Who Do You Think You Are?* Series 11 Episode 2 of 10, broadcast 28 August 2014. http://www.bbc.co.uk/programmes/b04dw11r.

Any Person, taking a Boy or Girl from the Workhouse, will be held responsible to the Board of Guardians for the proper care of such Boy or Girl and their clothing, for which they will be required to sign a receipt.[230]

In 1877, it was stated that eleven of the "best boys" and eight of the "most intelligent girls" from Eastville Workhouse had been placed out of the institution to be servants over the previous year.[231]

Older children, over the age of 14, were classed as 'adults' and were encouraged to leave the workhouse and take employment wherever and whatever that might be. In 1867, the Clifton Union Board of Guardians stated in reference to employment of their children:

We resolved if possible to find situations for them, one having expressed willingness to take a situation in the South Wales mines[232]

It wasn't until the Factory and Workshop Act of 1878 that children under the age of ten years were banned from employment. A series of Education Acts in 1870, 1880 and 1891 eventually led to compulsory schooling for all 5-13 year olds.

Whether forced to labour long hours in the workhouse, put-out for factory work or domestic service, boarded-out, sent to farms in Canada or to Naval Training Ships, life was clearly harsh for workhouse children. This is not to suggest that their lives were *always* miserable; in some cases there were improvements in their living conditions through some of these schemes, particularly boarding-out. Similarly, it would also be wrong to portray the philanthropists behind these programmes as the 'villains of the piece'. Most thought they were doing a great service to the children in protecting them from "baleful influences" whether their 'immoral' families or a 'life of crime'. However, what is abundantly clear is that most of the philanthropists shared views about the working-classes derived from their privileged backgrounds in Victorian society; that is, salvation for the workhouse child lay in segregation from their parents and backgrounds, strict discipline and hard labour to serve the needs of Empire. This 'year zero' policy was predicated on the idea that the poor were a product of the poor, rather than victims of the inequalities of the Victorian economic system. Thus workhouse children became pawns in an authoritarian process managed by the well-to-do and over which they or their parents had little control.

230 *Clifton Poor Law Union Statement of Accounts, 1874* BCRL Ref. PR2 Pamphlet Box: Societies IV B2401 pp. 35-6.
231 *Western Daily Press* 6 October 1877.
232 *Bristol Mercury* 15 November 1867.

Incarcerating 'Lunatics, Imbeciles and Idiots'[233]

Maudsley writing in 1873-4 noted some are born so defective "all the education and training in the world will not raise them above the level of brutes." For others, no care "will prevent them being vicious, criminal or becoming insane." Idiocy was attributed to parental transgressions like drunkenness, reinforcing inherited nervous instability. Children of low intelligence were born to women who violated natural law by being educated.[234]

A cursory inspection of the plans of Eastville Workhouse (see Figure 6) shows that by the turn of the 19th century the institution was catering for the 'insane', 'imbeciles' and 'epileptics' in specifically designated wards. This was certainly not the original intention of the 1834 Poor Law Amendment Act (PLAA), which clearly prohibited the detention in a workhouse of 'any dangerous lunatic, insane person or idiot' for more than fourteen days.[235] Prior to the introduction of the New Poor Law the mentally ill, those with learning difficulties, dementia or brain injury who had little or no means of support resided in terrible conditions in prisons or workhouses with a lucky few in public hospitals. Two acts of parliament in 1828 created the Metropolitan Lunacy Commission and encouraged the construction of county asylums which were intended to become the repository for 'lunatics'.

However, after 1834, despite the efforts of the Lunacy Commission to transfer these unfortunates from workhouses to the new county asylums their numbers in the Poor Law system were growing. More than ten years after the PLAA in 1844 it was estimated that only 25% of 'lunatics' in metropolitan areas were placed in asylums with the majority still in workhouses, boarded out or in licensed houses, often in appalling conditions. This stubborn pattern was

233 These outmoded terms are described by Ayers: "At this time [1867], the terms' lunacy' and 'insanity' were loosely used for the whole of what is now termed 'mental disorder', whether of the nature of mental illness or of mental sub-normality. Further, the terms 'imbecile' and 'defective' were used, equally loosely, for conditions associated with weakness of mind, and therefore applied to states of senile dementia and the end-results of mental illness, as well as to congenital defectiveness. Only the term 'idiot' was reserved definitively for the more severely subnormal". Ayers, G. M. *England's First State Hospitals* (Wellcome Institute of the History of Medicine, 1971) Chapter 4. http://www.sochealth.co.uk/national-health-service/hospitals/englands-first-state-imbecile-asylums/
234 Munson-Barkshire, A. *The Production and Reproduction of Scandals in Chronic Sector Hospitals 1981* MSc Dissertation in Sociology, Polytechnic of the South Bank 1981. Chapter II. Retrieved from: http://www.sochealth.co.uk/national-health-service/democracy-involvement-and-accountability-in-health/complaints-regulation-and-enquries/the-production-and-reproduction-of-scandals-in-chronic-sector-hospitals-1981/.
235 The Poor Law Amendment Act of 1834 — *An Act for the Amendment and better Administration of the Laws relating to the Poor in England and Wales* Section 45.

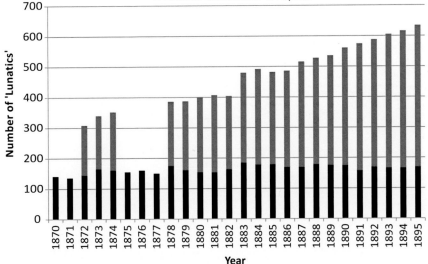

Figure 29: Number of 'lunatics' housed in Eastville Workhouse and asylums by the Clifton/Barton Regis Poor Law Union (1870-1895).

to continue through the rest of the century, with around a quarter of all pauper 'lunatics' residing in workhouses whilst the numbers of paupers registered as mentally ill in England and Wales rose rapidly from 31,000 in 1859, to 57,400 in 1876.[236] Regardless of the wishes of the Lunacy Commission and social reformers, as late as 1906 it was estimated that 11,500 inmates of 'unsound mind' were still in workhouses.[237]

This national trend was mirrored locally by the number of 'lunatics' who were retained in Eastville Workhouse by the Clifton/Barton Regis Poor Law Union as against those who were sent to the county asylum in Gloucester or, from 1860, the new borough asylum in the parish of Stapleton. Figure 29 shows the overall numbers of 'lunatics' placed in the workhouse and in the asylums for a selection of years between 1870 and 1895.[238]

236 The fraction of pauper 'lunatics' in workhouses are for 1859 (23%), 1870 (25%) and 1876 (26%). Ayers, G. M. *England's First State Hospitals* Chapter 4.

237 Longmate, N. *The Workhouse* p. 220.

238 Figure 29 was created from data from the following sources: Archer, I., Jordan, S., Ramsey, K., Wardley, P. and Woollard, M. 'Poor Law Statistics, 1835-1948' in Wardley P. (ed.) *Bristol Historical Resource* (Bristol: UWE, 2000) Table 15, *Clifton Poor Law Union - Statement of Accounts 1872-75* BRO Ref. 22936/129, *Barton Regis Poor Law Union – Statements of Accounts 1881-1889* BRO Ref. 22936/130, TNA Ref. MH 12/4036, MH 12/4040, *Western Daily Press* 5 January, 2 November 1878, 30 August 1879, 18 December 1886, 27 August 1887, 29 September 1888, 2 August 1890 and *Bristol Mercury* 24 December 1880, 29 October 1892, 30 December 1893, 15 December 1894. Data for the numbers of 'lunatics' in the asylums is not available for the years 1870-71 or 1875-77.

Designation	Number	% of total workhouse population	Notes
Imbecile	92	8.6	The Victorian definition of 'Imbecility' referred to what we would label today as moderate or severe intellectual disability usually as a result of a congenital condition or dementia. In the workhouse those afflicted were defined as a less severely deficient group, unable to protect themselves against moral and mental dangers.
Lunatic/ Insane	45	4.2	The Victorian definition of 'Lunacy' or 'Insanity' referred to a person who had episodes of mental illness without a possibility of recovery.
Idiot	20	1.9	The Victorian definition of 'Idiocy' referred to what we would label today as profound intellectual disability usually as a result of a congenital condition. In the workhouse those afflicted were defined as the most deficient, unable to protect themselves against basic physical dangers.
Total	157	14.7	

Table 5: Numbers of 'lunatics', 'imbeciles' and 'idiots' in Eastville Workhouse (1881 census).

Clearly a considerable group of people labelled 'lunatics' were being housed in Eastville Workhouse for decades, despite the existence of asylums. The designation 'lunatic' actually masks a series of sub-categories which are exposed in more detail in the 1881 census. Table 5 gives a breakdown and definition of the 15% of the 1,064 resident paupers classed as either 'lunatics', 'imbeciles' or 'idiots'.

So why despite the remit of the 1834 Poor Law to exclude these groups from the workhouse did their numbers persist for so long? As ever, cost was central to the decisions of the Poor Law Guardians who resisted pressure from reformers and Poor Law and Lunacy Commissioners to relocate pauper 'lunatics'. Ayers explains:

As the cost to the guardians of maintaining insane paupers in the workhouse was less than paying for their care elsewhere…these patients were retained in the poor law institutions, despite the absence of suitable accommodation and care, and in disregard of central recommendations, injunctions and statutory directives.[239]

This crucial fact allied with delays in building county asylums and specialised institutions for similar fiscal reasons condemned the mentally ill and those with severe intellectual and learning disabilities to the harsh regime of the workhouse, often for a life sentence.

The national picture was reflected in Bristol, where the shortcomings of the designated lunatic asylum, part of the workhouse at St Peter's Hospital (on Castle Park), were becoming clear as early as the 1820s. Complaints in the 1840s by the Lunacy Commission concerning overcrowding, subsequent high mortality rates due to T.B. and the inability to classify patients in the institution had fallen on deaf ears amongst the Bristol Justices. It took an executive order from central government in 1853 to try to force the penny-pinching Corporation to build a new asylum to the specifications of the Lunacy Commission. However, even this directive was resisted by vacillation and stalling for another four years, until finally a site was found adjacent to the existing Stapleton Workhouse. The Bristol Lunatic Asylum was finally opened in December 1860 and to the relief of the Corporation and wealthy rate-payers it was claimed that it would be "one of the cheapest in the kingdom".[240]

However, 'cheap' is a relative term, especially for the Poor Law Guardians who were already calculating the cost of managing 'lunatics', 'imbeciles and 'idiots' in their workhouses against the charges in the county and borough asylums. For example, when the new Lunatic Asylum in Stapleton opened in 1860 its cost per patient per week to a given parish was 12 shillings. This was nearly three times the cost to house an inmate in Eastville Workhouse. Consequently, in order to save money, the Clifton Board of Guardians deliberately flouted the PLAA directives prohibiting the retention of 'lunatics' in workhouses.[241] In 1862, the Lunatic Law Amendment Bill was

239 Ayers, G. M. *England's First State Hospitals* Chapter 4.
240 Bristol Lunatic Asylum became a military hospital during WW1 and is now the University of West of England's Faculty of Health and Social Care (BS16 1DD). Large, D. *The Municipal Government of Bristol 1851-1901* (Bristol: Bristol Record Society, 1999) pp. 151-158.
241 One tactic used by Poor Law Boards was to interpret the statement prohibiting the detention for more than 14 days in the workhouse of "any dangerous lunatic, insane person or idiot" in Section 45 of the PLAA as meaning those, in their opinion, who were not dangerous could be incarcerated.

launched in Parliament which aimed to take the jurisdiction for pauper 'lunatics' out of the hands of the Poor Law Unions and pass it to the Lunacy Commissioners. Fearing that the Commissioners would remove all 'their lunatics' to the costly Asylums, the Clifton Guardians petitioned against the Bill claiming that:

> at considerable expense, [they had] provided separate accommodation and attendants for such persons as may be of unsound mind, within their workhouses.[242]

To circumvent this repeated pressure from the Lunacy Commission to pass these unfortunates onto more appropriate facilities and care in the new asylum in Stapleton, in 1867 the Guardians ordered the construction of two dedicated 'lunatic wards' in the Eastville institution at a cost of £2,000.[243] This may have seemed a large sum to invest. However, a simple calculation shows that the savings accrued by housing a group of 170 long-term 'lunatics' in these wards (see Figure 29) rather than sending them to the asylum, allowed the cost of the new buildings to be met in less than one year. The new 'lunatic wards' also allowed the Guardians to claim they had specialised facilities available for the insane in an attempt, once again, to placate the Lunacy Commissioners. According to Ayer this particular financial scam was fairly common amongst parochial Poor Law Boards in metropolitan areas and he adds that these so-called 'insane' wards were:

> generally ill-equipped and poorly staffed, and were created merely to avoid the extra expense of sending mental cases to other institutions.[244]

Records of a meeting of the Barton Regis Board of Guardians in 1877 explicitly demonstrate the nature of these fiscal manoeuvrings.[245] In 1874 the government had introduced a subsidy of four shillings per patient per week to help parishes pay for paupers sent to county asylums. This was presenting a significant threat to the financial strategy the Guardians were operating. According to the Board the cost of accommodating a 'lunatic' in Eastville Workhouse had risen to six shillings and nine pence per week (as against five shillings and six pence for a 'typical' pauper). As the cost in Gloucestershire

242 *Bristol Times & Felix Farley's Bristol Journal* 19 July 1862.
243 *Western Daily Press* 16 March 1867.
244 Ayers, G. M. *England's First State Hospitals* Chapter 4.
245 *Western Daily Press* 15 December 1877.

Asylum was ten shillings per 'lunatic' per week and twelve shillings in the Bristol Asylum, the four shillings subsidy was undermining their plan. It was now costing more to keep the 'lunatics' in the workhouse than the county asylum and nearly as much as the borough institution. Consequently, along with other Poor Law Unions (who were no doubt operating the same scam), they planned to complain to the:

> Local Government Board, calling their intention to the *injustice which they were of opinion was done to the Guardians*, and asking them to devise a scheme by which it might be remedied.[246]

The irony of this is statement is astounding when the conditions in the workhouse for the mentally ill, those with congenital learning difficulties, dementia and the like are considered. For the first few decades after the introduction of the PLAA, despite their special needs, these groups which included the psychopathically violent to the pathetically vulnerable were thrown in with regular paupers who, as we have seen, included young teenagers. Ayer states:

> In the late 'fifties, many such patients were still being warded with sane inmates and attended by fellow paupers. Although forbidden by the Lunacy Commissioners, the use of mechanical restraints was tolerated because workhouse staffs could not manage without them.[247]

The use of such backward methods for controlling 'lunatics', imbeciles' and 'idiots' was predicated on 18th century notions:

> that madmen were beasts requiring restraint, force and fear was taken for granted, "… the madman was not a sick man… unchained animality could be mastered only by discipline and brutalizing" not appeals to reason. Such beliefs provided a useful smokescreen for the needs to contain costs, resulting in overcrowding, few attendants and the necessity for mechanical restraints and coercion. Many buildings were unsuitable, insanitary, the stench overpowering[248]

246 The Guardians were quite happy to claim this grant; by the 1880s it was worth several thousand pounds to them each year.
247 Ayers, G. M. *England's First State Hospitals* Chapter 4.
248 Munson-Barkshire, A. *The Production and Reproduction of Scandals in Chronic Sector Hospitals 1981.*

There are several cases in Eastville Workhouse which demonstrate that such measures were being employed to deal with the mentally ill and those with dementia or epilepsy. The evidence generally only appears in the public record after a death had occurred and details were submitted to the Gloucester Coroner's office to determine if an inquest was required. However, these reports point towards conditions and practices that were in place in the institution.

In May 1867 a 48 year old gas worker James Frost who was acting in a "confused" and "desponding way" was admitted against his will into Eastville Workhouse. He was diagnosed by the Medical Officer as being in a state of depression, with "mania and disease of the brain". During a visit from his wife a few days later, Frost complained that he had been tied to his bed in the sleeping ward and that 'they' only untied him when he had visitors. This was later corroborated by the testimony of the head nurse, Medical Officer and pauper nurses who claimed he had been noisy at night, "struggling violently" and thus had been restrained. Frost's health rapidly (and mysteriously) deteriorated after his admission and he died several weeks later. A post-mortem ordered by the Coroner revealed that Frost had, apart from substantial bruising to his face and chest, four broken ribs on his right side, one of which had punctured his lung, and a further three fractured ribs on his left side. The surgeon, Henry Grace, stated that:

> the ribs must have been broken many days, seven or eight, at least before death...[the] deceased must have been in great pain from the fracture of the ribs and particularly from the piercing of the lung. I consider such injuries could not have been occasioned by a common fall...I think that the violence occasioning the fracture of these ribs must have been applied when he was lying on his back...I don't think any force of his own could have done it...I could imagine it might be occasioned by a man jumping on him.

Clearly, Frost had been violently assaulted, probably while he was tied down, suffered major trauma and had subsequently suffered a slow and agonising death. His misery had lasted more than a week and his serious injuries appeared to have gone unnoticed by workhouse staff and the Medical Officer, Dr Mayor (Jnr). An inquest was held which branded Frost an "imbecile inmate" and which came to the conclusion that there was no evidence as to the cause of his injuries.[249] The same session of the Coroner's Court dealt with a second death in Eastville Workhouse. On the very same day that Frost had passed away, John Sargent, described as "being an epileptic and subject to fits":

> was then and there suddenly and unobserved seized with a violent fit of epilepsy and whilst in such fit turned on his face on the…bed and was…suffocated and smothered in the clothes of the…bed and there instantly did die.

Evidence given by witnesses of bruising around the deceased's neck was ignored by the coroner and jurors and they gave a verdict that Sargent had "accidentally, casually and by misfortune come to his death and not otherwise".[250]

There are several other similar deaths and injuries of 'lunatics' reported amongst the inquests and in the press concerning Eastville Workhouse, though it should be noted that these are certainly the exceptions that made it into the public domain.[251] The majority of incidents may never have been investigated in any detail and the cases highlighted here may merely represent where the systematic use of force and restraints against 'lunatics' became lethal. In any case, from the evidence of the workings of the Coroner's Court from this one day in June 1867, it seems unlikely the real cause of death would be determined

249 GA Ref. CO1/I/13/B/24. A week after the inquest and having studied the evidence given, the Lunacy Commissioners wrote to the Poor Law Board demanding an inquiry into the incident and even named a pauper nurse as being John Frost's killer. An internal inquiry was held by the Clifton Union Board of Guardians at Eastville Workhouse in late June 1867 but failed to come to any significant conclusion. As a result of the incident the Workhouse Medical Officer Mayor (Jnr) was scapegoated by the Guardians and resigned in July. A number of workhouse staff involved in the case left over the succeeding months. TNA Ref. MH 12/4013.

250 GA Ref. CO1/I/13/B/26. A more detailed discussion concerning the treatment of workhouse inmates with epilepsy can be found in Caldicott, R. *Bedminster Union Workhouse and Victorian Social Attitudes on Epilepsy: A Case study of the Life and Death of Hannah Wiltshire* Bristol Radical Pamphleteer #35 (Bristol: BRHG, 2016).

251 See for example the cases of William Ridd (1869) GA Ref. CO1/I/15/D/6, CO1/N/15/142 and William Harse (1874) GA Ref. CO1/IN/20/C/21, CO1/IN/20/D/2. Another case in 1880 demonstrates that such practices were continuing. William Parsons on admission to Gloucester Lunatic Asylum from Eastville Workhouse was found to have "extensive and severe bruises upon his chest and very great sensitiveness in a particular spot over one of his ribs". The Asylum Superintendent in a letter to the Barton Regis Board of Guardians stated that "These bruises are evidently the result of violence" but added "his mental condition is too weak for me to be able to accurately ascertain from him in what manner the injuries were inflicted. The patient is in a somewhat precarious condition". The Guardians admitted they had been using both physical violence and restraints on Parsons but absolved the officers of the workhouse of any blame and as an afterthought added "the man's skin would bruise at the slightest touch". *Bristol Mercury* 24 January 1880.

whether by neglect or violence, and even less likely that the culprits in the workhouse would be brought to justice.[252]

The systematic use of restraints and force against those branded 'lunatics' in Eastville Workhouse may have also served another function; that of disciplining inmates who were sane but resisting the punitive regime. Visiting Lunacy Commissioners would often point out in their reports supposed 'lunatic' inmates who they considered to be sane.[253] For example, during an inspection of the lunatic wards in 1870 one Commissioner noted:

> George Batish, a black, seems to be one of questionable insanity. He is very excitable & impatient of confinement, & uses violent gestures & threats, but Mr Bernard [the Workhouse Medical Officer] was not satisfied that he was insane, & would further watch him.[254]

There are a number of cases where those incarcerated as 'lunatics' in Eastville Workhouse claimed that they were of 'sound mind'. In 1886, Thomas Luke, who had been confined in the lunatic wards at Eastville for more than four years wrote a neat and articulate letter of complaint to the Home Secretary, in which he stated:

> I am without a mortal friend. I have taken the liberty to ask you. Is it lawful to detain a sane man in an Insane men's Ward simply because he was illegally arrested on the eleventh of March AD 1880. I have

252 The death of a 'lunatic' Robert Spence in Belfast Union Workhouse in 1894 is interesting as it demonstrates the increasing awareness of the dangers of restraint and incarceration of the mentally ill in workhouses. At the inquest for Spence the "coroner reminded the jury that use of such restraint was illegal in workhouses – any dangerous inmate should be transferred to a lunatic asylum for proper care…The jury recorded their strong protest against the illegal system of restraint used in the workhouse lunatic department. They also condemned the transferring of patients to the lunatic department without proper medical consultation into their mental state" Higginbotham P. *Grim Almanac of the Workhouse* (Stroud: The History Press, 2013) 1 June 1894.

253 According to the Lunacy Act of 1853 pauper 'lunatics' could be detained in institutions such as workhouses and asylums on the so-say of a Justice, a clergyman, an Overseer, or the Relieving Officer (under the Poor Law), along with a medical certificate signed by "One Physician, Surgeon, or Apothecary, who shall have personally examined him not more than Seven clear Days previously". In the case of non-paupers the medical certificate required a signature by not one, but two physicians, surgeons, or apothecaries. http://themaskedamhp. blogspot.co.uk/2012/05/stroll-down-memory-lane-lunatic-asylums.html.

254 *Report of a visit made by the Commissioners in Lunacy* 18 October 1870 TNA Ref. MH 12/4015 Clifton Union, Bristol quoted in Hawkings, D. T. *Pauper Ancestors: A Guide to the Records Created by the Poor Laws in England and Wales* (Stroud: The History Press, 2011) p. 268.

enclosed an Unvelope for a reply, if you will please grant it at your earliest convenience, you will kindly oblige a Conservative Working Man, one trained to work from his youth.[255]

Luke's request was refused and in general this appears to have been the norm with the decision to free inmates falling to the Board of Guardians acting on the advice of the workhouse Medical Officer.

Sometimes the retrospective branding of an inmate as being a 'lunatic' allowed the workhouse management and the Poor Law Guardians to escape censure, particularly with regard to suicides, as the following examples demonstrate.

In 1867, Michael Ryan, a "healthy" sixty-six year old man, returned to Eastville Workhouse "on the ground of destitution" having been forced into the institution several years previously. Ryan quietly worked picking oakum for a few weeks, kept himself to himself and then cut his own throat with a razor in a toilet. Whilst bleeding Ryan confessed to a nurse that "I'd soon be dead as alive here" and he added that he wished the razor had been sharper. Ryan died eight days later and his case went to an inquest where he was branded as "not being of sound mind, memory and understanding but lunatic and distracted" despite the fact that he had not displayed any of these behaviours when admitted to the workhouse.[256]

Thomas Walsh was a thirty-three year old labourer who had been an inmate of Eastville Workhouse for nearly two years before he hanged himself in July 1887. It was stated at the inquest that Walsh "suffered from fits and was an inmate of one of the imbecile wards" and had apparently "had been in a despondent state of mind". The jury returned a verdict that Walsh "committed suicide whilst in a state of temporary insanity". This was despite the fact that the Workhouse Medical Officer, Dr Bernard, had stated in his evidence that Walsh was "an epileptic, but *not* insane".[257]

These and other cases suggest that the designation 'lunatic' sanctioned the confinement of inmates against their will and the use of restraint and force, sometimes to lethal effect. In addition, retrospective branding provided a useful mechanism for dealing with the most extreme outcome of the effects of workhouse life on the mental health of its inmates, namely suicide. In this manner the responsibility for these unfortunate cases apparently lay neither with the workhouse system nor its managers or overseers, but merely with the 'lunatic'.

255 TNA Ref. MH 12/4029.
256 GA Ref. CO1/I/13/D/17.
257 *Western Daily Press* 9 July 1887 and TNA Ref. MH 12/4030. Our emphasis.

Violence surrounding the confinement and control of lunatics was not all one way; the dangerous consequences of the decision by the Guardians of Eastville Workhouse to "send all cases of insanity to the workhouse in the first instance instead of to the asylum"[258] had been demonstrated explicitly by the case of Ann Richards in 1860. Richards, a 23 year old servant had been admitted to Eastville Workhouse on the basis of a medical certificate claiming she had 'hysterical mania'. Richards, clearly in distressed state, tried to escape from the workhouse receiving rooms and was locked in by a porter. Upon the arrival of the matron and assistant matron a violent scuffle broke out during which Richards struck the matron, Mrs Hunt, who collapsed and died of a suspected heart attack.[259] This particular case was used by the Lunacy Commissioners to condemn the practice of retaining 'lunatics' within the workhouses. It appears, however, that despite the violent death of a leading overseer of the Eastville institution, their criticisms fell on deaf ears as far as the Guardians of the Clifton Union were concerned.

Incidents of violence by 'lunatics' against workhouse staff and inmates were not unusual in Eastville Workhouse, however they apparently did not spur major changes in policy regarding the confinement of the mentally ill. Instead, they had a gradual effect, filtering the 'lunatic' population in the workhouse of its more troublesome and unruly elements. Clues to this process can be found in the annual reports of the inspections of Eastville Workhouse by the Lunacy Commissioners. Although these documents often comment on overcrowding in the lunatic wards, the use of restraints and other sub-standard conditions, they also note where the environment is clean, orderly and peaceful. Furthermore, the Commissioners make recommendations to the Guardians for the removal of violent 'lunatics' to the County or Borough asylums. Although, as we have seen, the Guardians were often reluctant, or refused to carry out these proposals on the basis of cost, as the century wore on they began to realise that the growing number of people with congenital or acquired mental health problems, necessitated some filtering between workhouse and asylum. The basis of this sifting would be the ability to labour, the cost and the nuisance, rather than care for the inmates or concern for the staff. As Longmate noted:

> The real reason why many unions were unwilling to send their able-bodied but weak-minded paupers into special institutions was… "a good many are often found useful in the laundry and other domestic work of the institution" and many workhouses would have had difficulty in getting the household chores done without such help.

258 Large, D. *Bristol and the New Poor Law* p. 15.
259 *Western Daily Press* 31 March 1860, 3 April 1860.

Eastville Workhouse was no exception: in 1870 'lunatics' were reported as being engaged in needle work, net making, oakum picking and labouring on the land; by 1892 these tasks included domestic labour in the lunatic wards.[260] Super-exploitation of the labour of 'feeble-minded' inmates was common in workhouses even into the 20th century with Guardians gleefully stating that the value of their work "exceeded the cost of their keep".[261] In contrast, if the cost-benefit calculations for seriously violent, disobedient or unproductive pauper 'lunatics' did not add up, then the Boards would happily consign them to the asylums, which due to Government subsidies were now a more attractive proposition. As a result, by the early 1890s, Lunacy Commissioners visiting Eastville Workhouse noted that the majority of inmates with mental health issues were an apparently docile workforce made up principally of 'imbeciles' and 'idiots'. Consequently they recommended that *none* of these inmates should be moved to the asylums.[262]

For nearly fifty years, principally on a cost basis, the Guardians of Eastville Workhouse successfully manipulated the numbers of people with congenital or acquired mental health issues in their institution and the facilities and conditions they experienced. This was despite the recommendations and pressure from the Lunacy Commission and the alternatives provided by the new asylums. They achieved this whilst at the same time disregarding a central tenant of the 1834 New Poor Law; that the workhouse was *not* a repository for the 'dangerous lunatic, insane person or idiot'. The consequences of this policy for both workhouse inmates and staff on a day-to-day level were far-reaching and sometimes tragic.

---

260 *Report of a visit made by the Commissioners in Lunacy* 18 October 1870 TNA Ref. MH 12/4015 Clifton Union, Bristol quoted in Hawkings, D. T. *Pauper Ancestors* p. 269 and TNA Ref. MH 12/4037.
261 Longmate, N. *The Workhouse* p. 219.
262 TNA Ref. MH 12/4037. This is reflected in the ratios of 'lunatics', 'imbeciles' and 'idiots' shown in Table 5.

Crime and punishment inside the workhouse

The one effect her wanderings had produced in her was a deadly hatred of workhouse officials... She was not sure of going to "heaven," but she felt sure she should meet many of these her tormentors in hell, and "then," she said, "I'll heave bricks at 'em!" I couldn't help suggesting "hot bricks" as appropriate, and then talked to her about "loving her enemies." "I can't help it," she said, "if it keeps me out of heaven, I hate 'em — I hate 'em all!"[263]

Numerous accounts of the workhouse support our 21st century understanding of such institutions as being part of the Victorian punitive regime; where poor people were penalized for being poor, forced into the workhouse and punished as a result. In the workhouse not only was there the daily regime of segregation of families, grim conditions and long hours of hard labour; there were extensive punishments, including imprisonment for minor 'crimes'.

In 1847, the year Eastville Workhouse opened, the Poor Law Commissioners issued the *Consolidated General Order* which compiled over two hundred regulations or 'articles' which were to govern workhouse operation and administration for the rest of the century. Within these articles the section Punishments For Misbehaviour Of The Paupers[264] gives clear instruction on the types of misdemeanours and the expected penalties. These rules would, by decree, have adorned the walls of the Eastville Workhouse dining-hall for all to see.

The following offences were considered to be 'disorderly' conduct:

ART. 127.—Any pauper, being an inmate of the Workhouse, who shall neglect to observe such of the regulations in this Order as are applicable to him as such inmate ;

Or who shall make any noise when silence is ordered to be kept;
Or who shall use obscene or profane language;
Or shall by word or deed insult or revile any person;
Or shall threaten to strike or to assault any person;
Or shall not duly cleanse his person;

---

263 Oral history from Higgs, M. *The Tramp Ward* (1904) See Higginbotham, P. *The Workhouse* http://www.workhouses.org.uk/Higgs/TrampWard.shtml accessed 2015.
264 Articles 127-147 in the *Consolidated General Order* (1847) can be viewed at Higginbotham, P. *The Workhouse* http://www.workhouses.org.uk/gco/ accessed 2015.

Or shall refuse or neglect to work, after having been required to do so;

Or shall pretend sickness;

Or shall play at cards or other game of chance;

Or shall refuse to go into his proper ward or yard, or shall enter or attempt to enter, without permission, the ward or yard appropriated to any class of paupers other than that to which he belongs;

Or shall climb over any fence or boundary wall surrounding any portion of the Workhouse premises, or shall attempt to leave the Workhouse otherwise than through the ordinary entrance;

Or shall misbehave in going to, at, or returning from public worship out of the Workhouse, or at Divine service or Prayers in the Workhouse;

Or having received temporary leave of absence, and wearing the Workhouse clothes, shall return to the Workhouse after the appointed time of absence, without reasonable cause for the delay;

Or shall wilfully disobey any lawful order of any officer of the Workhouse;

Typically the above 'disorderly' offences were punished by a reduction of the already meagre diet for up to two days to a small amount of bread, potatoes or rice and the withdrawal of all food 'luxuries' (sic) such as butter, cheese, tea, sugar, or broth.

Repetitions of the above offences or more serious transgressions were considered to show 'refractory conduct':

ART. 128.—Any pauper being an inmate of the Workhouse, who shall, within seven days, repeat any one, or commit more than one, of the offences specified in Art. 127 (above):

Or who shall by word or deed insult or revile the Master or Matron, or any other officer of the Workhouse, or any of the Guardians;

Or shall wilfully disobey any lawful order of the Master or Matron after such order shall have been repeated;

Or shall unlawfully strike or otherwise unlawfully assault any person;

Or shall wilfully or mischievously damage or soil any property whatsoever belonging to the Guardians;

Or shall wilfully waste or spoil any provisions, stock, tools, or materials for work, belonging to the Guardians;

Or shall be drunk;

Or shall act or write indecently or obscenely;

Or shall wilfully disturb other persons at public worship out of the Workhouse, or at Divine service or Prayers in the Workhouse;

These offences could be punished by the withdrawal of food *and* solitary confinement for up to 24 hours in a 'refractory' cell which typically was underground in one of the workhouse cellars (see Figure 30).[265]

It is clear that the comprehensive rules of the workhouse which ranged from dealing with violence against the person and theft through to playing cards, swearing and breaking enforced silences gave great licence to the Masters and Matrons to create a punitive regime, which accounts suggest were encouraged and widespread. It is, though, interesting that the Consolidated General Order gives us plenty of clues to as to the uncontrolled horrors of workhouse system in the years before these generalised regulations were issued. For example, consider the following new rules:

ART. 109.—If any pauper require the Master or Matron to weigh the allowance of provisions served out at any meal, the Master or Matron shall forthwith weigh such allowance in the presence of the pauper complaining and of two other persons.

ART. 113.—No pauper in the Workhouse shall be employed or set to work in pounding, grinding, or otherwise breaking bones, or in preparing bone dust.

ART. 119.—No written or printed paper of an improper tendency, or which may be likely to produce insubordination, shall be allowed to circulate, or be read aloud, among the inmates of the Workhouse.

These three articles refer respectively to managerial corruption through short diets, the Andover scandal of 1845 where starving workhouse paupers were forced to eat the rotting bones they were crushing[266] and the Anti-Poor Law and Chartist agitation of the early late 1830s and early 1840s.

Interestingly, as late as the 1860s the latter article was used by the Eastville Workhouse Master to ban all newspapers on the basis that they encouraged 'insubordination'. In a heated meeting of the Board of Guardians in January

265 The 'refractory cell' at Eastville Workhouse is referred to in the report on the Board meeting of the Clifton Poor Law Union in the *Western Daily Press* 21 July 1866.
266 Higginbotham, P. *The Workhouse Cookbook* pp. 61-64.

Figure 30: A typical workhouse refractory cell.

1861, the Master was questioned by a Mr Bush as to the reasons for the ban and the Board had to be reminded by Bush that a:

> Union was not a prison, and that poverty was no crime… they did not live under despotism, and he hoped they would not treat the paupers like the serfs of Russia or the slaves of South America.[267]

According to the Master "paupers sometimes wasted hours in crowding down in corners reading newspapers" and as far as he was concerned he was the ultimate censor when it came to publications entering the Workhouse. This power also extended to which inmates should have access to them. The Board broadly agreed with his position, stating, however, that 'aged and good sort of persons should not be deprived of newspapers'. It appears the Master's ban had been enforced even more harshly because of critical articles about his authoritarianism in the local press,[268] though it should also be noted that simultaneously there was also a dispute in the media about 'short diets' in Eastville Workhouse as compared to other Union institutions in the Bristol area. This may have been the real source of the worries the Master and Guardians had of insubordination by inmates in their institution.

267 *Western Daily Press* 12 January 1861.
268 *Western Daily Press* 8 January 1861.

In addition to restrictions on access to papers and publications in the General Order, there were a tranche of new rules (Articles 135-142) specifically dealing with punishment of paupers, particularly young adults and children. These were clearly directed at proscribing overt sadistic violence and sexual abuse of minors, of which there are numerous accounts in the workhouse system.[269] This of course did not mean prohibition of corporal punishment for minors; it was quite acceptable to beat male children (defined as less than 7 years of age) and boys and girls (over 7 years of age) with weapons 'approved of' by the Guardians.

Crime and punishment outside the workhouse

For 'misbehaving' inmates this daily authoritarian regime was not the only concern. After the internal system of punishment came the external; workhouse Masters could refuse the right to leave and hold an inmate for longer than 24 hours in solitary confinement if they decided to put them before the magistrates. In order to make this decision miscreant paupers were sometimes were brought before the Board of Guardians acting as a 'kangaroo court'. A typical case from Eastville Workhouse in 1867 reported in the local press demonstrates both this process and the attitude of the Board to minors:

> The Master complained that three girls had torn a couple of leaves out of a book which was for the use of inmates of the ward to which they belonged. The Rev. F. Burges suggested that the girls should be taken before the magistrates. The Master was afraid there was a difficulty in proving that the girls did the mischief. A Guardian proposed that the girls should be brought before the Board – they might admit the charge. The three girls were a few minutes afterwards introduced to the guardians.

> The Chairman: Which of you girls broke out the leaves of the book?

> First Girl: We all three did it.

> The Chairman: Do you two others admit that you had a share in it?

> Second Girl: Yes, sir.

269 A number of disturbing accounts are provided in Longmate, N. *The Workhouse* and Higginbotham, P. *A Grim Almanac of the Workhouse* (Stroud: The History Press, 2013).

The Chairman: What does the last one say? Did you do it too?

Third Girl: Yes, sir.

A Guardian: What did you do it for?

Mr Giles: No matter what they did it for. I move that they be sent before the magistrates and prosecuted for destroying the property of the Union.

Rev. F. Burges: I second it, and hope they will have a very severe punishment. (Hear, Hear.)

The resolution was put and carried unanimously.

Mr Giles: Let them see how they like the inside of a gaol.

The Master stated that the first girl had been in a Reformatory. When she first entered the workhouse she pretended to be dumb. He suggested to the doctor, after the lapse of a fortnight, that a shower bath might be of some use. The shower bath was tried and was the means of restoring her speech. (Laughter)[270]

Once before the magistrates sentences given to workhouse paupers could be very harsh, as the following examples covering various misdemeanours in Eastville Workhouse demonstrate.

Refusing to work was a serious offence:

An insubordinate pauper - William Jones, an inmate of the Clifton Union Workhouse, was charged with refusing to work. The master proved the case and the bench sentenced the prisoner to a month's imprisonment with hard labour, the Chairman telling him it was shameful that the public should be called upon to pay for idle scoundrels such as he had proved himself to be.[271]

In 1875 James Bright failed to break the requisite weight of rocks (1.5 metric tonnes) for three consecutive days and was sent by the Guardians to the

270 *Western Daily Press* 7 December 1867.
271 *Western Daily Press* 19 May 1876.

Magistrates. He was found guilty and imprisoned. Bright wrote a letter to the Local Government Board in London complaining that:

> As a pauper in the Clifton Union Workhouse I beg respectfully to ask your Honourable Board if it is legal for the Master to order me to break 30 cwt of stone…For not performing this task I have been sent to prison for seven days. I believe the Act of Parliament does not specify any amount of Work for Inmates, and for that reason I have ventured to address your Honourable Board.[272]

Needless to say his protests were ignored. Bright was returned to Eastville Workhouse from prison. He again failed to complete the allotted stone-breaking task and was immediately sent to face the bench once more.

Leaving the workhouse without permission was also treated very severely through the penalty of theft of the uniform:

> William Smith was charged with stealing a cost, waistcoat, trousers, shoes… property of the Clifton Union. The master stated that the prisoner, who was a pauper in the house, absconded… taking with him the clothes of the Union-house. The magistrates committed him for six weeks.[273]

> Richard Mordan, charged with absconding from the Clifton Union Workhouse and wearing away a complete suit of clothes, value 30s, was sentenced to a month's hard labour.[274]

> Charles Wash, a pauper, charged with absconding from the Clifton Union, and taking away a suit of the Clifton Guardians' clothes, value £1 5s, was sent to prison for three months, with hard labour.[275]

> George Sweeting was charged with absconding from the Barton Regis Union Workhouse, and taking with him a suit of clothes, the property of the guardians.…His excuse was that he wanted to leave the house to seek employment, and took the clothing as he had none of his own. He was committed to Bristol gaol for three weeks' hard labour.[276]

272 30 August 1875 TNA Ref. MH 12/4019.
273 *Bristol Mercury* 11 September 1847.
274 *Bristol Mercury* 26 November 1870.
275 *Bristol Mercury* 30 November 1872.
276 *Bristol Mercury* 5 March 1880.

And our reluctant stone-breaker who appealed to the Home Secretary reappears:

James Bright was charged with escaping from Barton Regis Union Workhouse, and leaving his four children chargeable to the common fund. Prisoner, an old army reserve man, said he only went out to get work and inquire why he had been discharged from the army reserve. Previous convictions for similar offences having been proved, Bright was sentenced to ten days hard labour, the Chairman remarking that the authority of the officers must be maintained.[277]

Even with permission to leave, arriving back late or staying out overnight would mean a referral to the Board of Guardians for punishment:

William Bann… who had been a pauper in the Union Workhouse, obtained leave… to go out for a few hours, and instead of returning at the proper time he remained out all night. This morning he applied to… [the relieving officer] for an order for re-admission, which [he] refused, telling him his case must go before the board. Shortly afterwards the [relieving officer] was passing down the garden, when [Bann] struck him across the face with a stick, saying he only regretted that the stick was not a heavier one…magistrates fined him £5, and in default of payment committed him [to prison] for two months.[278]

Theft of minor items from the workhouse also drew significant sentences:

William Morgan, a pauper in the Clifton Union, was charged with having a quantity of pillow-casing in his possession, the property of the Workhouse authorities. Mr Workman, the master of the Workhouse, stated that on Saturday last the prisoners had brought him a message from another pauper, when he discovered some of the Workhouse property protruding from his pocket. He immediately pulled it out, and found that it was part of some pillow-casing… The Magistrates sentenced the prisoner to one month's imprisonment.[279]

In May 1863 a man was charged with stealing a pair of boots; he had applied for his discharge from the workhouse and the master had been suspicious, so he had asked the police to watch the outside of the workhouse and at 10 pm that

277 *Bristol Mercury* 19 November 1878.
278 *Bristol Mercury* 13 January 1855.
279 *Bristol Mercury* 30 June 1860.

night a pair of boots were thrown over the wall. John Phillips was arrested and imprisoned for 6 months.[280]

Disorder and violence within the institution almost always led to imprisonment, usually with hard labour:

> Charles Rees, Joseph Rees, and William Hazell were charged with disorderly conduct at the Clifton Union Workhouse, and Charles Pugsley with assaulting the master, Mr Rogers. The prisoners, with others, were proved to have behaved in a very disorderly way and to have disturbed the house by their misconduct. Hazell was discharged with a caution; the two Reeses were committed for fourteen days hard labour; and Pugsley, being a notorious offender, was sent for trial at the sessions.

Pugsley (34) later received an eight month sentence for assault.[281]

Youth or gender provided little defence in front of the Magistrates:

> Mary Ann Vaughan, a young woman, was charged with assaulting Harriet Wheeldon, the female superintendent of labour, and using threatening language towards her, at the Clifton Union Workhouse. She was committed to Bristol gaol for 21 days hard labour. Elizabeth Powell, another pauper, was charged with assaulting Mr. Rogers, the master of Clifton Union Workhouse, and using threatening language towards him, and Miss Wheeldon... The magistrates sentenced her to 21 days imprisonment in Bristol gaol. The prisoner, to the Master - "I'll give thee summat when I come out: all thy beard shall be off thee". Major Castle - "Stop a bit young woman, we had in mercy only intended to... Prisoner - "I han't had a fair trial. Major Castle - "We have determined to give you 28 days, instead of 21". The prisoner as she left the dock, shook her fist at Miss Wheeldon, and exclaimed, "I'll give thee summat, too".[282]

> Four girls, named Martha Ryan, Elizabeth Davis, Elizabeth Jenkins, and Mary Ann Gay, inmates of the Clifton Union workhouse, were severally charged with riotous behaviour. Ryan and Jenkins were sentenced to 21 days' hard labour each, and Gay and Davis to 10 days' hard labour.[283]

280 *Bristol Mercury* 9 May and 4 July 1863.
281 *Bristol Times & Mirror* 4 February and 19 March 1869.
282 *Bristol Mercury* 18 September 1869.
283 *Bristol Mercury* 31 December 1870.

Eliza Sledge, Fanny Jarvis, Flora Daw, Sarah Macey and Emma Taylor, five young girls, were charged under a warrant with wilfully damaging 135 panes of glass, value £2 10s, the property of the guardians of the Clifton Union, at the workhouse. It appeared from the evidence of Mr. D. Rogers, the master of the workhouse, that about half-past six o'clock yesterday morning Sledge came to him and demanded her discharge. As her conduct had been disorderly in the former part of the week, he refused to accede to her request, telling her he intended to take her before the justices. She left the ward where this conversation took place, and in a few minutes afterwards the master heard a great noise. On going to ascertain the cause he found all the prisoners engaged in smashing the windows with brooms and other articles, destroying not only the glass but the lead framework as well. They made a complete wreck of seven windows. The noise caused by their yelling and screaming, and the crashing of glass was fearful, and Mr Rogers declared he never recollected another such riot in the workhouse. Mrs. Nash, assistant-matron, and the matron, Mrs. Rogers, were called, and corroborated the master's statement. Sledge, who appeared to have been the ringleader, told the bench, with considerable effrontery, that Mrs. Rogers had systematically aggravated her and driven her to do what she had done. Taylor and Macey were sent to gaol for a month's hard labour each, no previous conviction having being proved against them; but Sledge, Daw and Jarvis, who had several times been convicted, were sentenced to two month's imprisonment with hard labour.[284]

Even fairly minor offences such as swearing and 'dirty' protests by young teenagers, could lead to severe punishments:

Mary Riggs, a girl of about 14, was brought up for disorderly conduct in Clifton Union Workhouse. Mr. Rogers, the master of the house, said the accused was incorrigible. When admitted into the workhouse, about two years since, she pretended to be deaf and dumb, and it was only when a cold shower-bath was administered that she recovered her speech and hearing. Since that time she had used her tongue rather too freely, occasionally uttering the most disgusting language. It was stated that she and other inmates of the house were in the habit of blacking their faces, to annoy the officers, and it was because she was ordered to wash the dirt from her face that the offence with which

284 *Bristol Mercury* 9 September 1871.

she was now charged was committed. Prisoner brought recriminatory charges against one of the officers who appeared against her; but as she had been twice previously convicted for like misconduct, she was sent to prison for a month's hard labour.[285]

And gay sexual activity, even based on hearsay, was brutally punished:

John Veale, 22 and William McCarthy, 16, paupers were indicted for an unnatural offence at Clifton Union Workhouse, Stapleton, on 21st February last. The facts of the case were spoken by George Porter... and a youth named Sandford. Both prisoners were found guilty of the attempt, and they were sentenced to three years' penal servitude.[286]

A spell inside a Victorian prison was no laughing matter; by the mid-century the notion of the prison as a place of punishment was being standardised into the penal system. Central to this concept was the separate system, which entailed solitary confinement, absolute silence and preventing the prisoners seeing each other anywhere in the prison. In Bristol, in the Common Gaol,[287] this system was:

practiced... with "complete strictness"... Prisoners wore bags over their heads down to their shoulders to prevent recognition of their features and were moved about the prison with a warder in front and behind them.'

The Governor boasted that:

the prisoners "very much dislike our gaol" and that "the discipline is more severe in our gaol, perhaps, than in any other prison".[288]

Prisoners were engaged in hard labour which in Bristol entailed endless hours on tread mills raising water from wells, building work on the prison itself or picking oakum. This harsh regime allied with punishments such as bread and water diets and flogging for the recalcitrant left many inmates half-mad and physically crippled upon their release.

285 *Bristol Mercury* 17 April 1869.
286 *Bristol Mercury* 11 April 1863.
287 The 'Common Gaol' was situated on the Cumberland Road. It was built in 1832 on the site of the 'New Gaol' which was destroyed by rioters in 1831.
288 Large, D. *The Municipal Government of Bristol 1851-1901* pp. 98-99.

However, some people appeared to have preferred prison to the workhouse. Catherine Reynolds, before the courts in 1882, said that she preferred gaol to Eastville Workhouse as "in the latter she was three quarter starved and worked to death". The Board of Guardians responded to the adverse publicity this had generated by claiming in their meeting:

> The guardians knew that paupers in that house were treated as well as they were in any workhouse in England. It was through their being treated so well in that workhouse that there were so many candidates for relief (hear, hear). He thought the paupers may be treated worse than they were, and even then not treated badly enough.[289]

The underlying sentiments of the Guardians were clear.

Juveniles, crime and the workhouse

> In some villages, large painted boards were fixed up: warning all persons who begged within the district, that they would be sent to jail. This frightened Oliver [Twist] very much, and made him glad to get out of those villages with all possible expedition[290]

Prior to the Victorian period there was no specific limit to the age at which you could be sent to prison. Children were subject to similar legal sanction as adults, were often incarcerated with them and were executed as young as twelve years-old. In the 1840s there was considerable concern amongst 'reformers' that placing children with adult criminals was likely to lead them into future lives of crime. As a result in the 1850s Reformatory and Industrial schools were sanctioned by acts of parliament.

Reformatory schools were private institutions (often run by religious organisations) endorsed by the state and linked directly to the prison system. They were places of detention for convicted juvenile offenders who were first required to spend two weeks in adult gaol. Parents of offenders were forced to pay for their children's upkeep in these institutions. In the Bristol area, Kingswood Reformatory School was opened in 1852 by social reformers Russell Scott and Mary Carpenter.[291]

289 *Bristol Mercury* 9 December 1882.
290 Dickens, C. *Oliver Twist* (Oxford: Oxford University Press, 1994) p. 51.
291 The later (1892) buildings of the Kingswood Reformatory School still exist and are currently the site of the Creative Youth Network on Britannia Rd (BS15 8DB). Higginbotham, P. *The Children's Home* website http://www.childrenshomes.org.uk/BristolKingswoodRfy/ accessed 25 April 2016.

Industrial schools dispensed with dealing only with the convicted, sweeping up wider groups of young paupers found to be homeless, begging or wandering the streets, or whose parents were considered morally unfit to look after them.[292] Effectively they acted as juvenile workhouses. Reformers argued that both of these institutions were better than sending children and teenagers to adult prisons. However, this did not mean that these 'schools' were benign; strict disciplinarian regimes allied with frequent beatings were accepted practice. Poor Law Unions often ran such institutions as adjuncts to their main workhouses. For example, the original Clifton Union Poorhouse, in Clifton Wood, was converted for use as a boys' Industrial School in 1859.[293]

So, as alluded to by Oliver Twist, the urban streets and rural byways of Victorian Britain were seriously unsafe environments for children and teenagers alike. Apart from convictions for petty theft, minors could be picked up for begging, wandering, vagrancy, 'frequenting with thieves' or if considered 'uncontrollable'. Those convicted under the age of sixteen could only avoid a long spell in adult prison on condition that they were committed to Reformatory School for a period of 2 to 5 years. Consequently, once a juvenile was in trouble with the law, despite the protestations of parents, the outcome could be literally life-changing, as this sample of cases from the 1860s demonstrates:

Mary Barker, ten years of age, daughter of a hatter, was charged with stealing 5s. worth of coppers from a basket at the Workhouse, Pennywell-road… the prisoner was apprehended in Little Ann-street by Mrs. Sutton, who found the money in the prisoner's skirt pocket. The bench sentenced the prisoner to the Fort-road Industrial School for five years.[294]

Robert Godfrey, a little boy, charged with begging in Charlotte St, was sent to Park-row school for three years.[295]

292 This could mean for example, children whose parents were considered to be alcoholics, criminals or prostitutes.

293 Higginbotham, P. The Children's Home website http://www.childrenshomes.org.uk/boardingout accessed 25 April 2016.

294 *Bristol Mercury* 29 June 1867. The Bristol Industrial School for Girls was established in 1866 in a small house and garden on Royal Fort Road, off St Michaels's Hill. Higginbotham, P. *The Children's Home* website http://www.childrenshomes.org.uk/BristolGirlsIS/ accessed 25 April 2016.

295 *Bristol Mercury* 26 July 1862. The Park Row Industrial School for Boys was established in 1859 by Mary Carpenter, founder of the nearby Red Lodge Reformatory for Girls. The original buildings have been demolished and the Bristol University Chemistry Department now stands on the site (BS8 1TH). http://www.childrenshomes.org.uk/BristolParkRowIS/.

Charles James, a little boy, was charged with stealing a pair of boots, value 2s 6d, from a shop door in the Lower Arcade…The boy, although only 13 years of age, had been previously convicted of felony. The magistrates committed him to hard labour for 14 days and five years confinement in a Reformatory School.[296]

Two urchins, named James Holbrook and William Thomas Nicholas were charged with stealing two cocoa nuts, the property of Mr Thomas Garmston, of 3, All Saints' Row….He saw the defendants and three or four other boys lurking about there…he also saw the two cocoa nuts drop between the two boys, who were in his warehouse. He detained them there, and gave them in charge. [Magistrates] said the defendants were two neglected children, and the Reformatory School was the best place for them. They were committed [to prison] for fourteen days, and ordered at the end of that time to be confined in the Reformatory School at Kingswood, Holbrook for two, and Nicholas, the younger boy, for three years.[297]

Although Reformatory and Industrial schools existed after the mid-1850s, magistrates could still take the option of sending child 'criminals' to the workhouse. For example, in May 1878 a boy was arrested by police and was sent to Eastville Workhouse by order of the magistrates because he had been found "sweeping a street crossing" and collecting a few pence to support his sick mother. This was regarded as illegal begging and is clearly a similar activity to the 21st century cleaning of car windscreens for a few coins at traffic lights.[298]

In 1880 the Clifton Union Board of Guardians unanimously rejected a proposal in Parliament that the workhouse be officially used as a place of incarceration for juvenile offenders, with one Guardian stating: "To make a gaol of the workhouse seemed to be one of the maddest ideas ever entertained". However (and unsurprisingly) this rhetoric from the Board was driven by the extra costs for buildings and staffing that would be required to house the young criminals, rather than any real concern for either the inmates or potential interlopers. Despite their feigned anxiety for the "injurious consequences that might arise in the commitment of young children to [adult] prison" they were quite happy to leave them there, as in their own words "they had too many of that class already to deal with".[299]

296 *Western Daily Press* 28 May 1866.
297 *Western Daily Press* 10 August 1861.
298 *Bristol Mercury* 11 May 1878.
299 *Bristol Mercury* 4 December 1880.

Positive aspects

After all this misery, it is worth pointing out that it was not the case that the workhouse was always utterly grim, unpleasant and worse than the life of the urban poor on the 'outside'. As we have seen, towards the end of the 19th century, the composition of Boards of Guardians was being seriously challenged by women candidates; by 1885 fifty had been elected nation-wide and the numbers grew rapidly as the century came to an end. This was also true of working-class men in general and specifically both working-class and middle-class radicals and socialists. These interlopers began to transform both the composition and attitudes of Boards of Guardians as Longmate explains:

> In these areas [towns and cities], for the first time in their history, the 'Guardians of the Poor' really came to merit that proud title and instead of being eager practitioners of 'severity' and 'deterrence' became their most implacable opponents.[300]

Following this trend in social reforms, the harsher aspects of workhouse life were mollified by some concessions and improvements in conditions for the paupers as the following examples from Eastville Workhouse demonstrate.

Relatives and friends of paupers were allowed to visit paupers on the first Wednesday of the month for two hours at lunchtime.[301] In May 1878 the Bristol Guardians reported that a Mrs. Procter had distributed toys for the children, the surplus of which had been sent on to Eastville Workhouse. Proctor had also enquired "whether the inmates had been supplied with a library",[302] though this only appeared nearly twenty years later in the Bristol Institution.

At various religious festivals the workhouse would be decorated (such as at Harvest festival) and Christmas became more visibly celebrated. However, even 'charitable actions' within the institution were often wincingly patronizing. At Christmas 1882 the *Bristol Mercury* reported:

> The Guardians with their customary liberality provide the necessary viands, the orthodox repast of roast beef and plum pudding. The little ones are given presents of oranges by Mr. Dodge the master. The numerous wards are gaily decorated, the rooms occupied by the female imbeciles being especially noticeable. Amongst the inscriptions on the walls are:

300 Longmate, N. *The Workhouse* p. 268.
301 *Clifton Poor Law Union Statement of Accounts, 1874* BCRL Ref. PR2 Pamphlet Box: Societies IV B2401 p. 22.
302 *Bristol Mercury* 4 May 1878.

God Save the Queen
Long Life to our Guardians
Prosperity to our Guardians
Long life to our master and matron

The newspaper concluded that the inmates would be able to enjoy their festivities as well as "those more favoured by fortune".[303] In 1893 the house was again "prettily decorated", the children given oranges donated by the public and a Mr. Billing (a Guardian) presented the boys with a football. It was almost a full house, of the 1180 'inmates' the house could accommodate, 1043 were present for Christmas.[304]

Special trips out of the institution for children became more common, sometimes becoming annual events. In 1886 a summer treat was organised, the Guardians advertised that the trip would cost £25 and asked for donations from the public. One hundred and sixty children had an outing to Weston-Super-Mare. On arrival at the town hall "Each child received a large bun and were allowed to scamper at will about the beach". A "good substantial dinner" was followed by the distribution of a hamper of pears and a ride in the "balloon swing, which they enjoyed very much".[305]

In 1892 the same event for 170 children involved a dinner of "Mutton pies, bread, lettuce and cheese with lemonade" and the children had three hours of "boundless freedom on the beach". On arriving back at the workhouse:

> the party arranged themselves round the entrance to their home and gave three hearty cheers for the Guardians and their friends, through whose generosity they had once more been enabled to spend such a happy day. Then after singing the National Anthem, the tired youngsters made their way indoors to bed.[306]

As we can see the Board of Guardians and the managers of Eastville Workhouse made great play in the newspapers of their beneficence and the supposed adoration of their charges. However this sometimes backfired on them, as the introduction of occasional concessions such as Christmas parties, trips to the seaside or drinking alcohol were interpreted by some rate-payers as being soft on the paupers. Typically trips and rare treats such as toys at

303 *Bristol Mercury* 24 December 1881.
304 *Bristol Mercury* 26 December 1893.
305 *Bristol Mercury* 27 August 1886.
306 *Bristol Mercury* 27 July 1894.

Christmas for the children were funded by public donations, consequently angry rate-payers focussed on drinking.[307]

The consumption of alcohol for medical purposes was widespread in the early 19th century, but the rise of scientific medicine from the 1850s onwards slowly undermined this practice. In the workhouse, Medical Officers had to sanction its use for sick patients and watchful rate-payers often focussed on the annual bills for alcohol. In 1877 there was a complaint about the volume of alcohol consumed in Eastville Workhouse. Guardians responded by pointing out that the number of sick people in the institution had more than doubled over the previous five years and that had led to an increase in the consumption of beer.[308]

In the 1880s and 90s the rise of the temperance movement caused large reductions in the consumption of alcohol in workhouses, especially after 1884 when the Local Government Board made Masters personally financially liable for any drink that was consumed outside of medical supervision.[309] Criticism of the workhouses in the Bristol area is reflected by a cartoon from 1904 (Figure 31) which drew attention to the supposed drinking culture of the paupers.

However, it appears in Eastville Workhouse the regime was very strict, with Guardians refusing even to countenance a single pint offered to paupers for their Christmas dinner by a charitable local brewery in 1879.[310]

On occasion the reports of the board meetings show some compassion and regret for the economic context in which they were operating. In the depths of the 'long depression' in October 1879, after complaints about the rising cost of relief, one perceptive Guardian noted that:

> He knew that there had been a recent and complete examination of all the outdoor paupers in the various parishes of the union by all the guardians, overseers, and clergymen, and he thought all would bear him out in his statement that there had *not been one case of imposition or fraud discovered.* There were…4,000 outdoor poor, generally aged

307 A flyer from 1888 denouncing the local Poor Law Unions for the levels of alcohol consumption in the workhouses can be viewed here: http://www.brh.org.uk/site/articles/eastville-stapleton-workhouses/.
308 TNA Ref. MH 12/4021.
309 Alcohol was banned in workhouses by the New Poor Law of 1834 with a concession made for Christmas in 1848. However, some workhouses allowed able-bodied male workers to drink after manual labour. In addition, workhouse management and staff were renowned for consuming large amounts of alcohol. The annual costs of alcoholic drinks per inmate for each workhouse were recorded and showed large variations as a result. It is unclear that these figures include that consumed by workhouse management and staff. Higginbotham, P. *The Workhouse Encyclopaedia* (Stroud: The History Press, 2012).
310 *Western Daily Press* 20 December 1879.

SURPRISE VISITS AT THE WORKHOUSE!
Arranged for by the Bristol Board of Guardians.

Figure 31: The Bristol Magpie October 13th 1904.

persons, cripples, or widows with young families, who the guardians were obliged to relieve, and it was often felt that a little more relief should be recommended…The poor people came into the district in prosperous times, when manufactories were busy, in search of work, and when there was a reverse they were thrown upon the rate-payers, and so increased the burden of relief.[311]

Several months later that winter it was reported to the Barton Regis Board of Guardians that the weather was very severe and, combined with the economic recession, had prevented many men from working; farm workers, quay workers and masons labourers were unable to get employment. In the freezing conditions there were real fears that 'respectable' working men and their families might starve to death. One Guardian testified that there was:

311 Our emphasis. We*stern Daily Press* 18 October 1879.

More distress than he could ever remember, people parting with their goods to obtain the necessities of life and people turned away from obtaining relief, men with tears in their eyes. In house after house, people say "We have not worked, we have parted with everything and here we are starving". People who cannot obtain out relief and will not come into the workhouse, with their families almost starving. Amongst the working class of England there are countless thousands who, rather than throw themselves upon the parish and receive pauper relief, would endure any amount of poverty and suffering.[312]

The sentiment of this statement is clear, but its irony was perhaps lost on the Guardians. The fear of the workhouse, the degradation, loss of control of their own lives, separation of families and punitive regime was so immense that many people were desperate to avoid it and would almost starve rather than pass through its gates. Fear of the workhouse, of being in its grip and the obverse working class pride in self-reliance, were always strong emotions and remain part of the collective memory of the institution to this very day.

312 *Western Daily Press* 11 January, 13 January, 1 February 1879. Not all the Guardians were sympathetic to these horrifying reports; some argued that working men had spent outdoor relief monies on alcohol whilst others claimed that the terrible conditions were exaggerated.

4. Death in Eastville Workhouse

In sum, one suspects that few of us would have survived long either on indoor or outdoor relief in the first generation of the new Poor Law.[313]

This chapter considers the increasing role that Clifton/Barton Regis Poor Law Union and Eastville Workhouse took in dealing with the sick in the absence of proper healthcare for the working-classes in the Victorian period.

Public health and the Clifton/Barton Regis Poor Law Union

He strongly believed... that improving the morals and behaviour of the poor was as important as changing their physical environment. Thus, unless "the social elevation of the poorer classes"... could be guaranteed there was no point in taking action on housing conditions.[314]

It is claimed that Bristol had in the mid part of the 19th century the third highest mortality rate in England; with its slums, overcrowding, poverty and sewage from the Frome flowing into the tidal Avon.[315] How this serious problem was perceived amongst the well-off of the city, those who had the wealth to do something about it, is reflected in their reaction to the 1832 cholera epidemic. This had an enormous impact on particularly the poorer sections of the population of Bristol with over six hundred deaths.[316] However, the unpleasant symptoms, allied with the unpleasant smell made "Victorian gentlefolk" think the poor were inferior both physically and morally.[317]

As with the increasing numbers of paupers created by the economy they

313 Large, D. *Bristol and the New Poor Law* p. 29.
314 David Davis, Medical Officer of Health for Bristol (1873-1886) discussed in Malpass, P. and Whitfield, M. *Public health in Victorian Bristol: the work of David Davies, Medical Officer of Health* ALHA Books No 19 (2015) p. 38.
315 Large, D. *The Municipal Government of Bristol 1851-1901* p. 102. This claim has been recently challenged 'Bristol was actually fourth in a list of ten large towns, chosen for their size rather than their high mortality' in Malpass, P. and Whitfield, M. *Public health in Victorian Bristol* p. 4.
316 Munro Smith, G. 'Cholera epidemics in Bristol in the 19th Century' *British Medical Journal* July 10 1915.
317 Hardiman, S. *The 1832 cholera epidemic and its impact on the city of Bristol* (Bristol: Bristol Historical Association, 2005). Some historians argue it was only when the wealthy began to die in outbreaks of infectious disease that the holistic public health approach to epidemics became part of the state apparatus in dealing with them.

supported and benefitted from, for the bourgeoisie, the problem lay not with themselves or their economic system, but solely with the "morally degenerate" poor. This ideological position was reflected in the approach to public health in the Victorian period which saw conflicts between the emerging science of epidemiology and:

> Medical men such as James Kay [who] could still insist that idleness and recklessness lay behind the incidence of much disease, reinforcing the belief that long term prevention lay not with medicine but with moral rectitude, and even suggesting that disease appeared a Malthusian check on the proliferation of those deemed morally weak.[318]

In addition, there was an almost religious obsession amongst some municipal reformers for public sanitation predicated on the idea of the poor as the source of disease rather than as victims of their conditions. Although successful in reducing the effects of some contagious diseases, concentration on this aspect of public health to the exclusion of nutrition, housing and health care provision was to limit its effectiveness. Finally, there were significant divisions amongst the middle classes over the increasing role of the state as a collectivist force and established Victorian principles of individualism. These debates had a significant impact upon the use of coercive measures to further the interests of public health.

When the second major cholera outbreak of the 19th century in Bristol occurred in early 1849, the Corporation (effectively, the City Council) appeared to take little interest in measures to prevent the spread of the disease. Partly as a result, amongst the three Poor Law Unions (Bristol, Bedminster and Clifton) nearly 1,500 people died.[319] The responsibility for the care of most of the victims of cholera and other infectious diseases (such as typhoid, typhus, smallpox, tuberculosis and scarlet fever) technically lay with the Poor Law Unions. However, the incessant drive to reduce the costs of relief, the associated reluctance to bear the financial burden of creating proper 'fever' hospitals for the poor, allied with the rivalry between the three bureaucracies, led to refusals to take responsibility for epidemics. This sorry state of affairs was borne out by an outbreak of smallpox in the last quarter of 1864 which claimed 180 lives in the parishes of the Clifton Union and 107 in the Bristol Corporation.[320] Amongst 632 Registration Districts, these death rates placed Clifton and Bristol respectively eighth and ninth worst in

318 Archer, I., Jordan, S., Ramsey, K., Wardley, P. and Woollard, M. 'Health Statistics, 1838-1995' in Wardley P. (ed.) *Bristol Historical Resource* (Bristol: UWE, 2000) Chap. 3.
319 Large, D. *The Municipal Government of Bristol* p. 123.
320 *Letter to the Clerk of the Clifton Poor Law Union* 20 April 1871 TNA Ref. MH 12/4015 Clifton Union, Bristol quoted in Hawkings, D. T. *Pauper Ancestors* pp. 360-1.

Registration District	Population 1861 Census	Small Pox Mortality (1864)	Death Rate %	Death Rate 1/x	Rank
Dudley	130,000	420	0.32	310	1
Walsall	59,000	166	0.28	355	2
Porsea Island	94,000	228	0.24	412	3
Stourbridge	68,000	157	0.23	433	4
Birkenhead	61,000	133	0.22	459	5
Prescott	73,000	151	0.21	483	6
Wolverhampton	126,000	244	0.19	516	7
Clifton	**94,000**	**180**	**0.19**	**522**	**8**
Bristol	**66,000**	**107**	**0.16**	**617**	**9**
Leicester	68,000	104	0.15	654	10
West Bromwich	92,000	121	0.13	760	11
West Derby	225,000	272	0.12	827	12
Sheffield	128,000	152	0.12	842	13
Birmingham	212,000	232	0.11	914	14
Liverpool	269,000	272	0.10	989	15
Islington	155,000	126	0.08	1230	16

**Table 6: Top-ranking smallpox mortality for 632
Registration Districts in 1864.**

the country, finishing *above* cities with serious levels of poverty such as Liverpool, Birmingham and Sheffield (see Table 6).[321]

In January 1867, the Local Board of Health (LBH)[322] in Bristol (primarily responsible for water supply and sanitation) wrote to the central authority for Poor Law Unions in London, the Poor Law Board (PLB), complaining that

321 *Letter to the Clerk of the Clifton Poor Law Union* 20 April 1871 TNA Ref. MH 12/4015 Clifton Union, Bristol quoted in Hawkings, D. T. *Pauper Ancestors* p. 360.
322 The 1848 Public Health Act created the Central Board of Health and although it was abolished 10 years later, the Act also encouraged local Boards of Health to be set up. These were obliged to appoint a Medical Officer, provide sewers and inspect lodging houses. The 1866 Sanitary Act made local authorities responsible for sewers, water and street cleaning through these sanitary authorities.

despite their efforts to remove the conditions that created epidemics, infectious diseases were:

> kept alive and propagated in certain poorer parts of the District… which lie in the Clifton Union by reason of there being no proper place provided by the Guardians… to which paupers suffering such diseases may be removed.[323]

Despite increasing pressure from both the LBH and PLB on the Clifton Union to provide a 'fever' hospital, the Guardians refused to move. In June the LBH provided the authorities in London with an extract from a report of the Medical Officer of Health for Bristol, David Davies:

> I have now the painful duty to report the death of an intimate friend - the Medical Officer of the Clifton Union in St Philips of Maculated Typhus. This is the 2nd Medical Officer which that Board has lost within the last two years of the same disease through the non-removal of Typhus patients. To attend Typhus Fever in the badly ventilated houses of the poor is certain death sooner or later to the Medical attendant…I now once more beg to remind your Committee that there is not in St Philips (without) a place for the removal and isolation of fever patients, this fact is in itself a source of danger for the whole city and more especially so when the germs of this disease are already in that district.[324]

Even when faced with the deaths of two of their Medical Officers to typhus, and a potential threat to the whole city, the Guardians of the Clifton Union continued to ignore both the LBH in Bristol and the PLB in London. Nearly eight months later, in January 1868, a letter to the PLB stated that at Eastville Workhouse:

> Fever has now made its appearance in the Boys' School and a bad case of typhoid fever is at the present time under treatment in one of the sick wards in which there are other patients. The provision of suitable wards for the treatment of fever and infections has therefore become of urgent necessity, and I beg to recommend the Board [PLB]…issue an order at once, requiring the Guardians to erect the Fever Wards.[325]

323 TNA Ref. MH 12/4013 18 January 1867.
324 TNA Ref. MH 12/4013 6 June 1867.
325 TNA Ref. MH 12/4013 27 January 1868.

It appears from the evidence that the threat of an epidemic breaking out in Eastville Workhouse was not the driving force behind the Guardians' decision to finally sanction the construction of an isolation facility to deal with epidemics. Instead the threat of an executive order from the PLB galvanised them into action and by the end of 1868 they had a 'fever' hospital "adjacent to, but unconnected to the [Eastville] workhouse".[326]

By 1871, the Clifton Union Guardians were confidently claiming that they had "sufficient accommodation to cater for all infectious diseases among their paupers"; but as the LBH suspected, this was both far from true and a statement that carried a deadly caveat, as Large points out:

the Sanitary Committee…realised this did not mean that there was any provision for cases… "amongst those persons who are *not* paupers but who might desire to be removed to a hospital or the inconvenience of whose homes might render their removal necessary to prevent the spread of the disease"[327]

The LBH continued to criticise both Bristol and Clifton Unions for failing to protect their large populations from disease through incomplete vaccination and lack of specialised facilities, claiming the same year that:

there was a serious cause to fear that Small-pox would soon be dispersed through the City. They had to look at the fact that a large proportion of the city had not been vaccinated, and to the necessity of having some place provided for the accommodation of parties infected with the disease…[328]

Despite the repeated warnings and rebukes from the LBH, the reluctance of the Clifton/Barton Regis Poor Law Union Guardians to take full responsibility for epidemics outside of the workhouses in their parishes and certainly if they were located in another Union (such as Bristol) continued until the end of the century.

This sad state of affairs was borne out by their reaction to a further smallpox epidemic in 1893-4 which produced several hundred cases and thirty

326 Letter from Eastville Workhouse Medical Officer, Dr David Bernard to the PLB. TNA Ref. MH 12/4013 23 December 1868. The standard of the building erected is unclear in the sources; the speed of the construction suggests a wooden structure.
327 Large, D. *The Municipal Government of Bristol* p. 132.
328 *Letter to the Clerk of the Clifton Poor Law Union* 20 April 1871 TNA Ref. MH 12/4015 Clifton Union, Bristol quoted in Hawkings, D. T. *Pauper Ancestors* p. 360.

or so deaths in the city and its environs.[329] A dispute broke out between the Barton Regis Guardians and the Sanitary Authority of Bristol in the autumn of 1893 after the latter declined to take a patient into their overcrowded smallpox hospital in St Philips and instead passed them onto Eastville Workhouse. As a result of the conditions in the workhouse infirmary a mini-epidemic broke out in the male and female insane wards at Eastville with 28 cases and four deaths within a few weeks.[330] In a tit for tat reaction, when requested by the Sanitary Authority to take the overflow of smallpox cases from growing epidemic in the city into the workhouse infirmary, the Barton Regis Guardians refused on the grounds that:

> they had been good in the past…[but] had given the city notice that they were not going to be good anymore *at their own expense* in the future.[331]

This refusal to isolate the infected allowed the smallpox epidemic to spread into otherwise untouched parishes with additional deaths and disfigured survivors. Despite scathing criticism from the Medical Officer for the city, the Barton Regis Guardians remained unmoved and even claimed that their intransigence had forced the Sanitary Authority to provide new facilities for smallpox victims at Novers Hill outside the city.[332] At no point did the Guardians consider that their financially-driven decisions had actually killed people or that, as the more responsible medical officers understood, epidemics didn't respect fiscal issues, Poor Law Union boundaries and, to a degree, social class.

Similar confusion along with ideological conflicts reigned in Bristol over the question of vaccination against smallpox, the only epidemic disease which had an effective vaccine in the period. Voluntary vaccination programmes were initially funded through the Poor Rate and administered by the Poor Law Unions. However, take-up was poor so the authorities made vaccination compulsory in 1853 by Act of Parliament. This legislation required that parents vaccinate their children within three months of birth and vaccination registers were retained by local registrars. A further Act in 1867 strengthened the law handing direct responsibility to Poor Law Guardians and by 1871 vaccination

329 Large, D. *The Municipal Government of Bristol* p. 133.
330 From the death records we can ascertain that three of the dead were Henry Ward (32), John O'Connor (36) and Mary Sealey (74); all of whom are buried in Rosemary Green. BRO Form T 30105/3/4 (1889-98). The mini-epidemic eventually spread outside the workhouse into the immediate neighbourhood of Eastville producing 76 cases by February 1894. *Bristol Mercury* 17 January 1895.
331 *Bristol Mercury* 27 January 1894. Our emphasis.
332 Large, D. *The Municipal Government of Bristol* p. 133-4.

officers were being officially appointed by Guardians. Vaccination officers were generally medical officers from workhouses who also assumed responsibility for keeping the records. Half-yearly registers of the newly born that had not been vaccinated were submitted by the registrar to the vaccination officer, which meant that parents could be prosecuted for non-compliance.[333]

According to reports from central government medical inspectors, prior to 1864 the record of smallpox vaccination programmes administered by Poor Law Guardians in Bristol and its environs was mixed at best.[334] This comes as no surprise; the constant drive for cost reduction within Poor Law Unions allied with under-paid and overworked district medical officers given responsibility for upwards of 25,000 people[335] at any one time, was hardly going to inspire the comprehensive vaccination coverage needed to stamp out contagious diseases such as smallpox. However, there were additional problems of a more ideological bent which restricted the scheme. These were exhibited in frequent heated debates amongst the Guardians of the Clifton/Barton Regis Union concerning the usefulness of vaccination, the right of the individual to refuse it for their children and whether, as a result, the Union should press charges in keeping with the law.[336] Throughout the latter part of the 19th century there was vociferous opposition amongst the Board to vaccination, with claims that it was "proven" to be useless, perpetuated smallpox or had even led to the deaths of children.[337] As late as the mid-1890s this faction was being referred to as the "anti-vaccination side of the Board",[338] though it had been consistently opposed by a number of Guardians, including Mary Clifford, who brandished health statistics rather than platitudes.[339]

After 1864, fortuitously, the war against smallpox in Bristol and its environs was principally waged by the LBH and its successor in 1872, the Urban Sanitary Authority rather than the Poor Law Unions. As Large points out:

333 *Vaccination Registers & Certificates* http://www.genguide.co.uk/source/vaccination-registers-amp-certificates/51/.

334 Large, D. *The Municipal Government of Bristol* p. 133.

335 In 1871, of the six districts in the Clifton Poor Law Union, 1 (Clifton) and 3 (St James and St Paul out parish, Horfield and the City part of Westbury on Trym) had populations of over 25,000 and a single medical officer in each. *Clifton Poor Law Union - Statement of Accounts 1872-75* BRO 22936/129.

336 There was considerable public opposition to vaccination. Court cases and fines for parents who failed to have children vaccinated were fairly common. Examples include Sibly (*Bristol Mercury* 23 August 1883), Scott and Crossman (*Bristol Mercury* 18 December 1884), Billett (*Bristol Mercury* 9 November 1886) and Johnson (*Bristol Mercury* 18 August 1896).

337 See for example reports on meetings of the Barton Regis Board of Guardians in *Bristol Mercury* 12 January 1895 and 11 July 1896.

338 *Bristol Mercury* 9 May 1896.

339 See for example *Bristol Mercury* 6 January 1888.

That war seemed to be virtually won in the late seventies and early eighties when from 1877 to 1884 there was but one death from smallpox in the city. The key to stamping out the disease lay in vaccination – and revaccination – isolation of patients and, crucially, the M.O.H. [Medical Officer of Health] getting to know of or being notified of all cases so action could be taken.[340]

These three key issues in the fight against contagious diseases such as smallpox - vaccination, isolation and coordinated action to halt epidemics - had all been problematic for the competing Poor Law Unions in Bristol. Rivalries between Unions, internal divisions, ideological imperatives and, as always, financial concerns had seriously limited their effectiveness. As a result, in the Victorian period, many Bristolians were condemned to early deaths.

Provision for the sick

The Chairman, while he sympathised with the poor woman, would remind the Board that on almost every occasion of the death of a child in the house, it was invariably asserted to be from secondary causes.[341]

A recent detailed study of the Leicester Poor Law Union between 1867 and 1905 states that the provision of healthcare in workhouses was often inadequate:

with sick wards originally provided simply for able bodied inmates who became ill. However the poor law rapidly became the main source of medical help for the poorest in the population, since sickness was a prime cause of poverty.[342]

This responsibility (or problem as most Boards saw it) was reflected in frequent debates amongst the Eastville Guardians concerning the insufficient number of beds to deal with the sick in the workhouse. For example in August 1878 there were "367 sick paupers in the house", over a third of all 920 inmates

340 Large, D. *The Municipal Government of Bristol* p. 133.
341 Meeting of the Clifton Union Board of Guardians faced with complaints of 'gross neglect' by the mother of Edgar Walbeoff a six-year-old boy who died in the Eastville Workhouse sick ward on 18th December 1860 and was buried in Rosemary Green. Her protestations were dismissed by the Guardians. *Bristol Mercury* 22 December 1860 and BRO 30105/3/1.
342 Negrine, A. 'Practitioners and Paupers, *Medicine at the Leicester Union Workhouse 1867-1905'* in *Medicine and the Workhouse* Eds. Reinarz, J and Schwarz, L. (University of Rochester Press, 2013).

at that time. Eastville Workhouse had been originally designed with space for only 120 'sick' beds. As a result another 27 beds had been squeezed in to the bulging wards and an extra 78 had been placed in "apartments not built for that purpose". By December of that year even this was not sufficient. However, the Guardians were concerned at the financial impact of building new accommodation for the sick; one worryingly noted that the projected cost of the "fever hospital" which they had been ordered to build in the 1860s had tripled by completion. Instead they proposed that they should "get rid of the lunatics", that is remove them to Gloucester Asylum, as their wards could then be converted for the sick at little cost.[343]

The problem of severe overcrowding in the sick wards at Eastville Workhouse was not the only reoccurring issue that faced the Guardians. As early as 1867 the *British Medical Journal* (BMJ) had conducted research into the Bristol Workhouse infirmaries. The Bedminster Workhouse was given a more favourable report but the Eastville institution was particularly criticised. Writing of the men's side of the workhouse, Dr Tibbits and the other authors explain that the second block is for able bodied paupers and two wards occupied by the sick:

> had neither bath-rooms, lavatories nor sculleries and were badly ventilated. The third block was for the infirm and included a lock-ward, an itch ward and a dayroom. The itch ward and the lock ward are locked at 7pm. The patients during that time have no means of communicating with anyone.

Those wards on the ground floor had no bathrooms. On the upper floor there were two bathrooms for three wards, but no lavatories or sculleries; plates and cups were washed in the bathrooms, which were extremely dirty. The same bucket was used for washing the ward and the patients' hands and faces.

> In the male department, the use of one basin and one towel a week were allowed for each ward.

If patients wanted to bathe any lesion or sore they had to use the chamber pots and Tibbits added:

> The great point that struck us was the total absence of any proper washing arrangements for the inmates.

343 *Bristol Mercury* 3 August and 5 December 1878. However, the accommodation for the 'lunatics' would not be available for another two years.

Figure 32: Children's washroom at Eastville Workhouse
(last used in 1922, Photo c.1960).

He went on to note that in the sick wards, one towel had to last a patient a week, there were 26 towels for 32 people, that patients with sores were lying in the wrong kind of bed and that chamber pots had been used as wash basins to wash people. Finally, he observed that the nursing was conducted by untrained pauper nurses.[344] The lack of cleanliness, inability of patients to summon assistance in the night and general poor medical care may have hastened many of the deaths of the workhouse inmates who entered the sick wards.

When the critical report on Eastville Workhouse was published in the BMJ in October 1867 the Clifton Board of Guardians exploded with indignation. They refuted the allegations claiming that they originated from untrustworthy "pauper nurses" and that in fact the wards were "clean, orderly... and satisfactory". Some guardians responded by calling Tibbits conclusions "erroneous" and "bare-faced lies"; others claimed that "some gentlemen consider that workhouses were to be turned into palaces" and that they:

344 Tibbits et al. 'Report on workhouse infirmaries of Bristol, Clifton and Bedminster' *British Medical Journal* October 6 1867.

had to consider the poor ratepayers, many of whom had not the comforts which the paupers in the workhouse possessed[345]

The Guardians also launched an internal investigation to find out how a "reporter from a medical newspaper" had managed to get access to the sick wards without notice. They soon turned on the recently-employed workhouse Medical Officer, David Bernard,[346] whom they suggestively claimed was "on terms of great intimacy with Dr Tibbits". The Guardians accused Bernard of allowing Tibbits to visit the institution on several occasions without permission and colluding in the damning BMJ report in order to force the Board to provide medical facilities and equipment that he had previously requested. Despite his protestations to the contrary, the humiliated Bernard was obliged to write a letter to the newspapers refuting the findings in the BMJ report.[347]

Several weeks later Tibbits and Bernard were requested by the Clifton Guardians to attend an 'inquiry' into the affair at Eastville Workhouse. The meeting commenced with the Board absolving themselves of any blame in the matter and, if there was to be any, placing it squarely upon the Master and Medical Officer of the institution. Dr Tibbits protested that:

> The board had already pronounced judgement, by stating that one portion of his assertions were wilful errors and the other barefaced lies, and he thought it was contrary to all forms of usage to meet together for an inquiry after they had passed judgement. He thought it would be much more satisfactory to the public and to themselves to have an *independent commissioner* to make the investigation.

Despite one or two dissenting voices (which were rapidly silenced by the chairman) this suggestion was swiftly dismissed by the Guardians and the so-called 'inquiry' continued with a parade of pauper nurses parroting statements refuting almost all of the observations Tibbits had documented in the BMJ report. Several witnesses denied having spoken to Tibbits, or even recognising him, and there were howls of laughter from the Guardians when it was suggested by one that he gained his information from an 'imbecile nurse'. The 'inquiry'

345 *Bristol Mercury* 2 November and 7 December 1867.
346 Bernard married Alice Rose Grace, sister of the famous cricketer W.G. Grace, a few weeks after this incident. W.G. Grace later became a medical officer for the Barton Regis Poor Law Union following in the footstep of his father Henry who held a similar post for the Clifton Union. Interestingly, Dr Henry Grace had accompanied Bernard and Tibbits on their fateful tour of the Eastville Workhouse sick wards in 1867. Tomlinson, R. *Amazing Grace: The Man who was W.G.* (London: Little, Brown, 2015) pp. 166-7 and *Bristol Times & Mirror* 13 December 1867.
347 *Western Daily Press* and *Bristol Mercury* 2 November 1867.

concluded with further merriment when one Guardian stated "that it was a very lucky thing that it was not the 1st of April, for Dr Tibbits had made fools of them all", thus compounding the humiliation of the interloping doctor.[348] It certainly wasn't a lucky day for him or, more crucially, for sick paupers in the wards of Eastville Workhouse.

From studying the scandal surrounding the Tibbits report, it is evident that the primary aim of the Guardians was to protect their public reputations as "humane men and Christians" rather than deal with any concerns about the treatment of sick paupers in the workhouse. This obsession with their public face even led them to consider refusing to introduce the medical equipment Dr Bernard had lobbied for, as it suggested an admission of guilt in the light of the critical BMJ article. Certainly their already low opinion of medical officers was compounded by the actions of supposedly troublemaking doctors-cum-journalists such as Tibbits and his collaborator Dr Bernard.

Testing relations between the Clifton Guardians and the workhouse Medical Officer were nothing new. The first workhouse doctor, E. H. Mayor who began his tenure with the opening of the institution in 1847, was forced to resign in 1862. The prevalence in Eastville Workhouse of infections such as 'bad eyes' (ophthalmia), skin diseases and parasites (scabies or lice) causing the 'itch' especially amongst children, were common knowledge in Bristol in the 1860s.[349] In February 1862, Thomas Rider, the Schoolmaster of Eastville Workhouse, penned a letter to the Guardians of the Clifton Union:

> Gentlemen, I hereby beg to resign my office...and in so doing allow me to state that, <u>among many other motives</u> the most decisive in leading me to take this step has been the dread of the Itch among the boys extending itself in an alarming manner as the warm weather of the spring & summer approaches.[350]

Although Rider had made it abundantly clear to the Guardians that there was a serious problem, several months of inaction passed before the issue of

---

348 *Bristol Times & Mirror* 4 December 1867.
349 Unfortunately, what was not fully understood was the relationship between lice and typhus. *Bristol Mercury* 14 June 1862. George Poole was brought to court in July 1862 for "deserting his wife and children, leaving then chargeable to the parish of St. Philip and Jacob". One of the magistrates, Bigg, noted that one of Poole's children present in the court "who had been in the Clifton Union, appeared to be suffering from bad eyes, upon which Mr. Bigg remarked that almost every boy that went to the Clifton Union got bad eyes. Mr. Alford [a relieving-officer for Clifton Poor Law Union]: I don't know what's the reason, I'm sure. Mr. Bigg: They ought not to let them use the same towels. It's a very odd thing they cannot get rid of the ophthalmia there." *Bristol Mercury* 26 July 1862.
350 TNA Ref. MH 12/4010 27 February 1863.

the numerous and perpetually unhealthy children was again brought to their attention by a member of the workhouse Schools Committee, Rev. J. Ludlow. In June 1862 they responded by blaming the introduction of the 'itch' on a group of children received from the Bristol Corporation and lack of isolation of the afflicted. Subsequently, Dr Mayor reported to the Guardians in a letter stating that parasites were spreading despite his best efforts, because children were kept in a "dirty state", were sharing beds and there was improper fumigation, effectively laying the blame at practices within the workhouse.[351] The Board were insulted by these comments and one member, a Mr Pope "thought the doctor had acted very disrespectfully towards the Guardians, not only on that but on other occasions" and suggested he had been finding excuses "in order to screen himself from neglect of duty".[352]

After an angry debate the Guardians summoned Dr Mayor to report in person to the next meeting; it appears they were looking for a scapegoat within the institution to deflect criticism away from the Board and events over the following weeks would bear this out. In the interim, unbeknown to Dr Mayor, a letter had been received by the Poor Law Board in London from an inmate of the Eastville Workhouse, George Evans. Evans claimed in his correspondence that he had asked Dr Mayor for medicine to deal with his "general nervous debility, accompanied by great exhaustion and depression of spirits" and had been refused. The letter continued:

> On my intimating my intention of applying to a higher quarter for redress, he [Dr Mayor] threatened to kick me down stairs…I am suffering with many more of my fellow-inmates, from his neglect. Mine is no exceptional case. I could relate dozens of a similar nature…

Evans went on to accuse the doctor of failing to give medical assistance to two workhouse inmates both of whom died in the previous few weeks. He concluded his letter by begging the authorities to carry out an inquiry into these matters.[353]

The combination of the Evans letter, the scandal over the 'itch' amongst children and a number of other accusations damned Dr Mayor; a resolution was passed by the Guardians in his absence requesting him to resign his office. However, during the fractious inquiry held by the Board into the accusations

---

351 *Bristol Times & Felix Farley's Bristol Journal* 14 June 1862. It "transpired that the room once used for fumigating the clothes of paupers had been converted into a tool-house". *Western Daily Press* 7 June 1862.
352 *Bristol Mercury* 14 June 1862.
353 *Western Daily Press* 21 June 1862.

against Mayor it became clear that the problems in Eastville Workhouse were worse than the Guardians imagined and were of a systemic nature rather than merely the failings of the Medical Officer.

Amongst the accusations, claims, counter-claims, contradictions and denials that marked the evidence given by workhouse staff including the Master and Matron, a number of facts emerged. Skin infections and infestations of lice were endemic and chronic, particularly amongst children. The procedures for fighting them such as fumigation and isolation had been largely disregarded and this had been the case for many years. Complaints by the workhouse Schoolmaster and the Medical Officer about the cleanliness of the children and the filthy state of the schools and insane wards were apparently denied or ignored. Finally, Dr Mayor had been continually overwhelmed, both in time and resources, with the sheer numbers of children suffering from the effects of the various afflictions. To cap it all, the ex-chairman of the Board, now ex-officio Guardian the Rev. Mirehouse exclaimed:

> He was not at all satisfied as to the state of things he had found there that day, but he saw where the mischief was – all the officers were at loggerheads, and did not pull together. A house divided against itself could not stand, and as long as the officers were quarrelling and jangling they could not have their house properly managed. He could not say he was satisfied with the doctor, nor with any one of the officers he had heard that day. He believed they were all to blame, every one of them.[354]

Despite this damning critique of collective practice in Eastville Workhouse, which it should be noted makes no reference to the responsibilities of the Poor Law Guardians for either management or funding, Dr Mayor tendered his resignation and effectively became the 'sacrificial lamb' in this sorry tale. This certainly suited the Clifton Guardians as they were well aware that if Mayor had resisted them, they probably would have been investigated by the Poor Law Board and that may have uncovered the dubious practices in Eastville Workhouse.[355]

After Dr Mayor had left the institution it was noted by the Guardians that he was not only functioning as Medical Officer for Eastville Workhouse, but also for District 2 of the Clifton Poor Law Union. District 2 comprised the parish of St. Philip and Jacob (without) which had a population of over 40,000 according to the 1871 census and was by far the largest in the Clifton Union.

354 *Western Daily Press* 28 June 1862.
355 *Western Daily Press* 5 July 1862.

In order to supplement the relatively low wage of £70 per year for administering to the workhouse (even some of the Guardians considered it "very small"), it appears it was normal practice for the medical officer to take on another district as well. Consequently, Dr Mayor's workload was immense and it is no surprise that he turned patients away and was unable to visit patients regularly or immediately attend to injured or dying inmates in Eastville Workhouse. In addition, some of the Guardians suggested that the rule imposed by the Union that doctors should supply their own medicines, should be rescinded on the grounds that:

> it seemed that many poor creatures came to that house [workhouse], suffering under a number of diseases, which required medicine the medical officer was not able to give from the salary he received.[356]

The idea that a doctor should be paying for medicines out of his own pocket and the consequences of this state of affairs for pauper patients was apparently lost on the Guardians, who turned down both an increase in salary and the proposal that the Poor Law Union should fund "expensive" medical supplies.[357]

If the Clifton Guardians thought that they could eliminate what were clearly systemic problems regarding pauper healthcare by merely sacking the workhouse Medical Officer, they were in for a rude shock. The new doctor, J. Mortimer Granville, was elected in August 1862. Five months later, he too was querying why vital medical equipment to halt the spread of parasites amongst inmates was endlessly delayed, asking for a large pay rise and for medicines to be funded by the Poor Law Union.[358] The Guardians ignored these requests and by the end of January 1863 the number of inmates with skin diseases had once again reached epidemic proportions with 110 cases and a growth rate of nearly 20 per cent per week![359]

Worse was to come for the Board. Granville had clearly reached the end of his tether with the intransigent Guardians. A few days later he wrote a letter to the local press containing a comprehensive and damning critique of conditions in the sick wards of Eastville Workhouse. Granville's primary criticisms centred on the complete lack of paid nurses, the use of unpaid pauper labour, overworked staff in general and an absence of medical equipment and drugs. His

356 *Bristol Times & Felix Farley's Bristol Journal* 19 July 1862.
357 It was estimated by one of the Guardians that the minimum cost of medicines would be more than half the current salary of the workhouse Medical Officer. *Bristol Mercury* 20 December 1862, *Bristol Times & Mirror* 19 July 1862 and *Clifton Poor Law Union - Statement of Accounts, 1872-75* BRO Ref. 22936/129.
358 *Bristol Times & Felix Farley's Bristol Journal* 13 December 1862.
359 *Western Daily Press* 31 January 1863.

outrage was compounded by the paucity of simple amenities that "decency and common humanity necessitate" such as curtains and screens between those inmates undergoing surgery or dying. Crucially he noted:

> I have yet to learn why paupers are to be treated as imposters every time they complain of highly probable aches and pains, and to be refused medicine because the medical officer has no ocular demonstration of their illness….But never will the Clifton Union Workhouse be a healthy establishment, or its inmates receive their just provision in the hour of sickness, until at least one paid nurse is provided, and some arrangement is made by which the supply of efficient medicines to the paupers may be possible.

Granville rounded off his condemnation of healthcare in Eastville Workhouse by stating that the obsession of some Guardians with penny-pinching micro-management was not only causing unnecessary suffering amongst inmates, but was at the same time financially inefficient in that it failed to prevent the spread of disease, which in turn lead to greater costs both in human and fiscal terms.[360] The outraged Clifton Guardians characteristically responded by proposing that Dr Granville resign immediately; two weeks later he complied with their request.

It is important to state that the cases of Doctors Mayor, Granville, Tibbits and Bernard[361] were not exceptions local to Bristol, as the context for similar disagreements and failures in Poor Law healthcare was in place across the country. The relationship between Guardians and Medical Officers was problematic as the costly appointment of the latter was frequently resented by the tight-fisted Boards and the quality of the service provided was consequently second class. Many doctors only took the relatively low-paid Poor Law Union appointments as it allowed them to develop networks of far more lucrative fee-paying customers.

360 *Western Daily Press* 4 February 1863.
361 Despite his rocky beginnings with regard to the affair of Dr Tibbits and the *British Medical Journal*, David Bernard was one of the longest serving Medical Officers at Eastville Workhouse serving from September 1867 to December 1873 and was reappointed in August 1876 at the age of thirty five. On the second occasion he replaced a Mr Hodges who had resigned because of accusations by the Guardians of "irregularities and negligence" and "very unsatisfactory discharge of his duties". It is unclear to what these statements referred as journalists present at the meetings of the Board deliberately obscured details of the investigation. However, if previous battles between the Board and its Medical Officers are anything to go by it should not be assumed that Hodges was necessarily guilty or that the Guardians bore no responsibility for these misdemeanours. TNA Ref. MH 12/4043, *Western Daily Press* 1 July 1876, 8 July 1876 and *Bristol Mercury* 15 July 1876.

As with most Poor Law Unions, the miserly Clifton/Barton Regis Guardians were fully aware of this unequal practice and acted accordingly. They resisted pay-rises, paying for medicines, medical equipment and the use of locums to save on cost whilst apparently failing to realise that Medical Officers might have given more time to their numerous pauper patients if they could actually afford to do so.[362] Similarly, spending money on preventing illness and the spread of disease within the workhouse, and providing even adequate nursing-care to those in the sick wards was resisted by the Guardians. This was despite the fact that it caused unnecessary suffering and often led to *extra* costs in the long-run. When information about bad healthcare practice in Poor Law Unions and their workhouses did leak to the public, the Guardians closed ranks, grudgingly held dubious internal 'inquiries', blamed overworked and underfunded medical officers, and if necessary silenced or sacrificed them. The care of paupers was, as ever, secondary to the considerations of the respectability of the Guardians and their fiscal responsibilities to the rate-payer.

Despite the furore caused by the healthcare scandals of the 1860s and the incessant overcrowding in the existing sick wards, the Clifton Poor Law Guardians resisted the construction of a purpose-built infirmary at Eastville. However, by the mid-1870s they were tussling with their own management in London in the form of the Local Government Board (LGB) over conditions for sick inmates. This was far more problematic than having to deal with snooping BMJ reporters or critical workhouse Medical Officers who could be easily intimidated or silenced. In 1877, LGB Inspector Long condemned the badly constructed and filthy sick wards and, to the annoyance of the Guardians, the recently reappointed workhouse Medical Officer Dr Bernard fully endorsed the report. However, this time the Guardians were forced to act as the LGB now controlled most aspects of local government administration and had quasi-judicial powers. They agreed plans for a new, dedicated infirmary with lying-in wards and began to make inquiries about borrowing the money to pay for it.[363]

Despite the pressure from the LGB, it took until 1880 before the new infirmary was completed. The buildings were situated on the south-east side of the institution in a somewhat ironic location overlooking the workhouse burial ground (see Figure 6). However, this was certainly not the end of the Board's problems in terms of provision of medical care. In March 1881 the Government Inspector's report noted that the health of children in Eastville

---

362 W.G. Grace was the medical officer for Barton Regis Union in the 1880s-90s. Despite serving a population of 25,000 for twenty years, the Guardians refused him a pay-rise and made it difficult for him to employ locums. Tomlinson, R. *Amazing Grace: The Man who was W.G.* pp. 167-9.

363 TNA Ref. MH 12/4021.

Workhouse "was not as good as usual" and the institution's Medical Officer concurred stating that:

> the children were suffering from a contagious skin disease which would be much lessened by children sleeping single, instead of two in a bed, and by allowing children a separate towel. He also suggested that they should be removed until they were quite recovered.

The chairman added:

> it was well known that the accommodation [at Eastville Workhouse] for children was very bad... he was of the opinion that children ought not be connected with the workhouse, for it was a great evil for them that they should be amongst paupers. They could not wonder at the increase of pauperism when by having the children there they were practically nursing pauperism.[364]

Despite the allusion to the 'poor creating the poor', the chairman suggested creating a separate institution for children in collaboration with the Bristol Board of Guardians. However, as we have seen, most suggestions of this nature were obstructed by the reluctance of Poor Law Unions to cooperate and were subject to tight cost restrictions which typically foiled them.

The culture of casual negligence amongst the Guardians with respect to care for the sick in Eastville Workhouse, even when confronted by shocking reports from their own Medical Officers, continued into the 1890s. In February 1890, during an outbreak of influenza in the overcrowded wards, it was suggested by the Chairman of the Board of Guardians, Major Rumsey that infected patients could be isolated by moving them to the wooden pavilion which provided extra space specifically for sick young children. The Medical Officer, Dr Bernard, stated to the meeting of the Barton Regis Board that:

> owing to the manner in which it was built, it was not warm enough. *The infant mortality had nearly doubled itself...*[the pavilion] is not fit for anything *(laughter).*[365]

It is far from clear what the assembled Guardians thought was funny about the huge rise in the infant mortality rate over several years which Bernard attributed

364 *Bristol Mercury* 30 April 1881.
365 *Bristol Mercury* 8 February 1890. Our emphasis.

to freezing conditions in the wards.[366] In any case, it appears the Board made no recommendations to improve the heating of the pavilions.

The reactive nature of actions by the Board of Guardians, that is they generally only did something when confronted by damning reports from outside bodies with some kind of clout, is backed up by evidence from the return visit of the BMJ inspectors in 1894 who found nursing arrangements still "shockingly defective".[367] Their main concerns centred on the extremely low staffing levels, calculating that 586 sick patients (including children) had no trained nursing supervision during the night at all, effectively leaving their survival 'at the best to chance and unskilled care'. They noted ominously that the:

> death-rate is rather over 3 a week, and many of these deaths, as is also usual, take place in the night, when the nurse is off duty.

The general lack of nursing care was also prevalent in the 'insane' and 'imbecile' wards and there were complaints concerning how cold the wards became in winter; this state of affairs had remained despite the protestations of the workhouse Medical Officer four years previously. The Inspectors also made an explicit recommendation that boys should not be allowed to mix with men in the infirmary as this "was likely to lead to moral harm". As a result, and confirming their purely reactive nature, the *Bristol Times & Mirror* stated in September 1894 that the Board of Guardians were to be congratulated on spending an extra £200 a year on nursing at Eastville Workhouse. However, the article also pointed out that some of the Guardians had "hesitated to incur the large expenditure", regardless of the shameful absence of nursing care exposed by the BMJ inspectors.[368]

Despite the recruitment of extra nurses, the pattern of neglect continued as the numbers of sick people who were forced to use the workhouse for medical treatment increased. In 1897 a report by a Local Government Board inspector was again very critical of the numbers and quality of nursing care quoting the workhouse Medical Officer:

---

366 The wooden pavilions were constructed in 1886. It is interesting to note that this particular meeting of the Barton Regis Board of Guardians included most of the philanthropists discussed in Chapter 2.

367 *Bristol Mercury* 8 October 1894 and 'Reports on the Nursing and Administration of Provincial Workhouses and Infirmaries, 1894-5 Barton Regis', *British Medical Journal*. The report can be read online at Higginbotham, P. *The Workhouse* http://www.workhouses.org.uk/BMJ/BartonRegis.shtml accessed 2015.

368 *Bristol Times & Mirror* 29 September 1894.

I am not satisfied with the state of the Insane sick wards, there are too many for one nurse and they are mostly so ill and helpless, no attendance will be satisfactory unless by people who have been taught to nurse. Neither is the general sick ward properly attended to.[369]

Despite this litany of scandals in Eastville Workhouse stretching back over nearly forty years, entry into the 20th century seemed to make little difference. In 1905 the Inspector of the Local Government Board, Mr W. Ethered stated that:

A large portion of accommodation for the sick at Eastville is of temporary nature, made of wood, a dining hall is lacking and the laundry arrangements are inadequate. The Guardians have been reminded of the need for providing one infirmatory building for all the sick poor and permanent quarters for imbeciles and epileptics.[370]

Exposés in the radical press

In all things is King Ratepayer's convenience to be considered rather than that of the slouching tramp or shifty professional pauper… not even toleration for him, but repressive punishment, and, if in mercy possible, extermination of him, root and branch, kith and kin.[371]

Having studied official inspections, reports and responses concerning care for the sick in Eastville Workhouse it is now worth turning to evidence we have from whistle-blowers within similar institutions. Serious deficiencies in workhouse medical care were exposed in a number of socialist publications in the late 19th century and these reports give us an insight from insiders into some of the more controversial practices. For example, *The Clarion*, a weekly from Manchester published a series of articles penned by an anonymous investigative reporter on life in the workhouse in 1892 which focused on the treatment of children, schooling and included interviews with workhouse masters and medical officers.[372] These testimonies, although not derived from the Eastville institution, guide us towards aspects of care for the sick which may not have been obvious to 'outside' inspectors.

Central to the condemnations of care for the sick in the workhouse

369 *Report of LGB Inspector Westland* TNA Ref. MH 12/4047.
370 Fisher, J. et al *Bristol Then and Now*.
371 'Life in the Workhouse: Chat with a Workhouse Master' *The Clarion* 2 July 1892.
372 *The Clarion* 2 July 1892, 16 July 1892, 10 September 1892.

highlighted by *The Clarion* were the effects of the economic austerity imposed by the Poor Law Guardians. Underpaid workhouse Medical Officers were criticised for making:

> the most of their workhouse pay by dispensing physic to the paupers upon severely economical principles – with a minimum of regard for the patient's health and a maximum regard for the practitioner's pocket.

These penny-pinching behaviours, the author suggests, were exacerbated by the patients being "old, ugly, decrepit, penniless, and uninfluential" and thus it was no surprise that "patients in the workhouse hospitals sometimes die before medical assistance can be procured".

Even more shocking in the article was the implication that workhouse paupers were experimented on by unscrupulous doctors. Animal vivisection was strictly controlled in Britain after the introduction of the Cruelty to Animals Act in 1876, so according to one doctor quoted in *The Clarion*, "somebody must bear the brunt of a new medicine or new form of treatment". That somebody, it was suggested, was the sick pauper, though the doctor added rather chillingly that "nothing is ever done to a patient except with the strongest grounds for belief in the beneficial effects of the treatment". The author of the article noted that:

> some men less scrupulous and less humane than my informant may occasionally seek to improve their knowledge by experiments which, in these insignificant, neglected, out-of-the-way union hospitals, could never be detected.

The criticisms of the practice of workhouse Medical Officers were matched by those concerning the number and competence of nursing staff. The author mentions one "short-handed" workhouse infirmary where a single nurse had to attend to 70-80 patients at any one time, which he argues was nigh on impossible. In comparison with Eastville Workhouse this seems to be relatively good; the BMJ inspectors in 1894 reported a ratio of 1:120 for day care and zero trained nurses for night care.[373] It is further insinuated by *The Clarion* exposé that untrained nursing staff were employed in workhouses, not just to save money, but also to act as housemaids for the master and his wife rather than attending to patients. The lack of trained nurses in the sick wards was compensated for by using the system of 'pauper-aid'; that is, using inmates

373 'Reports on the Nursing and Administration of Provincial Workhouses and Infirmaries, 1894-5 Barton Regis', *British Medical Journal*.

to care for the patients. *The Clarion* reporter is scathing about this practice, quoting an "experienced medical officer" as saying:

> There is another class of professional paupers... cringing and fawning to their 'superiors', they are spiteful, malignant, and cruel beyond belief in their dealings with those weaker and more dependent than themselves. The cases of 'accidental deaths' in workhouse hospitals always happen in the absence of the regular nurses, and whilst the victim is in the charge of pauper-aids. The vindictiveness of some of these fiends has astounded and horrified me many a time... They will torture and plague a helpless, speechless, agonised sufferer for mere spite and deviltry, upon his deathbed – torture him literally to death, without any conceivable motive against that of wanton, deliberate cruelty. And as the most cruel of such fiends are the most obsequious to all persons in authority, it usually happens that they get the promotion to the position of assistant nurses.[374]

This damning indictment of 'pauper-aid' may seem overdramatic but there is evidence for cruelty such as this in Eastville Workhouse. In July 1868, nine months after he had been appointed as the new Workhouse Medical Officer, Dr Bernard was requested by the Poor Law Board to complete a standard form reporting on the state of the sick wards. To the question "Is the nursing satisfactorily performed", he replied:

> The paid nurses work well. But the pauper deputies are extremely inefficient. They are, almost without exception ignorant and careless; frequently brutal in the treatment of patients. They seldom remain long enough in the House to learn nursing.[375]

It should be borne in mind that this was less than a year after the violent and agonising death of James Frost discussed in Chapter 3, which was almost certainly at the hands of a pauper nurse.

The series of shocking reports in *The Clarion* could be disregarded as sensationalist anti-workhouse propaganda, as many Boards of Guardians almost certainly did. However, the experience of similar institutions, prisons, detention centres, children's and care-homes in the 21st century should warn us to take note of the whistle-blowers rather than solely relying on official reports for evidence of day-to-day malpractice.

374 'The Workhouse Hospital: Its Insufficiency and Inhumanity' *The Clarion* 16 July 1892.
375 TNA Ref. MH 12/4013 4 July 1868.

For these… are nothing else but the water-babies who are stupid and dirty, and will not learn their lessons and keep themselves clean; and, therefore (as comparative anatomists will tell you fifty years hence, though they are not learned enough to tell you now), their skulls grow flat, their jaws grow out, and their brains grow small, and their tails grow long, and they lose all their ribs (which I am sure you would not like to do), and their skins grow dirty and spotted, and they never get into the clear rivers, much less into the great wide sea, but hang about in dirty ponds, and live in the mud, and eat worms, as they deserve to do.[376]

It is clear that there were serious deficiencies in the provision of care in Eastville Workhouse almost from its inception. These ranged from chronic overcrowding in infirmary wards (which was exacerbated by the mid-century city-wide epidemics), the consequent use of inappropriate and temporary buildings for sick wards, insanitary conditions, limited isolation of patients with infectious diseases, under-funded and overworked medical officers and crucially a lack of medicines and trained medical staff. It may be easy in hindsight to put these problems down to a lack of modern understandings of medical practice, but the fundamentals of sanitation, cleanliness and the transmission of infectious diseases were well understood certainly towards the end of the 19th century. In any case, various official and semi-official inspectors and even the Union Medical Officers made these deficiencies in care in Eastville Workhouse patently clear, time after time, report after report, scandal after scandal. Yet the Board of Guardians, lurching from outright resistance to grudging acceptance, remained reactive at best and rarely proactive. So what was going on?

It is certainly true that central to the intransigence of the Guardians lay the cost of indoor relief to the rate-payers and arguably the comparative worth of the pauper, whether adult or child. Large also points out that the original aim of the New Poor Law in:

disciplining able-bodied paupers meant that… the central authority right down to the late 1860s were reluctant to concede that a workhouse fashioned to deter the able-bodied from entering it was scarcely likely to be a caring institution for the sick, the disabled or maternity cases.[377]

376 Kingsley, C. *The Water-Babies: a Fairy Tale for a Land-Baby* (Project Gutenberg E-book, August, 1997).
377 Large, D. *Bristol and the New Poor Law* p. 15.

However, there may have been some deeper ideological reasons for the neglect of the sick in the institution, especially in late Victorian England. The ideas of Francis Galton, one of the most famous scientists of the 19th century and founder of eugenic theory, the concept that the 'genetic quality' of human populations can be engineered, were becoming dominant amongst the middle and upper classes in this period.[378] In particular, despite increasing scientific knowledge concerning 'germs' and the transmission of infection, popular understanding of disease and illness amongst these classes were being modified by eugenic ideas. As Arnold points out:

Tuberculosis, syphilis and nervous and mental diseases came to be seen by some as manifestations of a generalised degenerative heredity passed on by successive generations.

So rather than, for example, tuberculosis being treated as a contagious disease,[379] many believed it was passed on through birth and that this was related to the subject's position in the hierarchy of social class; as Arnold explains:

This understanding of biological determinism led to a common perception of paupers and the chronically sick as constituting a 'social residuum', a biologically distinct underclass, which it was argued, could not be cured or reformed and which posed a serious threat to the vitality of the national stock... This biological explanation of chronic sickness served to account for the growing contradiction between national prosperity and empire on the one hand and the persistence of urban poverty and disease on the other.[380]

These eugenic ideas, popular amongst the middle and upper classes (who more often than not made up Poor Law Boards of Guardians), were to have serious consequences for the provision of care for the sick poor. Arnold continues:

378 Famous British proponents of eugenics, which demonstrate its penetration into various political perspectives amongst the well-to-do, include Winston Churchill, H. G. Wells, George Bernard Shaw and John Maynard Keynes. Of course, Adolf Hitler was to incorporate eugenic theory into *Mein Kampf* in 1925 and both praised and copied U.S. programmes of forced sterilisation for 'defectives'. https://en.wikipedia.org/wiki/Eugenics#Supporters_and_critics.
379 In fact, when the *tubercle bacillus* was isolated in the early 1880s, *The Spectator* magazine bemoaned the fact that 'nature' would lose a potent weapon that 'sweeps away the feeble...the naturally weak would be preserved to rear up broods of children tainted with their inherent imperfections'. Arnold, N. *Disease, Class and Social Change* p. 25.
380 Ibid. p. 22-3.

Although it is difficult to discern how consciously... Poor Law functionaries withheld assistance from those they considered morally undeserving or constitutionally defective, a pattern of selective neglect often becomes apparent in their treatment of the destitute and chronically sick.

The idea of 'hereditary disease' took hold amongst the medical profession in the 1870s and by the 1880s:

sanitary medicine was increasingly challenged by a social-Darwinist ideology, according to which preventative medicine was seen as contribution to a weakening of the nation by keeping alive "degenerate stock" that would otherwise have naturally died out.[381]

So the socialists and reformers (particularly women) who were elected to the Boards of Guardians in late Victorian Britain in order to improve conditions in the workhouses were not just facing questions of cost but an ideological justification for neglect.[382] This may further explain the reluctance amongst the Eastville Workhouse Guardians to improve the provision of care, despite the repeated damaging reports by the various inspectors. The combination of covert planned neglect based on the unholy fusion of Social Darwinism and Eugenic theory combined with the harsh economic constraints of the workhouse system may explain why the disgraceful conditions in which the sick paupers were treated, were tolerated by the Guardians into the 20th century. This state of affairs almost certainly contributed to the high mortality rates amongst paupers in the Eastville institution.

---

381 Ibid. p. 24-5.

382 This is not to say eugenic theory was merely the province of reactionary liberals and conservatives. Social reformers such as Marie Stopes (pioneer of contraception) and William Beveridge (engineer of the welfare state) along with socialists such as J.B.S. Haldane (scientist) and those in the Fabian society were all pro-eugenics at one time or another. These issues are discussed in Stack, D. *The first Darwinian Left: Socialism and Darwinism 1859-1914* (Cheltenham, New Clarion Press 2003). Of course, eugenic theory was less popular after the horrors of the Nazi regime in Europe and Asia and further discredited by subsequent post-war scientific enquiry. However, the influence of eugenics upon the brutality and genocides of the colonial land grab in Africa and neglect by the British administration during famines which killed millions in China and India at the end of the 19th century is less well known. See for example Erichsen, C. and Olusoga, D. *The Kaiser's Holocaust: Germany's Forgotten Genocide and the Colonial Roots of Nazism* (London, Faber & Faber 2011) and Davis, M. *Late Victorian Holocausts: El Nino Famines and the Making of the Third World* (London: Verso, 2002).

Causes of death

Determining the most common causes of death amongst the inmates of Eastville Workhouse in the first two decades of its operation is not an easy task. In the mid-1870s the Registration of Births and Deaths Act began to compel the collection of statistics related to causes of death. These were then issued by the Medical Officer of Health (MOH) as reports with tables of data of which summaries were presented in the local press. By the 1880s this data was being issued quarterly and included statistics broken down by district as well as combined figures for 'Extra-Municipal Institutions'. These were the workhouses of Bristol and Clifton Union and the Lunatic Asylum. In the late 1890s, these statistics were refined once again with specific data provided for each of these institutions.

Table 7 gives causes of death, primarily in Eastville Workhouse, at the end of the 19th century.[383] Although the years 1898-1900 are just beyond the period of burials at Rosemary Green (1851-1895) they provide specific information on deaths in Eastville Workhouse, whereas the data for 1881 is a combination of similar institutions.

The first group of afflictions, the 'zymotic diseases' as they were known, were acute infectious diseases, marked by their "epidemic, endemic and contagious" nature.[384] Statistics concerning these particular diseases were of particular interest to Local Boards of Health formed in the mid-19th century who were engaging in sanitation and isolation to fight against epidemics, hence the detailed breakdown. However, it is noticeable that one of the biggest and persistent killers of workhouse inmates, phthisis (now known as pulmonary tuberculosis or T.B.), which it has been estimated led to the demise of four million people in 19th century Britain,[385] is still listed outside of the zymotic category. As already discussed, this was partly down to the erroneous belief in its hereditary nature and thus a reluctance to consider its eradication in the same manner as the contagious diseases.

These limited samples of statistics mainly cover the turn of the century. Although these figures show the effects of limited outbreaks of zymotic diseases, such as measles, scarlet fever, whooping cough, typhoid, typhus and dysentery, they are taken from the period where the worst of these epidemics was over. As noted previously Bristol, as with most major cities, was periodically ravaged

383 Data was collated from *Bristol Medical Officer of Health Quarterly Reports 1880-1888* and *Bristol Medical Officer of Health Annual Reports 1898-1901* both of which are available at the Bristol Central Reference Library.
384 The term which related to theories for disease based on fermentation fell out of favour with the rise of bacteriology in the early 1900s. https://en.wikipedia.org/wiki/Zymotic_disease.
385 Large, D. *The Municipal Government of Bristol* p. 140.

	% of total deaths by year				Notes
	1881*	1898	1899	1900	
Zymotic Diseases					
Smallpox	0	0	0	0	
Measles	1.0	0	0	2.4	
Scarlet Fever (Scarlatina)	2.4	0	0	0	
Diphtheria	0	0	0	0	
Whooping Cough	0	0.5	1.5	0	
Enteric Fever (Typhoid)	1.0	0.5	0.4	0	
Typhus	1.2	0	0	0	
Diarrhoea & Dysentery	2.7	2.0	2.3	0	
Cholera	0	0	0	0	
Membranous Croup	-	0	0	0	Bacterial/viral induced swelling of airway
Puerperal Diseases	0.3	0	0	0	Infection of the female reproductive tract
Erysipelas	0	0	0	0	Bacterial skin infection
Rheumatic Fever (Rheumatism)	0.3	0	0	0	Joint inflammation due to throat infection
Phthisis	9.8	10.2	11.8	10.0	Pulmonary tuberculosis ('consumption')
Bronchitis, Pneumonia, Pleurisy	11.7	11.2	10.3	21.4	
Heart Disease	5.2	11.7	12.2	11.4	
Brain Disease	10.3	-	-	-	
Urinary Diseases	1.4	-	-	-	
Syphilis	1.5	-	-	-	
Premature Birth	0.3	-	-	-	
English Cholera	-	0	0	0	Dysentery and food poisoning
Injuries/Violence	0.7	2.0	1.1	0.5	
Other	48.7	61.9	60.3	54.3	
Total (%)	**100.0**	**100.0**	**100.0**	**100.0**	

Table 7: Causes of death (% of total) in Eastville Workhouse 1881, 1898-1900. *Combination of Bristol and Barton Regis (Eastville) Union workhouses and the Lunatic Asylum.

by waves of these contagious diseases in the 19th century. Did these affect the death rates in Eastville Workhouse?

In order to study this question analysis of the death records for Eastville Workhouse was required. Unusual peaks in death rates for the period 1851-1895 were isolated through statistical examination and cross-referenced with historical sources.[386] Table 8 presents a series of probable epidemics amongst Eastville Workhouse inmates compared with outbreaks of disease in the wider city as a whole.[387]

Barring perhaps 1853, the evidence suggests during the early years of the workhouse (1840s-50s) the inmates may have been spared the effects of major epidemics (such as cholera, smallpox and scarlet fever) which periodically raged in Bristol and the parishes of the Clifton Union. This may have been due to the distance of Eastville Workhouse from the city centre, the isolation its walls provided from the rest of the population and that it had no dedicated provision for 'fever' cases. Ironically, the intermittent policy of the Clifton Guardians in refusing to provide assistance to other Poor Law Unions and the Board of Health when epidemics broke out may also have unwittingly protected the inmates. This was borne out by the smallpox outbreaks in 1887 and 1893, both of which were initiated by the Guardians allowing infected patients into their wards. In each case the disease spread rapidly from the sick and 'insane' to the able-bodied workhouse inmates and then out into the community of Eastville.[388] This is not that surprising considering the evidence of dubious nursing practices and lack of staff in the overcrowded sick wards in the Eastville institution.

Typhus was a chronic problem, particularly amongst the destitute, in Bristol and the Clifton Poor Law Union in the 1850s-60s. It was not until 1909 that the link with lice as the carrier of the disease was established and thus the requirement for de-lousing as a preventative measure. As we have

---

386 Potential epidemics were isolated from the data by averaging the burials in Rosemary Green for each month over ten year periods (1851-1895). Positive deviations of 50%, 100% and 150% from the mean were noted and weighted (1-3). Unusually high death rates were considered to be epidemics if they appeared as peaks greater than 100% in a given month, contiguous deviations of greater than 50% over three or more months or a score greater than 5 was achieved for a given year.

387 Major epidemics in Bristol for the second half of the 19th century are as follows: cholera (1849, 1853-4, 1866), measles (1861, 1894-5), scarlet fever (1858-9, 1863, 1870, 1875-6), typhus (1864-5, 1866, 1873, 1877), typhoid (1878, 1897), smallpox (1858, 1864, 1872, 1887-8, 1893-4) and influenza (1889-94). These are listed in Large, D. *The Municipal Government of Bristol* pp. 130-145. Detailed statistical information on causes of death in the Victorian period in the Clifton/Barton Regis Poor Law Union is available in Table 11 of Archer, I., Jordan, S., Ramsey, K., Wardley, P. and Woollard, M. 'Health Statistics, 1838-1995' in Wardley P. (ed.) *Bristol Historical Resource* (Bristol: UWE, 2000).

388 *Bristol Mercury* 24 April 1888 and 16 July 1894.

seen, procedures in Eastville Workhouse for dealing with parasites, such as the fumigation of inmates' clothes and uniforms, had lapsed in this period. Allied with cramped wards and the lack of isolation facilities for the sick, typhus was probably a persistent killer in the institution.

The 'splendid isolation' of the workhouse environment may have protected inmates from some external epidemics, but the closed workhouse environment could also be a death trap for the young, elderly and infirm. The bad diets, physical proximity of inmates and lack of nursing care could be devastating if a disease took hold within the institution. For example, as shown in Table 8, between March and May 1855, some virulent killer disease (probably whooping cough, measles, dysentery or diarrhoea) swept through the under-fives, killing nearly thirty children. It appears that there was little or no isolation of the infected as the workhouse death registers indicate that eleven of the victims were brothers and sisters, with the McCormack family losing two of their children (aged one and four) on the same day and a third (aged five) a couple of weeks later.[389] Similar internal epidemics of typhoid, measles and other 'zymotics' appear regularly over the next thirty years, killing eight infants in 1868 and more than thirty in 1882.

A major factor in the prevalence at Eastville Workhouse of waterborne diseases such as the bacterial infections typhoid and dysentery was the quality of its water supply and the infrastructure for sanitation. When the institution was constructed in 1847 a series of wells were excavated to provide fresh water and a crude sewage system piped waste via some old coal pits into the adjacent Coombe Brook, a tributary of the nearby River Frome. An injunction in 1855 by a local landowner who opposed the dumping of raw sewage into the stream, forced the Guardians to re-engineer the system to some degree, but significant problems remained.[390]

In 1878 the workhouse wells were analysed and found to have substantial faecal contamination, along with high levels of ammonia; indicating that the drinking water contained animal and probably human sewage. This revelation encouraged the Board to switch to piped water provided by the local water company, though there was opposition from some Guardians because of the extra cost. In 1879 a series of burst pipes led the Master of the workhouse, Daniel Rogers, to authorise a return to the contaminated wells. Almost immediately there was an outbreak of 'enteric fever' (typhoid) particularly amongst the child inmates. When confronted by the Guardians, Rogers claimed that "both the children and himself preferred the contaminated water" and this was backed up by another senior Guardian who "did not think it right to put the Union to

389 BRO Ref. 30105/3/1
390 TNA Ref. MH 12/4007 9 March 1855.

Year	Period of Workhouse Epidemic	Type of Workhouse Epidemic	Concurrent epidemic in Bristol?	Notes
1853	Feb	Not Known	Cholera	
1855	Mar-May	Not Known	No	Children <5 years in family groups, 27+ deaths
1855	Jul-Aug	Not Known	No	
1856	Jun-Nov	Not Known	No	
1857	Jan-Mar	Not Known	No	
1864	Jul	Not Known	Typhus & Smallpox	From 1856-68 Typhus was a significant cause of death in the Clifton Poor Law Union
1865	Jul-Sep	Typhus	Typhus	
1867	Aug-Dec	Not Known	No	
1868	Jun-Jul	Typhoid	No	Children <5 years, 8 deaths
1878	Aug	Not Known	Typhoid	Contaminated wells at workhouse
1882	Mar-May	Measles	Measles & Whooping Cough	Children <5 years, 30+ deaths
1887	Nov	Smallpox	Scarlet Fever & Smallpox	Smallpox outbreak in death register; 12 deaths
1891	Aug-Dec	Not Known	Influenza	
1893	Nov-Dec	Smallpox	Smallpox & Influenza	Second major outbreak of smallpox in workhouse

Table 8: Epidemics amongst Eastville Workhouse inmates based upon death statistics (1851-1895).

the expense of £100 a year for the company's water". Despite the outbreak of disease, the Board were undecided on the right course of action and passed it on to be dealt with by one of their numerous committees.[391]

Four years later, in 1883, it was reported to the Local Government Board that there were still "grave defects in the water supply" to Eastville Workhouse. A visiting Lunacy Commissioner reported that:

391 *Western Daily Press* 22 March 1879.

Since the last visit Typhoid fever has broken out here and in the lunatic wards. 1 man and 3 women were attacked and one woman died. At this time 7 or 8 women are suffering from diarrhoea. I was told that it was supposed that the defective drains caused the outbreak of typhoid, but these having been set right some other cause must be sought for…and I was not able to discover that the doctor or master had any theory on the subject.[392]

Considering the recent history known to both the Medical Officer and the Master of Eastville Workhouse, the latter statement seems surprising. Either way, inability or unwillingness to deal with serious issues surrounding the supply of drinking water and of sanitation by the purse-holders (the Board of Guardians) produced a chronically unwell workhouse population, and certainly hastened many of the younger and more elderly inmates to their graves.

Outside of the contagious killers, such as the zymotics and ailments of the lung (pulmonary tuberculosis, bronchitis, pneumonia and pleurisy), we are left in Table 7 with non-specific heart and brain diseases as well as the mysterious category 'other' which makes up half or more of our sample. After 1900 there is greater detail provided on deaths in the Eastville Workhouse, including categories under "diseases of the brain" such as meningitis, "softening" and "senile decay" (probably dementia), "paralysis" (strokes) as well as "cancer", "spinal", "gangrene" and "infant convulsions". However, without more evidence it is difficult to determine how much of the 'other' category these made up.

Three Acts, the pauper body and pauper burials

The New Poor-Law regarded the poor as being positively worth more when dead than living, insomuch as the Overseers could procure from the surgeons £2 12s. per corpse, and thus save the expense of burial.[393]

Three new pieces of legislation in the 19th century, the 1832 Anatomy Act, the 1834 Poor Law Amendment Act and the 1858 Medical Act made fundamental changes to the 'ownership' of bodies of workhouse paupers and the nature of their burial. The former allowed anatomists legal access, for an appropriate fee, to the corpses of paupers who had died in the workhouse and were unclaimed by relatives or friends within two days of their demise. These bodies were then typically dismembered and dissected in medical hospitals by

392 TNA Ref. MH 12/4026 29 May 1883.
393 Feargus O'Connor, Bradford Anti-Poor-Law Meeting, December 13 1837, quoted in Baxter, G. R. W. *The book of the Bastiles*.

students. The latter Act led to a significant growth of the medical profession, which in turn demanded more pauper bodies.

Since the 18th century, control over the deceased's body, especially of executed criminals had been highly contentious. Riots over corpses were a regular occurrence at public executions, as crowds often led by friends and relatives of the victim tried to retrieve the body from the scaffold before they could be whisked away by the hated surgeons for dissection.[394] People were not only fearful of losing control over the 'right and proper' burial of the body but that it would literally disappear; cut up into pieces, dispersed and then disposed of piecemeal without ceremony. These fears were clearly demonstrated on the streets of Bristol during the cholera epidemic of 1832:

> In the cholera-smitten districts the poor were in a state of panic. Unfortunately, there was a widespread prejudice against medical attendance, partly owing to some recent instances of "body-snatching". Early in August [1832], on a Sunday morning, whilst a boy who had died of the disease at St. Peter's was about to be buried… his mother, accompanied by a considerable mob, insisted on having the coffin opened, on the supposition that the body of her son had been otherwise disposed of. The demand under such circumstances was very properly refused, but no assurances would satisfy her, and, as she persevered in her determination, the coffin was forced open by the mob, when the corpse was exhibited in a very black and putrid state.[395]

Prior to the 1832 Act, only the bodies of executed murderers who had been designated by the court for dissection could be appropriated by medical schools. However, the increasing requirements of the medical profession and the shortage of corpses led to a rise in illegal body snatching. Essentially, with the 1832 Act, the state took over the body snatching role, by appropriating the bodies of not only criminals who had died in prison but also, controversially, of paupers.

Similarly, the remaining act of the three allowed the state through the Boards of Guardians to increase their control over the form of pauper burials. As with many of the 1834 Poor Law measures the aim was to make engagement with the relief system harsher (or "less eligible") than the already desperate conditions of the poor. Legal control over 'unclaimed' corpses in the workhouse was already in place; the next step of the Commissioners was, according to Longmate, to "wage

394 See Linebaugh, P. 'The Tyburn riot against the surgeons' in Hay, D. (ed.) *Albion's fatal tree: crime and society in eighteenth-century England* (London: Verso, 2011).
395 Munro-Smith, G. 'Cholera Epidemics in Bristol in the Nineteenth Century' *British Medical Journal* July 10 1915.

determined war" on the tradition of "modest but dignified pauper funerals".[396] As with the riots over the executed at the scaffold in the previous century, control over the demise of the pauper was to become a battleground in the 1800s.

Pauper funerals prior to the New Poor Law were governed by customary practice and organised by the parish. They typically involved preparation rituals such as washing the corpse, dressing in a funeral shroud and 'laying out the body'. The latter was important as it established to the community that the deceased had died 'naturally' and was thus entitled to be buried in consecrated ground. A simple wooden coffin and trappings such as palls and simple flowers were expected on the day of the funeral. The cask was borne to the churchyard by friends and family and rituals such as ringing the 'passing' or 'dead bell' to mark every year of the deceased's life were enacted followed by a simple Christian service. Typically a wake with some customary alcohol would take place after this basic ceremony.[397] So to a certain extent, burials remained within the control of the pauper's community, even if the relatives could not afford to pay for a private funeral.

After the 1834 Act these simple but dignified send-offs were regarded by the Poor Law Commissioners as 'extravagances' and in accordance with their requirements for harsher treatment of paupers they "required that every parish funeral should demonstrate the public disgrace which resulted from failing to provide for one's own old age".[398] The Commissioners encouraged Boards of Guardians to cease giving small grants to poor families to bury their dead and to take control of the burials and their location. All rituals and trappings were to be removed from pauper funerals both to save cost and to demonstrate "public disgrace" by the very absence of ceremony.[399] This was in complete contrast with the middle and upper-class English obsession with extravagant, symbolic and 'respectable' funeral rituals and trappings.[400]

Many of the public were outraged at the 'lack of decency' of the new regime, with the denial of rights of mourning, randomly chosen workhouse inmates in uniform as pall bearers and often little or no access to private burial grounds where the unmarked graves lay. The 'penny pinching' nature of such

396 Longmate, N. *The Workhouse* p. 148.
397 Hurren, E. and King, S. "Begging for a Burial': Form, Function and Conflict in Nineteenth-Century Pauper Burial' in *Social History*, Vol. 30, No. 3 (Aug., 2005) pp. 331, 335.
398 Norman Longmate, *The Workhouse* (Pimlico 2003) p. 148.
399 Laqueur notes that "Whether or not it was Chadwick or his rival Lewis [Poor Law Commissioners] who forbade Unions to pay for the ringing of bells at pauper funerals is not clear; the important point however is that the degree of shabbiness of the pauper funeral had become a question for administrative adjudication" Laqueur, T. *Bodies, Death, and Pauper Funerals in Representations*, No. 1 (Feb 1983) p. 122.
400 Strange notes that: "Victorian Britain witnessed funerals of unprecedented ostentation, such as that for the Duke of Wellington in 1852, a military spectacle which took three months to organise". Strange, J.M. *Death, Grief and Poverty in Britain, 1870-1914* [Cambridge Social and Cultural Histories] (Cambridge: Cambridge University Press, 2005) p. 3.

pauper funerals organised by Boards of Guardians was particularly commented on and is angrily satirised in the poem *The Poor Man's Burial* penned in 1841:[401]

> Ho! contract coffins for the parish poor.
> Eight shillings each, complete with shroud and nails!
> 'An please your Honour stop within the rails,
> Poor Simon's scarce will reach the big church door.
> Not take him into church! It will not hold,
> Tho' we have patch'd it up.' 'I hear no bell.'
> 'Your Honour, the New Laws won't have it toll'd.'
> 'What! stint a poor man's soul a parting knell?'
> 'Go, tell his Lordship that old Simon's dead,
> And now they bury him, whose honest hands
> Plough'd, sow'd, and reap'd—his Lordship ate the bread;
> Bid him repeal harsh laws, that Heaven his lands
> May bless—God's poor not unregarded sleep;
> Tell him new hands may sow, and God gave all to reap'

The outrage of the public over the 'disgrace' of pauper burials was followed by widespread protest and disorder in the 1830s-40s. Many Boards of Guardians, especially in the rebellious areas of northern England and Wales, continued with customary pauper burial practices despite the instructions from London and as a result there was some back-tracking by the Poor Law Commissioners in the mid-century. However, the creation of the Local Government Board in 1871 with the primary intention of cutting local government spending, particularly welfare provision, initiated another round of attacks on provision for pauper funerals, this time from a fiscal angle. One Board of Guardians in the vanguard of these 'cuts' even suggested that:

> if they eradicated all pauper burial provision and sold cadavers to regional anatomy schools… then the poor who claimed welfare could be made to repay their financial debt to society in death.[402]

The twin objectives of the Poor Law Commissioners (and, later, the Local Government Board) to make the Union-funded pauper funeral 'less eligible' and to reduce welfare costs was reflected in how dead and dying paupers were treated in the workhouse.

401 Quoted in Baxter, G. R. W. *The book of the Bastiles.*
402 Hurren, E. and King, S. "Begging for a Burial': Form, Function and Conflict in Nineteenth-Century Pauper Burial' p. 327.

Death and burial in the workhouse

Rattle his bones, over the stones,
he's only a pauper whom nobody owns[403]

The Consolidated General Order of 1847, effectively the regulations which governed Eastville Workhouse upon its opening, provided only one rule concerning care for inmates who were dying: "To take care that no pauper at the approach of death shall be left unattended either during the day or the night." However, Longmate notes that:

> this humane rule was constantly broken, or interpreted to mean that, instead of being left alone to die in peace, frightened and suffering patients spent their last hours in a crowded ward, a painful experience for all concerned.[404]

The lack of nursing care and the over-crowded nature of the sick wards at the Eastville institution made this scenario very likely. An examination of witness evidence at inquests suggests that dying patients were not removed from the wards and they often expired in serious pain over several days in the presence of many other inmates.

After an inmate had passed away, the immediate procedures were typically focused upon the bureaucratic. The Workhouse Medical Officer (WMO) would be informed, in order to confirm the death and provide a probable cause for the death certificate. It could, however, take a considerable length of time for the non-resident and over-worked WMO to attend the scene. There is also significant evidence that inspections of deceased paupers were cursory, and it was rare for cause of death *not* to be determined at this point.[405] In cases where cause of death was not immediately established, or where foul play or suicide were judged to have occurred, the police at the nearby St George station would be informed. Their report on the circumstances of the death, usually in the

403 Traditional saying taken from Noel, T. *The Pauper's Drive* (1842).
404 Longmate, N. *The Workhouse* p. 149.
405 The case of James Frost discussed in the section *Incarcerating 'Lunatics, Imbeciles and Idiots'* in Chapter 3 is a good example of this. The WMO, Dr Mayor (Jnr), apparently inspected the body of Frost but failed to notice the extensive injuries to his torso that had led to his agonising death that lasted more than a week. As ever, Dr Mayor provided a useful scapegoat for the Clifton Union Guardians who were concerned with the scandal that surrounded the death of Frost. After admitting his mistake in the internal inquiry that followed Frost's death and under pressure from the Guardians, Mayor resigned a few weeks later citing the "increase in workload" in his job as his reason for leaving. TNA Ref. MH 12/4013.

form of a letter, would be sent to the Coroner for the County of Gloucester who would then decide if an inquest was required. These letters often show a distinct irritation with any WMO who refused to give a cause of death for a workhouse inmate and thereby required the intervention of the police.[406]

It was not until the Coroners Act of 1887 that the authorities became more concerned with determining the circumstances and the actual medical causes of sudden, violent and unnatural deaths. This is reflected in the outcomes of those cases concerning the deaths of pauper inmates in Eastville Workhouse that made it to the Gloucester Coroner's desk. An analysis of all the inquests from the 1860-70s demonstrates that *none* produced verdicts other than suicide, accidental death or - the most common - 'visitation from God' which was a euphemism for natural causes. This is despite the fact that studying the witness evidence points towards cases of serious negligence, manslaughter and even murder.[407]

According to Poor Law regulations, having informed the WMO of the death of an inmate, officers were then meant to contact "the nearest relations of the deceased...who may reside within a reasonable distance", which was (as with many similar workhouse procedures) open to interpretation. It is also unclear exactly how workhouse officials were expected to track down relatives of the deceased and how diligent they were in exercising this task. The fact that during the Victorian period only a minority of those inmates who died in Eastville Workhouse were recovered by relatives for burial outside the institution indicates that this process was probably not very successful. Whilst supposedly searching for relatives of the deceased, workhouse staff were also obliged to provide an inventory of their clothes and possessions, provide a place of storage and then interment for the body and most importantly, complete all the paperwork, including registering the death and filling out the workhouse death registers.[408]

---

406 See for example the cases of Ruth Tranter GA Refs. CO1/N/16/D/33, William Purnell CO1/N/15/4 and Thomas Maize CO1/N/16/A/33. Dr Bernard, who served two long stints as Eastville WMO from 1867 to 1897, seems to be a regular offender as far as St George Police were concerned. The Board of Guardians also pressurised Bernard several times to provide causes of death in cases where he was clearly unsure. *Bristol Mercury* 10 December 1870. Other WMOs seem to have been more reluctant to instigate contact with the Coroner's Office perhaps due to similar coercion by the Guardians.

407 See for example the following cases, some of which are discussed in more detail in this book: GA Refs. George Rogers CO1/I/1/C/2, Phoebe Hunt CO1/N/6/A/28 & CO1/I/6/A/12, John Sargent CO1/I/13/B/26, William Ridd CO1/N/15/142 & CO1/I/15/D/6, Samuel Smith CO1/N/5/14, William Harse CO1/IN/20/C/21 & CO1/IN/20/D/2 and James Frost CO1/I/13/B/24.

408 These documents, known as Form T, provided the basis for the study of pauper graves at Rosemary Green. *Social Services Committee: Records of the Home for the Aged, Chronic Sick and Able bodied at 100 Fishponds Road (now closed), originally the workhouse of the Clifton Union at Eastville - Registers of deaths* BRO 30105/3/1-4 (1847-98).

In the late 1860s Eastville Workhouse had a dedicated storage facility for bodies, the Dead House (mortuary) though it was clearly unsatisfactory both in its location and condition. A report in the *British Medical Journal* in 1867 stated:

> the room, about ten feet square, used for the reception of the dead, had its window opening into the premises used by the convalescent patients, and its ceiling dilapidated, this being caused we are told, by the water from a bath above trickling down into it.[409]

From the available evidence it is difficult to gauge how the bodies of deceased paupers were treated in Eastville Workhouse, though the condition of the Dead House provides some indication. Longmate cites sources which state that bodies were stripped of their workhouse uniforms, placed naked on sawdust in un-planed wooden shells (open boxes) made of the cheapest materials and then perhaps covered in calico.[410]

Once a pauper had died relatives and friends had to move fast; if the body was not claimed within 48 hours then under the rules of the 1832 Anatomy Act the corpse could be "given to the medical school". Such markings in the margin of the death registers for Eastville Workhouse demonstrate that between 1872 and 1894, 118 bodies of paupers were recorded as being passed on for this purpose. These consisted of ninety-two males and twenty-six females.

However, it appears prior to 1872 no cadavers were given to medical science despite the fact that legally they could have been claimed for dissection. Elizabeth Hurren's study of pauper bodies passed to Cambridge University anatomical teaching school over the same period shows similar characteristics to Figure 33, with a large increase in 1873-4 and a significant fall in 1885.[411] Hurren explains these changes as being a result of the waxing and waning of the crusade against poor relief launched in 1871 by the Local Government Board, discussed in Chapter 1. The harsher administration of the New Poor

---

409 This comes from the report on Eastville Workhouse by Dr Tibbits, discussed in the previous section *Provision for the sick in Eastville Workhouse* and quoted in the *Western Daily Press* 10 November 1867. Dr Bernard on his appointment in 1867 had made a number of recommendations to the Clifton Union Board of Guardians concerning medical equipment and facilities including "that the situation of the Dead House be altered and 2 rooms of 10ft square each be built in the ash yard to be lighted from above and properly fitted under the direction of the Medical Officer, the present Dead House to be converted into a scullery for the sick wards". It is unclear if this alteration was undertaken. TNA Ref. MH 12/4013 27 November 1867.

410 Longmate, N. *The Workhouse* p. 149.

411 Hurren, E. T. *Protesting About Pauperism* p. 206, Figure 10.

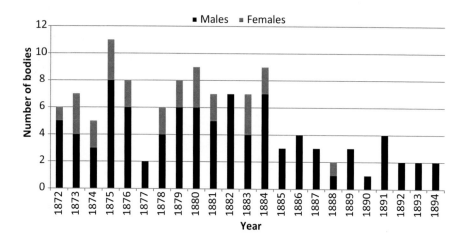

Figure 33: Eastville Workhouse: bodies recorded as passed to the Medical School per year (1872-94).

Law engendered by the anti-welfare campaign in the early 1870s produced more unclaimed pauper bodies due to cuts in funeral provision and encouraged the enforcement of the 1832 Anatomy Act in order to recoup costs through the sales to medical schools:

> Fee income was generated by passing on the costs of preparing, transporting and burying pauper cadavers to anatomists, thereby recovering some of the poor relief costs already paid out. These covert payments were not declared on central government returns and an illicit trade in pauper cadavers developed, which underpinned medical training[412]

According to Hurren, by the mid-1880s the anti-welfare crusade was beginning to subside, particularly in less zealous Poor Law Unions, which may have reduced the pressure to sell corpses to the medical schools. There may be another factor in that by the early 1880s the slow democratisation of Boards of Guardians, particularly through the influence of philanthropic reformers, may have stymied the practice to some extent. This is perhaps borne out by a meeting of the Barton Regis Board of Guardians in January 1882 when questions were asked about the practice of passing bodies to the medical school. The suggestion had been made a few days previously at the meeting of the Bedminster Board that bodies of paupers may have been sold for medical purposes and it was

412 Hurren, E. T. *Protesting About Pauperism* p. 207.

intimated that this had happened in two of the three Bristol Poor Law Unions. The Guardians of Eastville Workhouse responded that this was a disgraceful suggestion, that there was no truth in it and that if any officials took any money for corpses they would face a penalty of £5. The Master of the Workhouse Mr. Rogers backed this up by saying five years previously he had "received a warrant to hand over for medical purposes all unclaimed bodies" which he had complied with. We have to take the Master and Guardians' statements with a pinch of salt as semi-legal and illegal payments for bodies 'given to the medical school' were common throughout the Victorian period.[413]

Somewhere between 1 in 4 (25%) and 1 in 5 (20%) of deceased paupers from Eastville Workhouse are marked in the register of deaths as being "buried by friends". This usually meant that the corpse had been recovered by relatives or associates, who had enough money to transport the body and pay for a funeral elsewhere. The Master of the Workhouse was, of course, happy to let them go as it saved the costs of coffins and interment as well as space in the burial ground at Eastville. However, the majority of deceased paupers (greater than 70%), were neither removed by friends nor passed to the medical school. These bodies were technically unclaimed, but that did not necessarily mean that the deceased had no remaining relatives or friends, or that they did not care. Instead relatives or friends may have lacked the cash or perhaps the inclination to pay for a funeral outside the institution. It is hard to determine this ratio with the available data, but it would seem that the large expenditure involved in a funeral was beyond the capability of most poor Bristolians, despite the stigma attached to consigning a close relative, lover or friend to a pauper burial in an unmarked grave.

Once the body of a pauper had been left in the hands of the workhouse for burial, it was at the mercy of cost-cutting at best, and indifference and disrespect at worst. From cheap coffins, "a few rough planks joined together; the black initials, age and date" to the randomly selected "bearers in the grey frieze dress of the union... who forgetful of the occasion, seem glad of the opportunity of again mingling with their fellow creatures and breathing the air of freedom", to the burial service often conducted for multiple deceased inmates in "indecent haste", it was a miserable affair.[414] Even the lure of fresh

---

413 *Bristol Mercury* 21 January 1882. Elizabeth Hurren's research into the 'black market' in pauper corpses for medical science has demonstrated that it was widespread and lasted into the 20th century despite the practice being made technically illegal in an amendment to the 1834 Poor Law Act in 1844. Hurren, E. 'Whose Body Is It Anyway? Trading the Dead Poor, Coroner's Disputes, and the Business of Anatomy at Oxford University, 1885–1929' *Bulletin of the History of Medicine*, Volume 82, Number 4, (2008)

414 Longmate, N. *The Workhouse* p. 149; Laqueur, T. *Bodies, Death, and Pauper Funerals* pp. 121-22.

air and fraternisation were not enough to attract inmates who were sometimes invited to attend; sources suggest there was a reluctance to do so.[415]

On top of this, mistakes were common in workhouses with bodies mixed up, mislaid or even falling out of the cheap coffins. The fact that the burial ground for Eastville Workhouse was adjacent to the institution may have precluded the use of even cheap caskets for burial, which would have been a significant cost saving for the Guardians.[416] Testimony from the Foreman who excavated the burial ground in 1972 suggested that there was no substantial evidence of coffins associated with the human remains that were uncovered.[417] Intriguingly, a number of sources refer to workhouses employing reusable coffins merely for transportation of the corpse, with bodies in some cases merely wrapped in cloth, cardboard boxes or old newspapers on interment.[418] A letter in 1885 from a Poor Law Union official in Northamptonshire to the daughter of a deceased pauper reveals some aspects of this practice:

> The relieving officer informed... [her]... that if she could not afford a coffin and a funeral service she would have to do without one. He instructed her to claim her father's body from the infirmary, wash it, 'wrap it in a cotton sheet', 'sew the body in' personally and accompany it back to her father's parish. The body could then be buried in a communal grave.[419]

Wrapping bodies in cloth or other materials that degraded relatively rapidly may explain the lack of evidence of coffins during the 1972 excavations into Eastville Workhouse burial ground. The absence of coffins (and the association with communal graves) is a sign of the subordinate location of such interments within the already lowly position of pauper burials in the hierarchy of Victorian funeral practice.

In 1882 the Local Government Board wrote to the three Poor Law Unions in the Bristol area complaining that "unfortunate mistakes had been

---

415 Higginbotham, P. *The Workhouse Cookbook* p. 104.

416 *The Eastville Workhouse death register (1847-68)* contains tables of coffin prices for various districts of the Clifton Union for the years 1847-51. This would coincide with the removal of bodies to their parishes of origin. However, after this date and coincident with the opening of the burial ground adjacent to the institution, these tables are discontinued. This suggests that coffins may have been dispensed with. BRO Form T 30105/3/1 (1847-68).

417 Unrecorded interview with Mike Baker undertaken by R. Ball on 19 August 2015.

418 Higginbotham, P. *The Workhouse Cookbook* p. 104 and Kelly J. *The Graves Are Walking: The History of the Great Irish Famine* Chap. 10.

419 Hurren, E. and King, S. "Begging for a Burial': Form, Function and Conflict in Nineteenth-Century Pauper Burial' p. 335.

made" with regard to pauper burials. Sometimes paupers had been laid to rest under the wrong name, or a burial service had been performed over an empty coffin. They also complained of burials taking place in locations other than in the appropriate spot in the cemetery or of the workhouse mortuary being placed under the care of pauper inmates without proper supervision. They recommended that:

> There should be affixed to the shroud, immediately after the laying out of the body, two legibly written tickets, each bearing the name of the deceased, one on the outside of the coffin and one on the shroud. The bodies should be inspected by the Master, or someone who knew the deceased. Proper coffin plates should be affixed – where they cannot the particulars should be inscribed on the coffin.[420]

The Master of Eastville Workhouse arrogantly claimed that no mistakes had been made in his institution. Analysis of the death registers tells a different story; it is only in June 1855, some eight years after the institution was opened, that grave numbers associated with each body appear in the records.[421] This suggests that for several years burials in nearby Rosemary Green were somewhat disorganised with no direct connection between the record and the location of the body in an unmarked grave. This seems to have been rectified to some extent after 1855, but as we shall see in the following chapter, shortage of space in the burial ground led to a number of dubious interment practices. The potential mistakes in keeping track of the location of the deceased is reflected, for example, in the entry for a Benjamin Young who died in Eastville Workhouse on August 19th 1869, where there is no grave number recorded and a note merely saying "number on the box".[422]

In 1895 the Local Government Board again wrote to all workhouse Guardians to complain that there had been cases of a lack of proper supervision of burials. It seems the ineptitude was reoccurring over decades, or perhaps, as we have seen with many aspects of the Victorian workhouse, this was merely the result of a systemic lack of care for the welfare of the pauper in life or death.

---

420 *Bristol Mercury* 27 May 1882.
421 BRO Form T 30105/3/1 (1847-68).
422 BRO Form T 30105/3/2 (1868-78).

5. The Pauper Burial Ground at Rosemary Green

A brief history

They thought nothing of enlarging their burial ground, and thought nothing of seeing the mounds sticking up, and as soon as they (the poor) cropped up they would put them there.[423]

The late 1840s and early 1850s were an extremely difficult period for provision for the dead in Bristol. The cholera epidemics of 1832 and 1849 allied with lack of burial space in the city centre had produced a serious crisis by the mid-century. The Public Health Act of 1848 stipulated that all new burial grounds had to be approved by the General Board of Health and existing ones could be closed down if they 'were considered dangerous to health'. Subsequently, a damning report in 1850 sponsored by the Corporation concluded that the city's church and chapel burial grounds were:

utterly insufficient for the wants of the city being almost all full and surrounded by houses and quite unfit to be used as places of burial.[424]

Within a year of the new Burial Act of 1853 Bristol had been issued with "an elaborate Order in Council which closed or regulated the burial grounds of all sects in Bristol".[425] This bombshell set the Corporation and church authorities off in a desperate (though uncoordinated) search for burial grounds in the environs of the city.

It is not clear whether the Clifton Union Board of Guardians had considered the problem of where to bury deceased inmates from their new institution in Eastville, either during the planning phases or when it finally opened in 1847. The Clifton Board of Guardians may have been relying on there being provision for pauper burials closer to the city centre, however, after the 1849 epidemic this was difficult and by the 1854 graveyard closures this was clearly out of the question. It appears that for the first few years after the opening of Eastville Workhouse (1847-51) they resorted to returning bodies of inmates to the parishes from whence they came. However, there was a drawback to this system in that:

---

423 Quote from a protest meeting of 'working men' concerning treatment of paupers in the Clifton Poor Law Union. *Bristol Mercury* 19 January 1869.
424 BRO *Cemeteries and Burial Grounds* (Bristol: BRO, 2009) p. 2.
425 Large, D. *The Municipal Government of Bristol* p. 120.

the Guardians, and through them the ratepayers, were put to considerable expense in determining where paupers were properly chargeable; an outlay was incurred... in removing the bodies to remote places.[426]

In order to alleviate these costs the Guardians opted to keep pauper burials 'in house' by consecrating land adjacent to their institution, an area now known as Rosemary Green (see Figure 6).

The land was certainly not ideal for a burial ground despite it being pronounced "picturesque" by one journalist. It was variously described as being "on the side of a hill", "sloping very considerably from its highest to lowest part" and accessible "by a path along the base of the acclivity [upward slope]", bounded on the northeast side by the workhouse and the open Coombe Brook on the other.[427] The lower part of the site was clearly flood plain for the stream which was heavily polluted by raw sewage and the immediate area was particularly susceptible to major flooding.[428] However, despite the foresight of a clergyman critic of the 1834 Poor Law who had argued that the "poor... suppose they would be put in the workhouse dunghill" and that "no consecration of the bishop would change the workhouse dunghill into a burial-ground",[429] necessity, simplicity and primarily cost pushed the Eastville Guardians into proving him right on the first and wrong on the second.

There were essentially three phases of development to the site, all driven by the necessity of rapid disposal of the bodies of workhouse paupers. In April 1851 a quarter of the eventual area of the burial ground was consecrated[430] in a ceremony led by an entourage of church officials, followed by workhouse Guardians and in the presence of the Bishop of the diocese. Children from the workhouse concluded the religious proceedings with a hymn and then the "clergy and the guardians proceeded to the Union House, where a very handsome dejeuner was provided by the liberality of the Rev. Mr. Mirehouse". Needless to say the pauper children were not invited!

426 *Bristol Mercury* 26 April 1851.
427 *Bristol Times & Bath Advocate* 26 April 1851, *Bristol Mercury* 26 April 1851, 15 June 1861.
428 Landowners adjacent to Coombe Brook complained about the discharge of raw sewage from Eastville Workhouse into the stream and one even launched legal action against the Clifton Poor Law Union in 1855 TNA Ref. MH 12/4007. There were major floods in the area in 1882; *Bristol Mercury* 26 October 1882.
429 Rev. Thos. Sockett before the Poor-Law Committee, March, 1837 quoted from Baxter, G. R. W. *The book of the Bastiles*.
430 Conveyances and indenture documents BRO 42228/1/1/1, St PHosp/190, EP/A/22/CU/1a-c.

After the meal, Chairman of the Clifton Union Board of Guardians, Reverend Mirehouse 'took the chair' and made a short speech (quoted at length below), which is significant in that it alludes to some of the controversial changes to traditional pauper burials instigated by the 1834 Poor Law Act that are discussed earlier in this book:

> With respect to the ceremony at which he had assisted that day, he could not help thinking that his Lordship had conferred a very great benefit not only on the Clifton Union, but upon the citizens of Bristol and Clifton, by consecrating a piece of ground for the purpose of the burial of paupers. He knew very well that many of the Bishops were adverse to consecrating ground for that purpose, but thought that in the present age it had become eminently necessary, and he rejoiced to think that the Bishop had taken the same view. It was a very solemn and depressing thing to a see a funeral going through the streets of a crowded city, even where it was attended by all the accompaniments that art could invent, or luxury bestow; but more melancholy still was the humble and lowly pauper funeral, and far better was it that they should be interred in the quiet of the country, near where they had passed their last years, and far from the hustle and turmoil of the noisy and crowed city. In addition to this consideration he thought that the rate-payers ought to feel gratitude to his Lordship, inasmuch as by consecration of this ground a considerable sum per annum would be saved by the Union.[431]

The Chairman implies that resistance from the clergy to creating separate 'private' burial grounds for paupers is backward, that the ceremonial funeral procession through the neighbourhood is unnecessary and the bottom line is, as always, that this will be a saving for the rate-payers.

By 1860, the Guardians were well aware that they were running out of space for burials and began the process for conveying to the Church a second larger piece of land adjacent to the original plot in preparation for consecration. However, this was opposed within the Board of Guardians on the grounds that:

> the land would become vested in the incumbent of the parish; it would be placed entirely under his control, and he would be able to claim the burial fees; and there would be nothing to prevent him from burying any bodies he pleased there.[432]

431 *Bristol Times & Bath Advocate* 26 April 1851.
432 *Western Daily Press* 29 September 1860.

Despite this opposition, which was centred on the Clifton Union retaining complete control over the burial ground and led one non-conformist Guardian to state that "he thought it would be no benefit for people to be buried in consecrated ground", the conveyance went ahead. The ultimate decision was based more on the immediate requirement for burial space than theological debate. In a subsequent meeting of the Board in January 1861 it was noted that: "there was a speedy need of it, for at present there was no room for burying bodies in the usual ground, and the Master had some corpses unburied".[433] A second consecration ceremony was carried out in June of that year, with some adult workhouse inmates and local residents present.[434]

Finally in 1868 a third tranche of land was added by the Guardians to the ever-filling burial ground,[435] though only after a protracted argument with the registrar of the diocese over the "scandalous and disgraceful" consecration fee of £50. This may have been reflected in the Bishops' speech at the ceremony in December that year when he bluntly reminded them "that they would at some time die and require a burial ground". It is, of course, doubtful that the Guardians and Masters would be buried in the cheapest manner in unmarked graves on a hillside next to an open sewer which regularly flooded.[436]

Despite the expansions of the Rosemary Green burial ground in 1861 and 1868, within 10 years it was again close to full. In June 1878 in response to protestations by the workhouse chaplain concerning the need for additional burial space, the Building Committee recommended that:

burials in the old graves should be discontinued for the present, that interments take place in the footpaths of the burial ground – which would allow of 112 interments – and that no additional land be provided'.[437]

This is an interesting statement as it suggests that, due to the lack of available fresh consecrated ground, for some time the gravediggers (usually inmates from the institution) had been ordered to restart interments in older parts of the burial ground and perhaps, as the wording intimates, in old graves. Multiple burials, that is stacking coffins on top of each other in a single plot, although common practice for pauper interments and

433 *Western Daily Press* 8 September 1860, 12 January 1861.
434 *Bristol Mercury* 15 June 1861, BRO 42228/1/1/2, EP/A/22/CU/2a-b.
435 BRO 42228/1/8/3, EP/A/22/CU/3a-b.
436 *Bristol Times & Mirror* 17 October 1868, *Western Daily Press* 24 October 1868 and 5 December 1868.
437 *Bristol Mercury* 29 June 1878, our emphasis added.

overcrowded graveyards earlier in the 19th century[438] had become very contentious in Bristol after the epidemics and burial ground scandals of the 1840s and 50s.

In February of the same year, the Bristol Guardians had faced a serious problem in the nearby Stapleton Workhouse burial ground, when flooding caused recently buried coffins to be uncovered and were seen to be "floating about". Requests to "place three or four coffins over each other" rather than having "according to the Act... make every interment in fresh soil" were being seriously considered by the Bristol Guardians.[439] The pointed reference to legislation probably relates to the 1853 Burial Act, which not only forced the closure of city-centre graveyards but also restricted the practice of multiple interments in a number of burial grounds.[440] It appears however, that the Guardians of Eastville Workhouse were already, if not flouting the law, certainly ignoring its spirit. Whether they considered the health effects of tightly packing dead bodies both horizontally and vertically next to a flood-bound tributary of the River Frome is unclear; what is transparent is their reluctance to spend any more money or effort in expanding the existing burial ground as they had done in 1861 and 1868. Records suggest the tight packing and multiple interment practices continued until 1895, when the Guardians shifted workhouse burials to the nearby Ridgeway Park Cemetery.[441]

This marked the end of nearly half a century of usage of Rosemary Green as a pauper graveyard. Apart from being located as a "burial ground (disused)" on old Ordnance Survey maps[442] and some local people's memories, by the post-war period it was unrecognisable as the resting place of thousands of Bristolians. It was this resting place that Bristol Radical History Group sought to investigate.

---

438 For example, in the West Bromwich Poor Law Union burial ground at Heath Lane Cemetery it is claimed paupers were buried in mass unmarked graves "in many cases 20 people deep". http://www.west-bromwich-photos.co.uk/paupersworkhouses.htm.

439 *Bristol Mercury* 9 February 1878.

440 *Bristol Mercury* 4 March 1854.

441 The Ridgeway Park Cemetery was a private enterprise and opened in 1888 at the top end of Eastville Park (BS5 6QH).

442 *Old Ordnance Survey Maps Bristol* (Ashley Down & Eastville) 1902 Gloucestershire Sheet 72.09 (The Godfrey Edition).

Researching the burial ground

The research into Rosemary Green, principally carried out over three years (2012-15), had several purposes:

- To collect the evidence that the site was a burial ground for the Eastville Workhouse
- To establish the period of time in which it was in operation
- To determine the number and location of the burials
- To gather details of every man, woman and child who was laid to rest there[443]
- To analyse this data in order to determine causes of death, epidemics, seasonal variations etc.

It was a fairly easy task to verify that Rosemary Green was a burial ground associated with Eastville Workhouse, through a cursory examination of the *Know Your Place* website.[444] This demonstrated that the burial ground was unmarked on the 1840s tithe map layer prior to the construction of Eastville Workhouse, but appears on the 1880s epoch 1 layer as in use, and is marked "disused" on the 1900s epoch 2 layer. This suggested it came into use after 1840 and was disused by 1900. Subsequent examination of the surviving conveyance and consecration documents for the site established that the burial ground was made up of three pieces of land.[445] These were consecrated in three phases, in 1851, 1861 and 1868 as shown in Figure 34.

The consecration documents accurately marked out the burial ground to the nearest foot and also gave exact areas of the three pieces of land; which were calculated to be, in total, 5,414m².[446] Assuming a typical adult grave (6 foot by 2 ½ foot) would occupy approximately 1.39m², we estimated that the maximum possible number of single adult burials in Rosemary Green would be 3895. This seemed to be a very large number of burials in what appeared to be a small area of land, but in retrospect it turned out to be a fairly accurate initial estimate.

Whether some or all of the bodies were still present in Rosemary Green became one of the central questions of the research. Perhaps the most important piece of circumstantial evidence was the fact that despite the construction of

443 It was decided to include those inmates whose bodies were given to medical science in the data but, at this stage, not those who were 'taken by friends' to be buried elsewhere.
444 http://maps.bristol.gov.uk/knowyourplace/.
445 BRO Refs. EP/A/22/CU/1a-c, EP/A/22/CU/2a-b, EP/A/22/CU/3a-b and 42228/1/8/1-3.
446 The areas quoted on the consecration documents were as follows, 1851: 1 rood and 14 perches (1366m²), 1861: 2 roods (2024m²), 1868: 2 roods (2024m²).

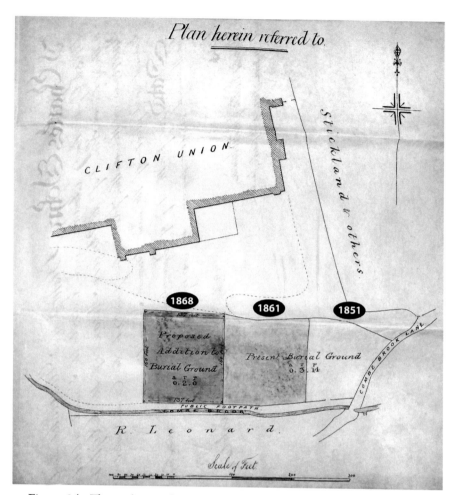

Figure 34: Three phases of consecration of the Eastville Workhouse burial ground (1851, 1861 and 1868).

the East Park housing estate in the early 1970s, Rosemary Green had been untouched and had remained curiously undeveloped ever since. At this point, the approach of the search switched to looking for evidence of the removal of bodies, rather than trying to prove they were still there. Correspondence in 1902 between Chancellor of Dioceses of Gloucester and Bristol and solicitors acting for the Bristol Board of Guardians concerning deep mine workings passing underneath Rosemary Green established that bodies had not been moved in the first few years after the burial ground became disused in 1895.[447]

Evidence after 1902 was, however, minimal, until some reminiscences

447 BRO Ref. EP/A/22/CU/4a-d.

from a teacher who worked at May Park School in the 1970s provided the first concrete eye-witness evidence of the existence of the burials in the post-war period. According to her account, after the demolition of the Eastville Workhouse buildings in 1972, pupils from the school had been entering the adjacent building site through a hole in the fence to look for Victorian bottles that had been turned up by the excavations for the new housing estate. Instead they returned with bags full of human bones. The teachers called the police and there was apparently a meeting with the contractors and then, silence. Searches of newspapers of the time yielded nothing and this tantalising piece of evidence remained unsubstantiated for more than a year until the Eastville Workhouse Memorial project became public in 2014.

After reports in the press and particularly the BBC TV programme about Rosemary Green there were several responses which supported the May Park teacher's statement. For example:

Circa 1972/3 I was working at Cavenham Confectionary Greenbank Bristol. I can recall a worker who had two skulls which he had taken from the site of 100 Fishponds Road. Apparently a lot of human remains were exposed during the ground works for the new housing estate.[448]

As a boy living in Coombe Road I remember the site being excavated before/during the demolition of 100 Fishponds Road. I am pretty sure some of the coffins, more like planks built into boxes, were dug up and removed. We used to dig around in the rubbish and I found a broken mug with the crest of the Bristol Guardians of the Poor...We dug up clay pipes, old glass bottles and various items that were thrown out. That must have been very late 1960s or early 1970s.[449]

The latter correspondent even provided photographs of the artefacts he found in the debris of the demolished Eastville Workhouse (see Figure 35) including a mug emblazoned with the Bristol Poor Law Union logo of a beehive and the Latin motto 'They labour in summer mindful of the winter'.[450]

448 E-mail to BRHG 20 January 2015.
449 J. Clevely E-mail to BRHG 9 February 2015. The respondent was probably referring to the timber boxes used to remove human remains from the site in 1972.
450 This symbol and motto has been associated with the Bristol Incorporation of the Poor since 1696 when the organisation was founded. Anon. *The Connoisseur: An illustrated magazine for collectors Vol. XXIX (January-April 1911)* Ed. Baily, J. T. H. (Forgotten Books, 2013) p. 89. Its presence suggests that the mug dates from after the 1898/1904 reorganisations of the Poor Law Unions when the Bristol Corporation took over the running of Eastville Workhouse.

Figure 35: Ginger beer bottle and mug from the Eastville Workhouse discovered in 1972.

These testimonies established for certain that bodies were present on the site in the 1970s and further searches for documentary evidence of their removal after the demolition of Eastville Workhouse seemed fruitless. In the autumn of 2014 Bristol City Council issued a letter to residents of East Park estate which stated that the location for a children's playground on Rosemary Green had been moved because "we have since discovered that the site had previously been used as a burial ground, over a hundred years ago".[451] Although the source of the evidence for their decision was not stated it appears that at least the planning department were now aware of mass burials at Rosemary Green.

In the summer of 2015 a local resident pointed researchers towards the company that had carried out the demolition of Eastville Workhouse in 1972. The Managing Director of the firm[452] who had been present remembered:

> … there were no graves but many bodies, many of which were buried very deep as if a pit had been dug. All uncovered bones were placed in timber boxes (some only skull or large bones) and reburied at a cemetery near the Feeder Road, Bristol[453]

451 G. Bryant, Neighbourhood Officer, Bristol City Council letter to East Park residents October 2014.
452 L.A. Moore Ltd. from Wells in Somerset.
453 T. Schroeder, Operations Manager, L.A. Moore Ltd. Email to EWMG 13 August 2015.

Subsequent interviews with those who had been present on the site began to unravel the story.[454] The company had been contracted to demolish the workhouse buildings and part of the arrangement was that they would clear the burial ground. This turned out to be a massive job, with excavations into what is now Rosemary Green lasting weeks in the summer of 1972. According to the Managing Director the operation was overseen by representatives from the church and carried out with considerable security in place. However, the care and consideration required for accurate disinterment of so many unmarked graves seems to have been of secondary importance.

The site Foreman recounted that excavations with mechanical diggers turned up huge amounts of human remains in some cases buried 15 to 20 feet (4.5-6.0 metres) deep, with evidence of multiple burials (i.e. they were stacked on top of each other). It was hard to estimate the number of bodies present as the remains were jumbles of bones, but certainly "more than a thousand and possibly thousands". Only major bones were collected (such as skulls, pelvic and leg bones) and placed in custom made timber boxes, "seven or eight skulls" in each, which were then loaded into a transit van and shipped off the site. The foreman remembered that there appeared to be no coffins associated with the remains and that there were a number of bodies of children. It was clear that delineating individual bodies was impossible due to the speed and crude method for disinterment that was employed. The remaining tens of thousands of skeletal fragments and small bones mixed with top soil and demolition rubble were then ploughed back onto Rosemary Green raising the ground level by several feet.[455]

According to the Register of Burials, in September 1972, one hundred and sixty seven boxes of human remains were recovered from the burial ground at Rosemary Green and deposited in three adjacent plots in a corner of nearby Avonview Cemetery in St George.[456] These 'common graves' containing the remains of thousands of people were completely unmarked (see Figure 36) and even with a detailed map of the burials at Avonview it wasn't clear exactly

454 Interviews with Les Moore and Mike Baker were undertaken by R. Ball on 19 August 2015.
455 This testimony was supported by evidence obtained from the installation of a memorial on Rosemary Green in November 2015. The hole that was dug to site the standing stone liberated human remains, including whole vertebrae, small bones and skull fragments. This was despite the fact that the memorial was located just outside the boundaries of the original burial ground. See Pike, B., Kopacka, Z., Longhurst, R., Kirby, Z., Oshana, M. and Yankovsakya, V. *100 Fishponds Rd* (Bristol: UWE, 2015) 6.00-6.10 http://www.brh.org.uk/site/articles/100-fishponds-road/.
456 The Register of Burials for Avonview Cemetery is held at Canford Cemetery & Crematorium Office, Bristol, BS9 3PQ. The address for Avonview Cemetery is St George, Bristol, BS5 8EN. The plot reference numbers are 1458/A/Light Blue/AA, 1459/A/Light Blue/AA and 1462/A/Light Blue/AA.

Figure 36: The final resting place of the human remains from Rosemary Green in Avonview Cemetery.

where they were. This state of affairs shocked us. Through our research we had uncovered the policies and attitudes of the Victorian Poor Law authorities to pauper death and burial. It appeared such attitudes to paupers had been replicated a century later in the 1970s.[457]

Having located the final resting place of the workhouse inmates we were keen to pin down who had made the decision to sanction the removal of the human remains from unmarked burials in Rosemary Green to the unmarked common graves at Avonview Cemetery. Once we had carefully studied the conveyance, indenture and petition documents for the consecrated ground at Rosemary Green we were confident that the dioceses of Bristol and Gloucester retained responsibility for the burial ground in the 1970s.[457] In fact, in 1902, a note had been added to one indenture clarifying this fact. It stated:

> an indenture dated the 14th day of April 1851 and made between the Guardians of the Poor of the Clifton Union in the City of Bristol of the one part and the Right Reverend James Henry Lord Bishop of Gloucester and Bristol of the other part A small plot of Ground…was granted unto the said Lord Bishop and his successors in trust that the said plot of ground should be forthwith consecrated and should for ever thereafter be separated and set apart from all profane uses and be devoted and appropriated by the said Guardians to the burial of bodies of persons who at the time of their respective deaths should

457 Bristol Archives Refs. EP/A/22/CU/1a-c, EP/A/22/CU/2a-b, EP/A/22/CU/3a-b, 42228/1/1/1-2, 42228/1/8/1-3, St PHosp/183-5, St PHosp/190, St PHosp/194 and St PHosp/198.

be chargeable to the said Union or to any Parish comprised therein and according to the Rites and ceremonies of the United Church of England and Ireland[458]

Having proved that the burial ground at Rosemary Green was both consecrated and held in trust by the dioceses and checked the legal requirements for disinterring bodies it seemed reasonable to assume that the church had taken the decision to allow the removal of the remains in 1972. In January 2016 we wrote to the Bishop of Bristol asking the diocese to verify the evidence for the disinterment, accept responsibility for this decision and suggesting they should mark the common graves at Avonview with a memorial.[459] Unfortunately, the responses were somewhat negative, to say the least. The Bishop claimed that:

checking the Diocesan Registry departments of both this diocese and the diocese of Gloucester has revealed nothing that connects the Church of England with the churchyard concerned. We have also heard that no ceremony was involved at the time the remains were dug up, and secondly, that this was done by a JCB-like bulldozer. I have to say, I think it is almost inconceivable that the church would have anything to do with such an outrageous approach...this really does have the feel more like property developers who may or may not have sought the proper permissions.[460]

The Bishop continued by offering a "without prejudice" contribution to the cost of a memorial.[461] In a subsequent letter from the Acting Archdeacon of Bristol their defensive position was reinforced:

I am sorry to confirm, however, that we cannot locate any records (either in this diocese, or in the diocese of Gloucester) which would support the building contractors' comment that the Church of England in any formal way 'oversaw' the events of 1972.

458 Bristol Archives Reference St PHosp/198.
459 Letter from Eastville Workhouse Memorial Group to the Bishop of Bristol, 22 January, 2016.
460 Letter from Rt. Rev. Mike Hill (Bishop of Bristol) to Eastville Workhouse Memorial Group, 29 January, 2016.
461 'Without prejudice' is a legal phrase which is generally used in correspondence between parties in out of court settlements. It supposedly makes any offer of monies inadmissible as evidence in court. In this case the Bishop was trying to deny any relationship between the diocese's donation and legal responsibility for the disinterment of the pauper burials at Rosemary Green.

Although it is clear that the site of Rosemary Green falls within what is now the Parish of St Anne with St Mark and St Thomas, Eastville, it does not appear to have been Church land (i.e. not a churchyard for which the local Parish Priest for example, would have had any responsibility) and the Diocese would not therefore have had any legal involvement in its sale or development for housing.[462]

The denial that the burial ground at Rosemary Green was a 'proper' graveyard, that is, in a church under the auspices of a "Parish Priest" carried significant historical irony. In 2016 the diocese were effectively claiming that the burial ground at Rosemary Green had no status as consecrated ground. This echoed the angry debates in the mid-nineteenth century about the status of "workhouse dunghills" and conveniently ignored the fact that the church had been paid significant sums, equivalent today to tens of thousands of pounds, for consecrating the site in the 1850s.[463]

For members of the Eastville Workhouse Memorial Group (EWMG) the refusal of the Church of England to take full responsibility for either the burial ground or the decision to remove the thousands of pauper bodies to Avonview Cemetery was demoralising. The question of who had made the decision to move the bodies remained unanswered and the prospects of memorialising the common graves at Avonview looked bleak. Despite all the years of work on the Eastville Workhouse project, it still felt incomplete. Consequently, in the autumn of 2018 EWMG agreed to approach the dioceses again. In the two years that had passed, the Archdeacon had retired and the Bishop had moved on. We resent the letters to the incumbents and, lo and behold, the evidence we were after finally turned up. In late October a meeting took place at Rosemary Green and Avonview Cemetery between members of EWMG and Michael Johnson the new Acting Archdeacon to discuss a proposal for a memorial. A few days later Johnson sent us a copy of a 'faculty' document from 1972, effectively a legal authorisation within the Church of England. This document sanctioned the City Engineer to carry out:

462 Letter from Venerable Christine Froude (acting Archdeacon of Bristol) to Eastville Workhouse Memorial Group, 9 February, 2016.
463 Using the GDP per capita conversion, the £50 consecration fee in 1851, 1861 and 1868 was worth in 2018 £63,370, £48,070 and £42,870 respectively. "Five Ways to Compute the Relative Value of a UK Pound Amount, 1270 to Present," MeasuringWorth, 2019. URL: www.measuringworth.com/ukcompare/.

The removal of human remains from the disused burial ground at 100 Fishponds Road Bristol and the reinterment of the human remains in Plot AA at Avonview Cemetery Bristol.[464]

The person who signed off the decision to move the bodies was David Charles Calcutt esq. Calcutt, a high flying establishment barrister, judge, Professor of Law and Master of Magdalene College, Cambridge was also Chancellor of the Church of England dioceses of Exeter and of Bristol from 1971-2004. Calcutt, who passed away in 2004, was described in his obituary as one whose:

> search for excellence was beyond compare, his determination was formidable, and his simple humanity was frequently unrecognised... Calcutt always had the common touch.[465]

It appears he failed to apply any of these traits to the treatment of the remains of more than 4,000 men, women and children buried at Rosemary Green, when in 1972 he consigned them to nameless oblivion in a forgotten corner of Avonview Cemetery.

Despite this rather ignominious end to the story of the pauper burials at Rosemary Green, by the end of 2018 most of the research questions had been answered.

Statistical analysis of burial data

The complete data on the men, women and children buried at Rosemary Green that was collected from the Clifton/Barton Regis Union death registers was published on the Bristol Radical History Group website in 2015 and is available for download.[466] Full details of these registers, the collation process and categorisations are given in Appendix 3. The accumulated evidence suggests that Rosemary Green burial ground was in continuous operation from May 1851 to Nov 1895, a period of more than forty-five years. In that time, more than four thousand interments took place. An overall summary of the burial data by decade for Rosemary Green is shown in Table 9.

464 St Thomas the Apostle, Eastville, Faculty No. 1716, 10 March, 1972.
465 Rawley, A. "Sir David Calcutt: Barrister in favour of controls on the press" *The Independent* 14 August, 2004. Retrieved from: https://www.independent.co.uk/news/obituaries/sir-david-calcutt-39022.html.
466 The data is available for download here: http://www.brh.org.uk/site/articles/rosemary-green-burial-ground-data/.

Age at death	Burials	% of burials
<1 month	115	2.8
<1 year	490	12.0
1-10 years	427	10.5
10-20 years	119	2.9
20-30 years	192	4.7
30-40 years	290	7.1
40-50 years	327	8.0
50-60 years	330	8.1
60-70 years	708	17.3
70-80 years	798	19.5
80-90 years	303	7.4
90-100 years	32	0.8
Unknown	68	1.7
Total	4084	100.0

Table 9: Eastville Workhouse burials at Rosemary Green by age group
(1851-1895).

Period	Burials at Rosemary Green			
	Male	Female	Unknown	Total
1851-59	223	229	13	465
1860-69	441	313	10	764
1870-79	612	484	17	1113
1880-89	636	458	16	1110
1890-95	359	268	5	632
Total	2271	1752	61	4084

Table 10: Summary of Eastville Workhouse burials at Rosemary Green
(1851-1895).

Figure 37 gives a breakdown by year of these burials with markers showing significant expansions of workhouse capacity and provision for the sick, both of which had an effect upon numbers of interments per year. In addition, based upon the analysis in Table 8, specific years where epidemics of disease within Eastville Workhouse have been isolated are marked in black fill along with their nature if known. After the expansion of the workhouse capacity in 1858 by about 40% there is a steadily increasing number of burials per annum until the construction of a dedicated infirmary in 1880. After this point, barring fluctuations caused by epidemics, the trend is more stable and, if anything, declining during the late 1880s and early 1890s.

Table 10 gives a breakdown of burials by age-group. The high proportions of infant (<1 year, 12.0%) and child (1-10 years, 10.5%) mortality are conspicuous, with nearly a quarter of all deaths in Eastville Workhouse associated with these age ranges. Deaths in the succeeding 10-20 year age group are less than a third of this level, demonstrating that survival was far more likely once a child had passed through the early years of vulnerability to disease, especially due to epidemics of the 'infant killers'; whooping cough, measles and diarrhoea. Improvements in municipal sanitation which helped reduce the number and impact of epidemics combined with better diets amongst the working classes in particular, produced increases in overall life expectancy as the century wore on. However, this was not reflected in mortality rates of infants which remained stubbornly high and static throughout the Victorian period in Bristol. Large explains that environmental and social conditions were most to blame for these high infant mortality rates in the poorer quarters of the city:[467]

> ... the offspring of the poorest and most disadvantaged were most at risk. Ill-nourished mothers, probably having low weight babies, living in very cramped conditions in poorly maintained housing, and having very little knowledge of child care, were sure to find combatting infectious disease or diarrhoea a real struggle... Dr Hugh Jones, the acknowledged expert in the 1890s was right in saying "most fatal cases (but not all) of infants suffering from diarrhoea are traceable to contamination of the food supply"'. The organisms which caused the condition were so often carried by flies flourishing in summer warmth buzzing around ill conditioned lavatories and settling on

---

467 A comparison of mortality of infants and young children in the 1880s and 1890s regularly shows poor working class urban areas (such as the parishes of St James, St Paul and St George) had death rates three or four times higher than wealthy areas such as Clifton or Westbury. *BCRL Bristol Medical Officer of Health Quarterly Reports 1880-1888* and *Bristol Medical Officer of Health Annual Reports 1898-1901.*

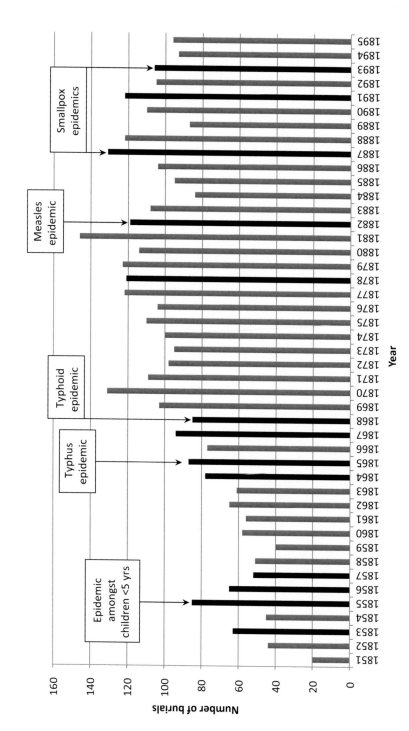

Figure 37: Eastville Workhouse burials at Rosemary Green 1851-1895 (known internal epidemics shown in black).

food, especially milk… the situation was not helped by the Water Company's practice of charging extra for connecting a lavatory to the water supply.[468]

The high rates of infant and child mortality are clearly mirrored in the analysis of burials at Rosemary Green and suggest that conditions in Eastville Workhouse were little better than those described by Large in the slums of Bristol.

Evidence for burial practices

Apart from statistical analysis, the Clifton/Barton Regis Union death registers give us some clues to the nature of burials at Rosemary Green.

From the opening of the burial ground in April 1851 until June 1855, no grave numbers are quoted in the registers, suggesting that interments were less regimented and consequently less sparing of space. After June 1855 there is clearly some planning in the use of the remaining area, with pre-numbered plots and separate areas of the burial ground designated for adult and child graves. This system seems to operate successfully until the end of 1860 when due to over-crowding the Guardians were forced to consecrate a second piece of land adjacent to the first in June of the following year. The use of the newly consecrated plot is corroborated by the words '1st in New Ground' written in the margin by the name Matilda Barnes, though significantly she died more than two months prior to the consecration suggesting that the body may have lain unburied for a considerable period of time.

Through the 1860s the regimented system of grave numbering appears to be effective until the autumn of 1868 when, once again, a lack of space causes a third and final consecration of new ground in December. By the mid-1870s space was once again at a premium and the death registers gradually become dominated by the words 'Buried in old ground'. This appears to be evidence of multiple interments; that is returning to previously used areas of the burial ground, re-excavating and stacking bodies on top of each other. Further confirmation of this practice is provided by the fact that from the mid-1870s onwards, grave numbers appear to be repeated, sometimes several times.

There are also a number of cases where inmates, particularly infants were buried in the same grave, contrary to typical practice.[469]

468 Large, D. *The Municipal Government of Bristol* pp. 136-7 & 146-47.
469 The placing of workhouse inmates, particularly infants or children, in the same grave was recently discovered in an archaeological dig at Kilkenny workhouse, in Ireland. See: http://www.archaeology.co.uk/articles/features/the-kilkenny-workhouse-mass-burials-an-archaeology-of-the-great-irish-famine.htm#.UW06GjNwZco.blogger.

¶ In February 1867 Fanny Hayes and James Brown, both two months old, died within days of each other and were given the same grave number.

¶ Twins, William and John Jones, who both died on 2 May 1870, were buried in the same grave.

¶ Emma Ward, an infant who died on February 16th 1879 had the same grave number as Thomas McDonald, another infant who died ten days later.

¶ On September 9th 1880 Sophie Ellen Burgess aged "seventeen days" was buried in the same grave with her mother Ellen who died a day later aged 26. The record notes 'Buried with mother'.

The nature of these burials suggests that a level of rationalisation was underway, probably to save space in the burial ground. An even more dubious practice appears in the case of very young infants who were born dead or died shortly after delivery. Within the death registers there are numerous examples of stillborn babies buried without grave numbers and a significant number of other interesting cases, including:

¶ On August 8th 1858 a baby known only as Willshire "lived about ½ an hour" and was buried without a grave number.

¶ Louisa Bevan, aged 1 year, died on January 25th 1863 and was charged to the "Union Fund" which suggests she was of unknown origin. She was buried without a grave number.

¶ George Brain lived seven hours after his birth on October 27th 1870 and was buried without a grave number.

¶ Thomas Tapp survived only five minutes before passing away on May 20th 1878. No grave number is quoted.

¶ Clara Thomas lived 21 hours and died on 1st February 1879. She was buried without a grave number.

¶ On April 10th 1881, Mary Evans lived for five minutes before dying. No grave number is quoted.

All of these examples share a similarity, that is, the babies and infants were almost certainly unbaptised and thus according to conformist Christian religious doctrine were ineligible for burial in consecrated ground. A significant clue to the fate of these unfortunates may lie in the case of George Theobald who died fifteen minutes after birth in Eastville Workhouse on 27th August 1880; his record in the death register is shown in Figure 38.

George Theobald was given no grave number in the same manner as many of the examples of the stillborn, foundlings and very young babies quoted

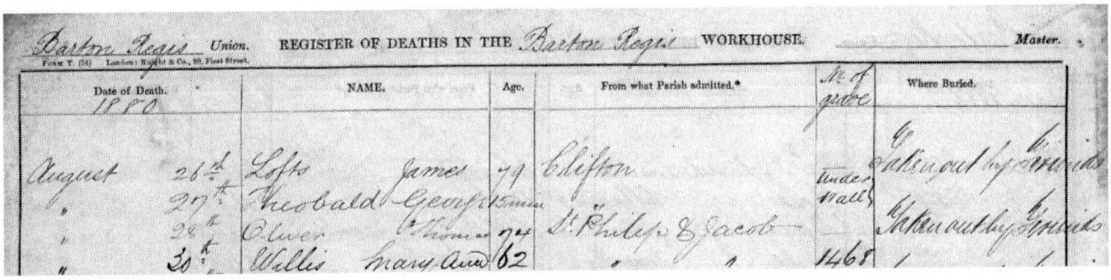

Figure 38: Record of George Theobald in the Barton Regis death register for August 1880.

above. However, the helpful workhouse scribe listed him as buried "Under Wall", suggesting that a significant number of unbaptised infants may have been buried outside of the consecrated turf of the burial ground at Rosemary Green. How many of these unbaptised infants failed to make it into the unmarked graves at Rosemary Green and where they now lie will probably remain a mystery.

This book began with some lines from Thomas Hardy: "So the baby was carried in a small deal box, under an ancient woman's shawl, to the churchyard that night, and buried by lantern-light, at the cost of a shilling and a pint of beer to the sexton, in that shabby corner of God's allotment where He lets the nettles grow, and where all unbaptized infants, notorious drunkards, suicides, and others of the conjecturally damned are laid".

And it is perhaps fitting that our research into the pauper burial ground at Rosemary Green should end with George Theobald.

Conclusion

The Victorian workhouse

The Victorian workhouse in popular literature is marked by horror stories ranging from punitive regimes and sadistic violence through to starvation and the misery of child labour.[470] It is easy to be distracted by these shocking representations, which although fictional, were often based on real cases. However, in order to understand what the workhouse was really about we have to leave the realm of the overbearing master, the sadistic overseer and the vicious schoolmaster, all of which, from one time or another, have been reduced by apologists for the workhouse to personalised examples of 'failures' within the system. Instead we need to consider what the New Poor Law was trying to achieve, what ideologies motivated its designers and managers and the unintended consequences it produced as a result.

The contradiction that confronted many social critics of the Victorian period (and is increasingly relevant today) is simply: why, when Britain was becoming the 'workshop of the world' and the British Empire 'ruled the waves', at the height of its immense power and creating massive wealth, were so many British subjects in various levels of poverty, from the abject to the chronic? This question certainly vexed the owners of land, factories and capital in the early 19th century. The problem was that their new-found wealth and consequent political power were based upon an economic system which had encouraged both enclosure and technological advance whilst simultaneously generalising the wage-economy. This had made people without property particularly vulnerable to under-employment, unemployment, low wages and price rises. Without access to land there was little or no means of subsistence for these new 'proletarians' to fall back on. The consequences were that even limited spells of unemployment or fluctuations in the price of food and fuel, could lead rapidly to malnutrition, destitution and homelessness. As a result the costs of 'outdoor relief', in particular, grew relentlessly.

By the 1830s, the situation was critical, with agricultural 'riots' led by desperate rural labourers, political unrest and insurrections over enfranchisement and the spectre of republican revolution raising its head again. It comes as no surprise that the propertied turned away from analysing and attempting to mollify the glaring contradictions of their 'free-market' economic system. Instead they headed towards the safer, though no less contradictory, shores of Malthusian ideas which emphasised the inevitability of 'natural' processes. So

470 The New Poor Law and the workhouse in Victorian literature are discussed in Moore, G. *The Victorian Novel in Context* (London: Continuum, 2012).

food-shortages produced by a lethal combination of bad harvests, export and speculation in the free-market became 'natures' way of redressing population imbalance. Low wages, under and unemployment became 'natural' phenomena of the fluctuating free-market economy and those amongst the poor who supposedly 'surrendered' to poverty became 'paupers' and were referred to as the "social residuum"; a type of human waste that reproduced itself, rather than being a product of economic circumstance.

As far as the bourgeoisie were concerned, there was a way out of this malaise for at least some of the poor and that was through moral self-improvement, based on hard work, frugality and self-discipline. In a world of the twelve-hour working day and six-day week in mills and factories, widespread child labour and no pensionable age, everyone had to be productive in the eyes of the manufacturers. Unwaged labour such as domestic work and looking after children which reproduced the workers was unrecognised. Those of the working-class who were unproductive, because they were injured at work, sick, infants, mentally ill, pregnant, elderly, infirm or disabled were certainly not considered to be the primary responsibility of the propertied or the state. To make matters worse, at the very time when traditional support structures for the rural working class - the community, extended family and patronage - were collapsing or had disappeared through displacement and industrialisation, the New Poor Law was introduced.

The primary objective of the Poor Law Amendment Act 1834 was to remove outdoor relief for the able-bodied altogether, reduce it for other dependent groups and at the same time intimidate the rural and urban working poor from claiming indoor relief by making workhouse conditions "less eligible" (less desirable) than those of an "independent labourer of the lowest class". This involved reorganising the existing relief system by creating an interconnecting net of coordinated Poor Law Unions across the whole nation with executive power centralised in the capital. The Poor Law Commission would enforce this new vision of a society without significant outdoor relief and with the indoor relief of the new workhouse system, characterised by segregation, harsh punitive regimes, minimal diets and hard labour.

Well, at least that was the plan. Despite attempts to terrify the poor, in the first decade their numbers in the workhouses seemed to increase rather than decrease, demonstrating the desperate situation of millions of proletarians. Political and physical resistance to the new 'Bastilles' was widespread and, regardless of numerous directives to dispense with outdoor relief from the Commissioners in London, the 'dole' remained a stubborn necessity across the country. The new Poor Law Unions, rather than collaborating, competed with each other both politically and financially and, as we have seen in Bristol, deferred important civic responsibilities concerned with epidemics and health provision, sometimes to devastating effect. To cap it all, the workhouse system was rocked by a series of scandals in the 1840s which shocked the public and eventually brought down the Poor Law Commission which itself was riven with internal strife. However as we have seen, these serious failings did not lead to reform; instead the Victorian ideologues of Malthus and the free-market forged on into the second half of the century with their flawed plan for the poor.

The basis of the workhouse on a purely economic level was unsound from the very beginning, as the value of the commodities it produced was minimal compared to the costs of its operation. In order for the New Poor Law plan to succeed on a fiscal level the overall costs of relief had to be shown to be falling; unfortunately it became clear fairly quickly that it cost more to keep a pauper in the workhouse than to pay outdoor relief. As Rose points out:

> Here indeed was the crux of the problem. If a pauper was sent to the workhouse, the Guardians would be forced to pay the full cost of maintenance of the pauper and his family. If outdoor relief was granted, however, this was no longer the case. Few Boards of Guardians paid sufficient outdoor relief to enable the recipient to maintain himself and his family without income from some other source.[471]

Consequently, on a cost basis and concerned about social protest, various forms of the minimal outdoor relief were retained by Guardians around the country despite objections from London. At the same time the drive to decrease the cost of the workhouse system became paramount, with the inmates taking the brunt of these constant cuts. From short diets, freezing wards and a lack of doctors and nurses to 'fake' lunatic wards, cheap burial grounds such as Rosemary Green and multiple interments, the pressure to reduce costs was relentless and sometimes lethal for the men, women and children within the institution. In death, unlike the pet dogs of the wealthy (see Figure 39), paupers from the workhouse apparently did not deserve even the simplest marker of their final resting place. Instead, consummate with the bureaucratic fiscal culture of the Victorian workhouse, they are merely accounted for in the Union death registers.

Ultimately there was a cruel irony to the workhouse system which had set out in the 1830s to discipline the supposedly recalcitrant, able-bodied pauper. As the century wore on, it became clear that the institution was full of the 'unproductive' and most vulnerable sections of the working classes;

471 Rose, M. 'The Allowance System under the New Poor Law' *Economic History Review*. New Series, Vol. 19 No. 3 (1966) p. 613.

Figure 39: Gravestones in an Edwardian pet cemetery of the Smyth family at Ashton Court Estate, Bristol.

single mothers and their offspring, orphaned and abandoned children, the sick, elderly, physically and mentally disabled and those with mental illnesses. Rather than acting as a 'boot camp' for the 'lazy', the workhouse in the late Victorian period became merely a reflection of the complete lack of accessible health and welfare provision for the most deprived. It was these groups that were punished by the harsh regime of the workhouse and it is no surprise that those who controlled the Poor Law Unions absorbed and then propagated convenient pseudo-scientific theories to justify their bureaucratic indifference. The conjunction of Social-Darwinist and Eugenic theories, that were popular amongst the Victorian middle and upper classes, encouraged belief in race and class hierarchy, degeneracy and extinction. This ideological environment generated the psychological conditions for organised neglect.

It was in this climate that the 1870s *crusade* against outdoor relief was initiated by the increasingly powerful Poor Law authorities. Led by the 'free-market' ideas of a cabal of influential economists and politicians and realised through the anti-welfare policies of the Charity Organisation Society, the Local Government Board set to work in disciplining Poor Law Unions and squeezing paupers once again. Obsessed with the idea that Guardians had been too liberal with outdoor relief payments and that they had been duped by the 'undeserving' poor, harsh relief policies were introduced at the very point where Britain entered the longest depression in its economic history. The misery of late 1870s Bristol with starving and freezing 'able-bodied' working class families refusing to enter the workhouse was a reflection of both the restriction of outdoor relief due to the anti-welfare crusade and the fear that the institution engendered. In the short term the 'crusaders' had achieved their miserable objectives.

However, there were some rays of hope for the Victorian pauper. The increasing enfranchisement, particularly in relation to local government, allowed the involvement of some new social activists in the management and monitoring of Poor Law Unions. The election of well-to-do women philanthropists to boards of guardians allied with the interventions of medical inspectors, radical investigative reporters and whistle-blowing infiltrators began to challenge conditions in the workhouse from within and without. Brutality and neglect were exposed and contested and the reality that the workhouse population was far from its intended demographic became increasingly clear. However, philanthropic endeavours rarely challenged the basis of poverty rooted in the free-market economy and were almost always based on middle or upper-class people teaching:

> … the working class how to reform itself on the assumption that poverty was the result of a series of individual or community produced moral failings.[472]

It was thus no surprise that philanthropic efforts in the Victorian period ranged from old school solutions such as exporting the poor to labour camps in the countryside or their children to colonies of the Empire to the later temperance societies, anti-gambling leagues, thrift societies and sanitary associations.

As the century wore on, and especially during the 'long depression' of 1873-96 which affected wider sections of the working-class as well as respectable rate-payers, tenant farmers, artisans and small-businessmen, the ideological positons of the anti-welfare COS and LGB *crusaders* and the well-to-do philanthropists began to look increasingly archaic, incorrect and incapable of solving the 'problem of the poor'. How could the widespread poverty which engulfed late Victorian society be merely the result of 'moral failings', 'sin' or 'degeneracy' amongst the poor? How could paupers be responsible for national and global economic crises? And, how could the structural problems leading to poverty be solved by punishing the poor? Hurren states:

> In the 1880s there was an increased realisation that environment, social and physical, played a critical role in the fortunes of the poor, so much so that few could control their economic destiny.[473]

The rise of socialist ideas amongst the working-class in the 1890s, particularly in the labour movement, led to both closer monitoring and criticism of the Poor Laws and workhouse conditions. More crucially, socialists shifted the debate about the poor, which had been hitherto dominated by various shades of Victorian individualism, to a generalised critique of the prevailing economic

472 Kotouza, D. *Lies and Mendacity Mute* Vol 2, No.3 (2006) http://www.metamute.org/editorial/articles/lies-and-mendicity.
473 Hurren, E. T. *Protesting About Pauperism* p. 72.

system. In 1897 Frank Sheppard,[474] one of the first socialist city councillors in Bristol, reported on conditions at the Bristol Workhouse:

> The able bodied [pauper] is a most difficult class to deal with, many of them being the waste product of our competitive beggar-my-neighbour system and more to be pitied than blamed...The subjects of outdoor relief, lunacy and vagrancy so closely bound up with our unjust social system would require a paper to themselves.[475]

Statistical surveys of poverty at the turn of the century, such as those carried out by Booth and Rowntree which estimated that "around 30 per cent of the nation lived in pauperism not of their making",[476] provided empirical evidence for the socialists. Armed with this data, a coherent critique of free-market capitalism and with a new humanitarian approach, Sheppard and his allies set about reforming the workhouses in Bristol. Bryher, writing in the 1920s, recalled their initial objectives:

> First, the removal of the children from the workhouse; Secondly, the establishing of proper hospital accommodation for the sick, with resident medical officer, and a properly equipped paid nursing staff. Thirdly, the more humane and better payment to the outdoor poor, and also, should be added, the proper classification of the inmates and a complete revolution as to the treatment of the epileptic and imbeciles...the barriers to be broken down were formidable...no one, unless they knew what the poor law system was and what it is now can realise the revolution that has been effected.[477]

474 Sheppard, born in Weston-Super-Mare in 1863, was orphaned at nine years of age. A year later he was working as an apprentice boot and shoemaker. At fifteen he joined the National Union of Boot and Shoe Operatives, later becoming its president. In 1893, he was elected to Bristol City Council for the St Paul's ward and also became the first socialist Guardian on the Board of the Bristol Corporation of the Poor. "So great was his dissatisfaction with conditions and so keen his interest in reform that he gave up his council work in 1896 to concentrate on poor law activities". In 1917 he became Bristol's first Labour Lord Mayor. http://www.davidmcfall. co.uk/page79.html. More details of the activities of early socialists, such as J.A.Cunningham, C. J. Satterley, T. C. Lewis, G. Thompson, Mrs. Webb, Mrs. Lloyd, and Mrs. Tillett who were elected to Poor Law Boards in Bristol in this period can be found in Bryher, S. *An Account of the Labour and Socialist Movement in Bristol*. (Bristol: Bristol Labour Weekly, 1929).

475 Sheppard, F. *Second Monthly Letter of the B.T.C.L.E.A.* [Bristol Trades Council, Labour Electoral Association], *Notes on the Progress of the Bristol Board of Guardians by Frank Sheppard, Labour Member* (1897). Private collection of Mike Richardson and Sheila Rowbotham.

476 Ibid. p. 72. Booth, C. *The life and labour of the people of London* (1889-1903) and Rowntree, J. *Poverty: a study of town life* (1901).

477 Bryher, S. *An Account of the Labour and Socialist Movement in Bristol*.

Pressure from socialists at a local level meant that the urgent need for a health and welfare system became a social demand by the end of the Victorian period. The emerging Labour Party which championed this demand and the increasing strength of trade unions, especially during the pre-WW1 industrial unrest,[478] applied pressure to the Liberal government of the time. Consequently, 1912 saw the beginnings of a social security system providing unemployment, sickness and maternity benefit. The eventual mutation of workhouses into NHS hospitals and homes for children, the elderly and the disabled as part of the creation of the modern welfare state in 1948 was both a consequence of these reforms and a reflection of the systemic failings of the Victorian free-market economy.

So, a return to 'Victorian values'?

Over our dead bodies.

Figure 40: Eastville Workhouse viewed from a back garden (c. 1960s).

478 For details of this stormy period in Bristol see Richardson, M. *Bristol and the Labour Unrest of 1910-14* Bristol Radical Pamphleteer #27 (Bristol: BRHG, 2013).

Afterword: Oral history and the legacy of 100 Fishponds Rd

I will not go to the bloody Workhouse with an order from you. If you send me an order for the Dam Workhouse I shall put it into the fire. I would rather go to Jail than Workhouse. I don't care for the Buggers who tell you lies of me. Burn the Workhouse note into the fire. I shant go.[479]

The traumatic experiences of inmates in the Eastville Workhouse remained in the memory for lifetimes. In the 1990s researchers from the local history group 'Living Easton' interviewed women who had been incarcerated in the institution often merely for being 'single parents'. These experiences were paralleled by a legacy of fear in the collective memory of long-time residents of East Bristol. The Eastville Workhouse was recalled by many as a 'bogeyman'.

One woman remembered as a child when she asked what the large building on 100 Fishponds was, her mother replied 'that's the workhouse and if we spend our money on too many sweets that's where you will end up'.[480] Another resident recounted that her grandmother would regularly threaten 'You'll end up in 100 Fishponds Road'.

Stephen Dowle recalled "The address...100 Fishponds Road, was mentioned with a certain dread when I was a boy; for this was 'the workhouse', often invoked, at times when our family finances were under strain, as the place we would all 'end up in'".[481]

Pat James, reminiscing in 1989, stated "Another change for the better that I was pleased to see was the disappearance of 100 Fishponds Road, commonly known as the Old Workhouse. To end up there was the dread of the poor and elderly".[482]

---

479 Letter of complaint to the Poor Law Board from Charles Vale a deaf and dumb Mason's labourer living on Catherine St., Easton, Bristol in December 1874. Vale's wife had recently died; he was looking after his young daughter and had lost his job that summer. His small weekly outrelief payment of 2s 6d had been withdrawn by the Clifton Poor Law Union, probably as part of the anti-relief crusade of the 1870s, and he was being ordered by them to enter Eastville Workhouse. Vale appealed to the Poor Law Board in London "because I don't like to break up a home for my poor daughter's sake". His request was refused. *Letter to the Poor Law Board* 4 December 1874 TNA Ref. MH 12/4018 Clifton Union, Bristol quoted in Hawkings, D. T. *Pauper Ancestors* pp. 192-4.
480 Comments from Betty Morris, a resident of Eastville as a child (2010).
481 Comments associated with a photograph,
https://www.flickr.com/photos/fray_bentos/357367889.
482 *Bristol Evening Post* 7 November 1989.

Others, too young at the time to understand the significance of the workhouse, recounted that merely the words '100 Fishponds Rd' were a source of fear in school playgrounds. Clearly, the physical dominance of the complex of the 'Old Workhouse' buildings that overlooked Easton was only matched by the psychological domination the institution had over the working classes of East Bristol.

Epilogue

Putting things right

Our dead are never dead to us, until we have forgotten them[483]

For the small group of historians who first discovered the Eastville Workhouse burial ground at Rosemary Green, the fact that it was completely unmarked, without memorial or remembrance of any description, was surprising and disturbing in equal measure. Indeed, without prior knowledge it was hard to locate any sign that the adjacent East Park housing estate was the original location of a workhouse either. There was clearly a need to raise the profile and emphasise the historical importance of the site as well as to name and memorialise the more than 4,000 men, women and children who had been buried there. However, it was unclear how local residents might react to the news that their homes lay on the foundations of an infamous East Bristol institution or that their children were playing on a hitherto hidden burial ground.

REMEMBERING EASTVILLE WORKHOUSE

28th Aug - 7:30pm

St Anne's Church, St Leonards Road, Greenbank

Over the last two years local historians from Bristol Radical History Group (BRHG) have been researching an old burial ground that lies on Rosemary Green between Rosemary Lane and Greenbank View.

It appears that upwards of 3,000 paupers from the Eastville Workhouse were buried in unmarked graves on the site between 1855 and 1895. BRHG believe the graves remain on the site and we plan to commemorate these forgotten people in some public events in the autumn this year.

We are interested to find out your views, any memories or information you may have about the old Workhouse and any ideas about best to commemorate these people. This public meeting is a forum to discuss these issues and an opportunity to get involved. So come along and find out more about our local history and have your say.   Email: BRH@BRH.ORG.UK

BRH.ORG.UK

Figure 41: Flyer for first public meeting concerning the pauper burial ground at Rosemary Green (2014).

Rosemary Green is a well-used public space within the community of East Park housing estate and close to May Park Primary School, so it was obvious that community support and input were required to further the project. In August 2014 members of Bristol Radical History Group (BRHG) went door-to-door with flyers (see Figure 41) announcing a public meeting. It became clear that there were unpleasant memories of the workhouse particularly amongst older residents. A woman taking her grandchildren to May Park School read the leaflet with interest and said "My Nan used to say to me when I was young 'if you don't eat your sprouts, you will end up in

483 George Eliot quoted from Pike, B. et al *100 Fishponds Rd* 9:42 http://www.brh.org.uk/site/articles/100-fishponds-road/.

the workhouse"". She went off chuckling about this family reminiscence, but it demonstrated that there was a sense of fear about the institution at 100 Fishponds Rd.

It became apparent that there was significant local interest in the project when more than forty people turned up to the public meeting. Eastville Workhouse Memorial Group (EWMG) was founded at this event and it was here that historians from BRHG met Hazel Durn and Gloria Davey, two local community activists who have played such an important role in the project. Hazel and Gloria had been involved in numerous campaigns to improve facilities on East Park estate including the building of a much-needed children's playground.

It was agreed from the outset that EWMG should raise funds for a memorial to the forgotten paupers, and the group were approached by a local stone mason and sculptor, Matthew Billington, whose workshop backs on to Rosemary Green. Matthew's knowledge and expertise in preparing and carving stone memorials was invaluable. By the summer of 2015 EWMG had agreed on a basic design and a large donation to the project from the John James Bristol Foundation allowed the manufacture to begin. Matthew transported an 8.5ft (2.57m) high by 2.5ft (0.76m) wide slab of slate to Bristol from a quarry near Blaenau Ffestiniog in Wales. EWMG wanted the design to have community involvement so Matthew and historian Steve Mills visited May Park Primary School to run a series of workshops on stone carving and the history of the poor laws and workhouses. The pupils were very engaged and were asked to produce some designs relating to what they had learnt, some of which would be chosen to go onto the memorial (see Figure 42).

In the meantime, a new health centre was being built using the original gateway to the workhouse at 100 Fishponds Road as its pedestrian entrance (see Figure 20). EWMG approached the partners of East Trees Health Centre, to see if they would sanction and help fund a historical plaque to mark the location of Eastville Workhouse. After protracted negotiations it was agreed that a plaque, designed by local artist Mike Baker, creator of the Easton Time-Signs trail, would be placed on one of the pillars that made up the entrance to 100 Fishponds Rd (see Figure 43).

One overcast morning in November 2015 a crew from EWMG met Bristol City Council workmen at Rosemary Green to erect the newly carved standing stone. A mechanical digger was used to excavate a hole for the memorial and a large amount of pottery, glass bottles and other artefacts from the workhouse were uncovered. Amongst them were a scattering of human remains which were reburied, a poignant reminder that Rosemary Green was the resting place for thousands of people.

Figure 42: Sculptor Matthew Billington inscribing the memorial stone for Rosemary Green (2015).

Figure 43: Members of Eastville Workhouse Memorial Group with mock-up of the history plaque to mark the original entrance to Eastville Workhouse at 100 Fishponds Rd (2015).

Figure 44: Installing the memorial stone at Rosemary Green (2015).

Figure 45: Memorial unveiling ceremony at Rosemary Green (2015).

Figure 46: Detail of the standing stone memorial at Rosemary Green (2015).

Figure 47: Plaque to mark the original entrance to Eastville Workhouse at 100 Fishponds Road.

On 16th November 2015 several hundred people gathered on Rosemary Green for the unveiling of the memorial. Amongst them were local residents, some of the congregation of St Anne's church, more than a hundred pupils from May Park Primary School and members of the local press, radio and TV stations. A number of people spoke at the ceremony including a representative of the John James Bristol Foundation, Mike Payne of the GMB Union whose father was born in Newport Workhouse and Wendy Bull, three of whose relatives had died in Eastville Workhouse and were buried at Rosemary Green. The memorial was fittingly unveiled by local resident and campaigner Hazel Durn who stated:

> I moved onto Fishponds Rd when I was six months old and the house was next door to 100 Fishponds Rd so I could look over the wall and see everything that was going on all through my life. So it played a big part. I am very honoured to be asked to unveil this today and I hope that we never have these days again.[484]

Since the unveiling of the memorial on Rosemary Green in 2015, the EWMG have been engaged in other parts of the project including a memorial

484 Pike, B. et al *100 Fishponds Rd* 8:15-8:40
http://www.brh.org.uk/site/articles/100-fishponds-road/.

garden and history walks and talks with a number of local schools and history groups. At a well-attended ceremony in December 2016 the decorative plaque to mark the original entrance to Eastville Workhouse at 100 Fishponds Road was unveiled on the pedestrian entrance to East Trees Health Centre (see Figure 47). The plaque carries the following words:

Entrance to Eastville Workhouse, 100 Fishponds Rd (c.1892-95)

Opened in 1847 by Clifton Poor Law Union, Eastville Workhouse held more than a thousand inmates at a time. Over 80 years thousands of men, women and children passed through these gates, driven by poverty, great age or ill-health. Families were separated, endured hard labour and a punitive regime. Many died and were interred in unmarked graves in the burial ground at nearby Rosemary Green.

In 1948, as part of the Welfare State reforms, the workhouse became a home for the elderly. In 1972 the workhouse buildings were demolished to make way for East Park Estate. This gateway and walls are all that remain.

I hope that we never have these days again (Hazel Durn, local resident)

Bristol Radical History Group and Eastville Workhouse Memorial Group will continue to popularise knowledge of Eastville Workhouse and how the Poor Laws operated. Many of us feel that at present this is particularly important as we can see the poor, disabled, sick and vulnerable being targeted by politicians, held solely responsible for their own economic situation and being regarded as a drain on resources. So-called 'deficit reduction' seems to involve giving tax-cuts to the wealthy whilst blaming the poor for their poverty. There have been ominous warning signs in the collaborations between charities, private business and local councils in setting up welfare-for-work schemes and perhaps the first modern workhouses.[485] At the same time we see the potential demise of our National Health Service and the support structures within our communities, through privatisation by stealth and the apparently unchallenged needs of the 'market'.

485 In November 2014 Blackburn and Darwen Council purchased a bus depot in the city centre and then sold it to a private charity to run it as a recycling centre. The plan was to house ten itinerant people at the depot who would work for free with the money raised from the recycling operation going to provide training, education and employment. http://guerillawire. org/politics/the-first-of-the-new-workhouses/.

Putting things right...again

The last stage of our project was realised in 2019 with the memorialisation of the 'common graves' at Avonview Cemetery, the final resting place of the forgotten inmates of Eastville Workhouse. With financial support from Bristol and Gloucester dioceses, Bristol City Council and EWMG, stone mason Matthew Billington designed, sculpted and installed a gravestone in the location of the 'common graves' (see Figure 48). The memorial at Avonview Cemetery (Beaufort Rd, Bristol BS5 8EN) can be found in the north western corner, between Blackswarth Road and Beaufort Road. It is marked with a cross on Figure 50.

On 8th May 2019, the Lord Mayor Cleo Lake, Acting Archdeacon of the Diocese of Bristol Michael Johnson and the Deputy Mayor Asher Craig joined us and some relatives of those who were buried at Rosemary Green to unveil the memorial (see Figure 49). The weather during the ceremony was 'biblical' from start to finish, with thunder, lightning and then hail lashing down. Most of us thought it apt. However, we were left with a lingering thought: this couldn't happen again, could it?

BRHG/EWMG January 2020

Figure 48: Memorial stone to mark the final resting place of the Eastville Workhouse inmates at Avonview Cemetery.

Figure 49: Members of Eastville Workhouse Memorial Group, the Lord Mayor, Deputy Mayor and Acting Archdeacon of the Bristol diocese at the unveiling of the memorial in Avonview Cemetery, St George.

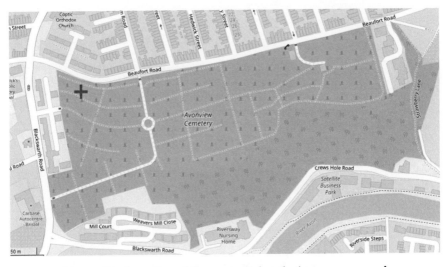

Figure 50: Location of the memorial at the 'common graves' in Avonview Cemetery.

Appendices

Appendix 1: A note on primary sources

The majority of administrative information concerning the Clifton/Union and Eastville Workhouse was, after the amalgamation of the Poor Law Unions in 1898, stored in St Peter's Hospital on Castle Park. Unfortunately a German air raid in November 1940 destroyed this building and the records stored within it. Luckily a significant collection of useful documents survived as they were stored at the Eastville institution, with the central authorities in London or elsewhere. These include:

¶ Registers of births, deaths and creeds for the Eastville Workhouse in the Victorian period [BRO]

¶ A set of half-year and annual statements of accounts for Clifton Poor Law Union (1872-75) and Barton Regis Poor Law Union (1881-2, 1884, 1889, 1897) [BRO]

¶ Numerous detailed plans of the buildings and grounds from the early years of the 20th century [BRO]

¶ Conveyance and consecration documents for Rosemary Green burial ground [BRO]

¶ Records of correspondence between Clifton (1838-1877) and Barton Regis (1877-1906) Poor Law Unions and the Poor Law Commission, Poor Law Board or Local Government Board in London [TNA]

¶ Correspondence and inquest documents concerning deaths in Eastville Workhouse (1859-1874) [GA]

The documents stored in the Bristol Record Office (BRO)[486] along with census records which provided further information on the inmates of Eastville Workhouse such as place of birth and occupation, allowed us to study the demographics of the inmates from gender and age, through to social class and ethnicity. Statements of accounts provided not only financial data but also information on the elected and un-elected Guardians, staff and Medical Officers, details of diets, types and hours of work, numbers in the casual and lunatic wards and policies on the boarding-out of children in the workhouse. The plans, maps and available photographic materials (both from the ground and the air) of the institution located in the BRO allowed the spatial layout

486 The two most useful guides to these documents are BRO *The Poor Law in Bristol* (Bristol: BRO, Dec 2013) and *Cemeteries and Burial Grounds* (Bristol: BRO, 2009). The half-year books are stored under *Clifton Poor Law Union - Statement of Accounts 1872-75* Ref. 22936/129, *Barton Regis Poor Law Union – Statements of Accounts 1881-1889* Ref. 22936/130, *Barton Regis Poor Law Union Annual Book 1897* Ref. 10900.

to be understood, tracked changes and additions to the buildings and helped determine the extent and form of the burial ground at Rosemary Green.

The National Archive (TNA) holds a wealth of information in the form of correspondence between the Poor Law Unions and central government. Although these numerous files cover accounting, audits and appointments in voluminous detail there were a number of other useful sources within them. Of most value were reports of inspections by the Lunacy Commissioners and Poor Law officials of Eastville Workhouse as well as debates over policy regarding epidemics, child emigration and boarding-out. Some of the most interesting and rare sources amongst the TNA files were letters of complaint sent by inmates and non-inmates of Eastville Workhouse to the Poor Law authorities about conditions in the institution.

The relevant material in the Gloucestershire Archives (GA) is primarily related to deaths in Eastville Workhouse. In cases where the workhouse Medical Officer was unclear about cause of death or where there were questionable circumstances, details in the form of 'notices of death' were sent to the coroner for the county of Gloucester. In some cases inquests were launched and these provide written transcripts of evidence given by witnesses, which include Eastville Workhouse staff and inmates.

A key source of statistical information was the Bristol Historical Resource CD produced by UWE (2000) which provided data on numbers in the Eastville Workhouse, costs of relief and health statistics for the for the Clifton/Barton Regis Poor Law Union. Further information on health in the workhouse was obtained from reports of inspections in the *British Medical Journal* and statistics on deaths in the Poor Law Union institutions from the *Bristol Medical Officer of Health Quarterly and Annual Reports*. The latter are available in the Bristol Central Reference Library.

Although the loss of official minutes of meetings of the Clifton/Barton Regis Guardians and similar documentation in the air raid was a significant shortcoming, local newspapers such as the *Bristol Mercury* (1716-1900) and *Western Daily Press* (1858-present) carried detailed accounts of the weekly meetings of the various Boards of Guardians, which included policy debates, financial statements, health records and particulars of elections for the various Poor Law Unions.[487] These newspapers were also useful in providing some social history via criminal cases involving workhouse inmates. Articles about workhouses in radical newspapers such as *The Clarion* delivered 'insider' information from investigative journalists which were backed up by accounts

---

487 Meetings of the Clifton Board of Guardians admitted reporters in 1860. However, this was only after a protracted campaign by local newspapers on behalf of rate-payers to gain access. See *Western Daily Press* 5 July 1858.

from social-reformer infiltrators who also published their experiences. Satirical magazines such as *The Bristol Magpie* provided comic portrayals of perceptions of the workhouse in the minds of angry rate-payers which were supported by some surviving flyers and posters for protest meetings.

Oral history was very useful in a number of ways, from determining the presence of burials at Rosemary Green and Avonview Cemetery through to understanding the changes that occurred in Eastville Workhouse due to the foundation of the modern welfare state and the considerable historical impact '100 Fishponds Rd' had on Bristolians for generations.

Appendix 2: Inmate numbers and expenditure on relief for the Clifton/Barton Regis Poor Law Union

Table 11 gives data on the costs of indoor and outdoor relief and numbers of recipients for the Clifton/Barton Regis Poor Law Union over the period 1858-1897.[488]

488 The data was derived from Tables 14 and 16 in Archer, I., Jordan, S., Ramsey, K., Wardley, P. and Woollard, M. 'Poor Law Statistics, 1835-1948' in Wardley P. (ed.) *Bristol Historical Resource* (Bristol: UWE, 2000).

| Year | Cost of Relief | | | Percentage of Total | | Av. No. Recipients | | Cost per head | | Ratio |
	Indoor £	Outdoor £	Total £	Indoor %	Outdoor %	Indoor	Outdoor	Indoor £	Outdoor £	Ind./Outd.
1858	4454	8584	13038	34.2%	65.8%	492	2577	9.05	3.33	2.72
1859	3897	8723	12620	30.9%	69.1%	467	2647	8.34	3.30	2.53
1860	3954	9431	13385	29.5%	70.5%	481	2803	8.22	3.36	2.44
1861	4550	10679	15229	29.9%	70.1%	504	3000	9.04	3.56	2.54
1862	4828	10619	15447	31.3%	68.7%	571	2903	8.46	3.66	2.31
1863	5246	10900	16146	32.5%	67.5%	605	2938	8.67	3.71	2.34
1864	5001	11353	16354	30.6%	69.4%	590	3161	8.48	3.59	2.36
1865	5101	12134	17235	29.6%	70.4%	558	3340	9.15	3.63	2.52
1866	5757	12657	18414	31.3%	68.7%	573	3559	10.05	3.56	2.82
1867	6526	13756	20282	32.2%	67.8%	652	3696	10.02	3.72	2.69
1868	6428	14178	20606	31.2%	68.8%	734	3642	8.76	3.89	2.25
1869	6044	13886	19930	30.3%	69.7%	737	3563	8.20	3.90	2.10
1870	6946	15354	22300	31.1%	68.9%	762	3725	9.12	4.12	2.21
1871	6970	14352	21322	32.7%	67.3%	684	3843	10.20	3.74	2.73
1872	6897	12859	19756	34.9%	65.1%	695	3454	9.93	3.72	2.67
1873	7182	12158	19340	37.1%	62.9%	680	3191	10.57	3.81	2.77
1874	7489	11762	19251	38.9%	61.1%	656	2858	11.42	4.12	2.77
1875	7584	12101	19685	38.5%	61.5%	716	3018	10.60	4.01	2.64
1876	7346	13237	20583	35.7%	64.3%	692	3136	10.62	4.22	2.52
1877	9101	14443	23544	38.7%	61.3%	846	3514	10.76	4.11	2.62
1878	10375	15228	25603	40.5%	59.5%	973	3774	10.66	4.03	2.64
1879	10611	16749	27360	38.8%	61.2%	1028	4113	10.33	4.07	2.54

| Year | Cost of Relief | | | Percentage of Total | | Av. No. Recipients | | Cost per head | | Ratio |
	Indoor £	Outdoor £	Total £	Indoor %	Outdoor %	Indoor	Outdoor	Indoor £	Outdoor £	Ind./Outd.
1880	11213	20257	31470	35.6%	64.4%	1091	4894	10.28	4.14	2.48
1881	10703	16931	27634	38.7%	61.3%	1086	4518	9.86	3.75	2.63
1882	10592	15828	26420	40.1%	59.9%	1031	4238	10.28	3.74	2.75
1883	11310	15358	26668	42.4%	57.6%	1056	4308	10.72	3.57	3.01
1884	10417	15199	25616	40.7%	59.3%	958	4263	10.88	3.57	3.05
1885	9124	14534	23658	38.6%	61.4%	913	4217	9.99	3.45	2.90
1886	9089	15000	24089	37.7%	62.3%	951	4267	9.56	3.52	2.72
1887	9159	14702	23861	38.4%	61.6%	976	4138	9.38	3.55	2.64
1888	9778	15505	25283	38.7%	61.3%	995	4268	9.83	3.63	2.71
1889	9873	15108	24981	39.5%	60.5%	933	4152	10.58	3.64	2.91
1890	9248	14787	24035	38.5%	61.5%	926	4053	9.99	3.65	2.74
1891	9258	15361	24619	37.6%	62.4%	920	4024	10.07	3.82	2.64
1892	9660	15645	25305	38.2%	61.8%	971	3981	9.95	3.93	2.53
1893	9317	16231	25548	36.5%	63.5%	1024	4087	9.10	3.97	2.29
1894	9912	16953	26865	36.9%	63.1%	1032	4319	9.60	3.93	2.45
1895	9988	18491	28479	35.1%	64.9%	1065	4504	9.38	4.11	2.28
1896	10339	18715	29054	35.6%	64.4%	1086	4573	9.52	4.09	2.33
1897	11687	18886	30573	38.2%	61.8%	1153	4503	10.14	4.19	2.42
			Min.	29.5%	57.6%				Min.	2.10
			Max.	42.4%	70.5%				Max.	3.05

Table 11: Costs of indoor and outdoor relief in the Clifton/Barton Regis Poor Law Union (1858-1897)

Appendix 3: Eastville Workhouse Death Registers

The details of the paupers buried at Rosemary Green were collected over a three year period from 2012-15 at the Bristol Record Office (BRO), mostly from microfiche, by three researchers from Bristol Radical History Group (BRHG). The records were first transcribed by hand and then transferred to Excel spreadsheets, where summaries and some basic statistical analysis were undertaken. In January 2015, the BRO made high-resolution images of the original sources available which enabled a collective checking process to be undertaken.[489] The same month the first issue of checked pdf versions of the data were released to the public online on the BRHG website in tandem with the broadcast of the BBC programme concerning Rosemary Green.[490] A second issue of the data with further checks, corrections and additions was made available in November 2015.

The data was gathered from the workhouse death registers which were formally introduced in July 1847, the year that Eastville Workhouse opened, as part of a General Consolidated Order issued by the Poor Law Commissioners. The order stated that one of the duties of the workhouse Master was:

> When requisite, to cause the death of every pauper dying in the Workhouse to be duly registered by the Registrar of Births and Deaths within five days after, the day of such death; and also to enter such death in a register kept according to Form (T.) hereunto annexed.[491]

The death registers (Form T) for Eastville Workhouse are held at the Bristol Record Office.[492] As the original documents were fragile and thus only available under special circumstances, the data collection process which originally began in 2012 was initially undertaken using microfiche copies of the death records.[493]

Although consecration documents provided evidence that the first phase of usage of Rosemary Green as a burial ground was after April 1851,[494] the end

---

489 This was undertaken by members of BRHG and local residents from the recently formed Eastville Workhouse Memorial Group (EWMG).

490 The data can be down loaded from http://www.brh.org.uk/site/project/eastville-workhouse/.

491 1847 *Consolidated General Order: Duties of the Master Art. 208* No. 17 Higginbotham, P. *The Workhouse* http://www.workhouses.org.uk/gco/gco1847.shtml accessed 2015.

492 *Social Services Committee: Records of the Home for the Aged, Chronic Sick and Able bodied at 100 Fishponds Road (now closed), originally the workhouse of the Clifton Union at Eastville-Registers of deaths BRO Refs.* 30105/3/1 (1847 Sep 27 - 1868 Sep 22), 30105/3/2 (1868 Oct 5 - 1878 Mar 25), 30105/3/3 (1878 Apr 2 - 1888 Dec 29) and 30105/3/4 (1889 Jan 4 - 1898 Jun 15).

493 BRO Refs. FCEW/D/1/1 (1847-1858), FCEW/D/1/2 (1858-1868), FCEW/D/2/1 (1868-1874), FCEW/D/2/2 (1874-1878), FCEW/D/3/1 (1878-1882), FCEW/D/3/2 (1883-1888), FCEW/D/3/3 (1888), FCEW/D/4/1 (1889-1893) and FCEW/D/4/2 (1893-1898).

494 Petition, act, sentence on consecration of land adjoining Comb Brook Lane, with plan BRO Ref. EP/A/22/CU/1a-c.

point of usage of Rosemary Green was less clear, until a detailed study of the death registers had been undertaken. It appeared that the Rosemary Green site became a disused burial ground on 20th November 1895.[495] After this point the death registers mark the new burial ground as the "Ridgeway" which is almost certainly the Ridgeway Park Cemetery located a few minutes' walk away at the top end of Eastville Park. This was opened by a private company in 1888.[496] This important piece of information provided evidence that Rosemary Green was in operation as a burial ground for the Eastville Workhouse for forty-four years between 1851 and 1895.

Figure 47 shows a sample of the Eastville Workhouse death register for January to February 1868 and Figure 48 shows the same data transcribed into the Excel spreadsheet format.

The categories of information concerning the deceased and how they were represented in the transcribed data are explained below:

Year/Month/Day: Date of death of inmate

Surname/Forename: Self-explanatory

Gender: This category does not appear in the death register but was, where possible, derived from the forename.[497] M = Male, F = Female and U = Unknown.

Age at Death: Ages at death were recorded in three ranges:

❡ Those aged 1 year or greater were rounded down to the nearest year. So, 18 months was recorded as 1.

❡ Those greater or equal to 1 month but less than 1 year were recorded as fractions of a 12 months rounded down to the nearest month. So, 6 weeks was recorded as 1/12 = 0.083.

❡ Those less than one month in age were shown as 0.001.

Parish: This column was stated as "To what parish chargeable" in the death registers, and referred to the parish within the Clifton/Barton Regis Poor Law Union responsible for the relief of the inmate (see Figure 4). Occasionally bodies were brought from other institutions for burial at Rosemary Green and were recorded under this category, these included Bristol Lunatic Asylum and Bristol Royal Infirmary. In other cases the deceased were marked as 'foundlings' or 'found drowned'.

Grave No: This referred to the plot allocated in Rosemary Green.

---

495 The final burial at the site appears to be Ann Evans who died on 20th November 1895 aged 41 and was buried in grave number 946.

496 It is located at Oakdene Avenue, Eastville, Bristol, BS5 6QQ. See also http://www.bafhs. org.uk/burial-data.

497 BRHG recognise the limitations of this approach but it was thought useful to get an overall approximation of male and female burials.

¶ It appears that over certain periods no grave numbers were allocated to plots at all.

¶ In other periods "In old ground" was stated in this column in the death register signifying a previous part of the burial ground was being employed, possibly for multiple burials.

¶ It was clear from the graveyard sequencing that children under the age of 10 were buried in separate plots to adults.

¶ In some cases very young babies were not given grave numbers and may have been buried outside the consecrated ground as they were not baptised before their deaths.

¶ The letter M refers to "Given to Medical School" (see below).

The data collection activity concentrated on those workhouse inmates who were believed to be buried at the Rosemary Green site, consequently there were some exclusions from the original death register data.

¶ A small proportion of those inmates who died in the Eastville Workhouse were listed in the death registers as "taken away by friends" or "buried by friends". This referred to bodies that were recovered by existing family and friends who paid for a funeral at another undisclosed location. These cases were excluded from the published data.

¶ The parish of a number of inmates was listed as "Bristol Incorporation" and there is no grave number stated in these cases. It is assumed that these inmates were not buried at Rosemary Green and have been excluded from the published records.

¶ A small number of entries are listed as being "Given to the medical school" denoting that the body was "donated" for medical science. It was decided to include these in the records, as there is apparently no final resting place for these inmates.

Notes: In most cases these are reproduced from the original death registers verbatim, but interesting conjunctions noted by researchers are also included.[498]

A note on legibility: The death registers are often unclear and consequently open to interpretation particularly with regard to forenames and surnames. Consequently the following designations have been added to the data by researchers:

U - Designates unknown, either illegible or cannot be determined (e.g. gender)

? - Researcher is unsure of interpretation of forename or surname

---

498 These include for example the deaths of several family members in a short period.

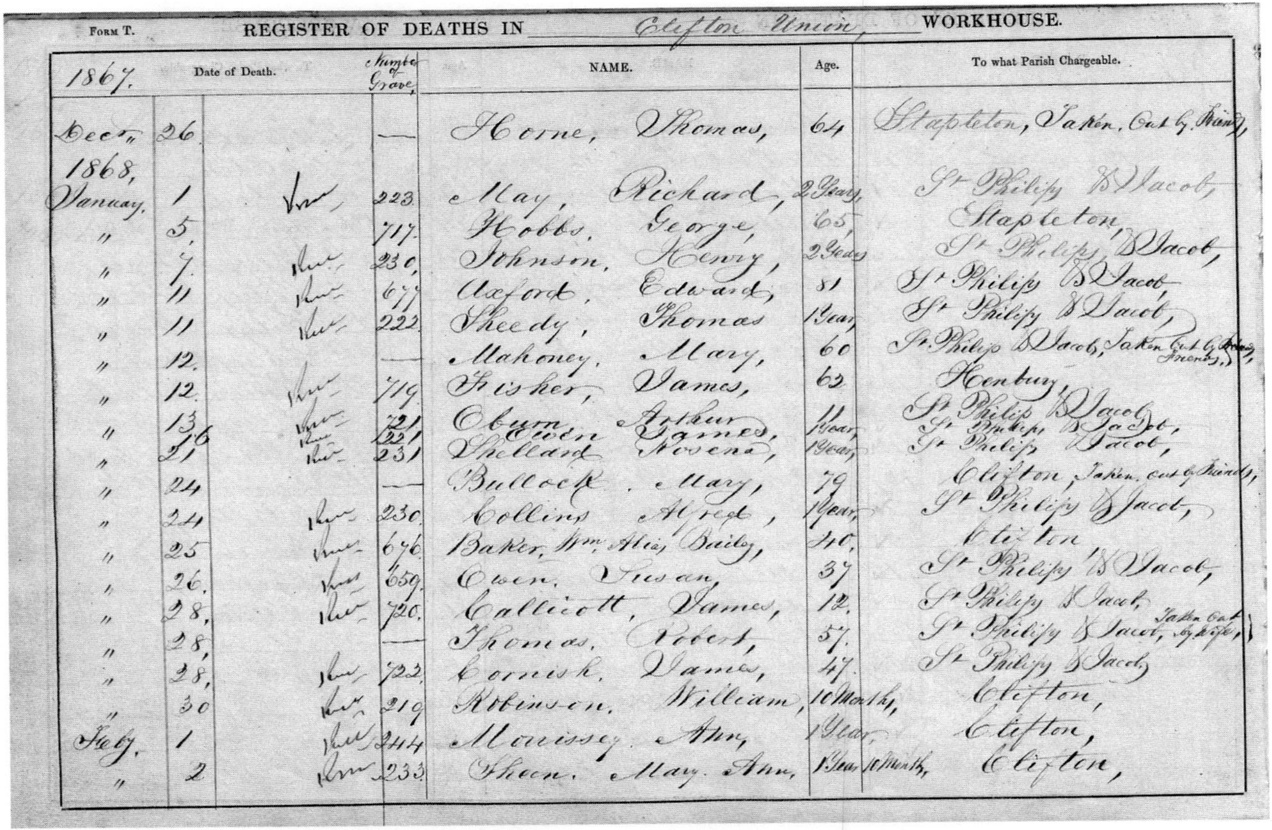

Form T. REGISTER OF DEATHS IN Clifton Union, WORKHOUSE.

1867.	Date of Death.		Number of Grave,	NAME.	Age.	To what Parish Chargeable.
Decr.	26.		—	Horne, Thomas,	64	Stapleton, Taken Out by Friends,
1868, January.	1	[illegible]	223	May, Richard,	2 Years,	St Philip & Jacob,
"	5,		717	Hobbs, George,	65,	Stapleton,
"	7.	[illegible]	230,	Johnson, Henry,	2 Years	St Philip & Jacob,
"	11	[illegible]	677	Axford, Edward,	81	St Philip & Jacob,
"	11	[illegible]	222	Sheedy, Thomas	1 Year,	St Philip & Jacob,
"	12.		—	Mahoney, Mary,	60	St Philip & Jacob, Taken Out by Friends,
"	12.	[illegible]	719	Fisher, James,	62	Henbury,
"	13	[illegible]	721	Oburn, Arthur	11	St Philip & Jacob,
"	16	[illegible]	221	Owen James,	1 Year,	St Philip & Jacob,
"	21	[illegible]	231	Shellard Rovena,	1 Year,	St Philip & Jacob,
"	24		—	Bullock, Mary,	79	Clifton, Taken out by Friends,
"	24	[illegible]	230.	Collins Alfred,	1 Year,	St Philip & Jacob,
"	25	[illegible]	676	Baker, Wm. Alias Bailey,	40,	Clifton
"	26.	[illegible]	659	Owen, Susan,	37	St Philip & Jacob,
"	28,	[illegible]	720.	Callicott, James,	12.	St Philip & Jacob,
"	28,		—	Thomas, Robert,	57.	St Philip & Jacob, Taken Out by Wife,
"	28,	[illegible]	722	Cornish, James,	47.	St Philip & Jacob,
"	30	[illegible]	219	Robinson, William,	10 Months,	Clifton,
Feby.	1	[illegible]	244	Morrissey, Ann,	1 Year,	Clifton,
"	2	[illegible]	233	Sheen, Mary Ann,	1 Year 10 Months,	Clifton,

Figure 51: Example of Eastville Workhouse death register for January to February 1868.

Year	Month	Day	Surname	Forenames	Gender	Age at death	Parish	Grave No.	Notes
1868	Jan	1	May	Richard	M	2	St Philips & Jacob	223	
1868	Jan	5	Hobbs	George	M	65	Stapleton	717	
1868	Jan	7	Johnson	Henry	M	0.001	St Philips & Jacob	230	
1868	Jan	11	Oxford	Edward	M	81	St Philips & Jacob	677	
1868	Jan	11	Sheedy	Thomas	M	1	St Philips & Jacob	222	
1868	Jan	12	Fisher	James	M	62	Henbury	719	
1868	Jan	13	Oburn?	Arthur	M	11	St Philips & Jacob	721	
1868	Jan	16	Owen	James	M	1	St Philips & Jacob	221	
1868	Jan	21	Shelland	U	U	1	St Philips & Jacob	231	
1868	Jan	24	Collins	Alfred	M	1	St Philips & Jacob	230	
1868	Jan	25	Baker	William	M	40	Clifton	676	Alias Bailey
1868	Jan	26	Owen	Susan	F	37	St Philips & Jacob	659	
1868	Jan	28	Callicott	James	M	12	St Philips & Jacob	720	
1868	Jan	28	Cornish	Sarah	F	47	St Philips & Jacob	722	
1868	Jan	30	Robinson	William	M	0.833	Clifton	219	
1868	Feb	1	Morissey	Ann	F	1	Clifton	244	
1868	Feb	2	Sheen?	Mary Ann	F	1	Clifton	233	

Figure 52: Transcribed death register information for January to February 1868 in Excel spread sheet format.

Sources and Bibliography

Archives

Bristol Central Reference Library

Bristol Medical Officer of Health Annual Reports 1898-1901
Bristol Medical Officer of Health Quarterly Reports 1880-1888
Clifton Poor Law Union Statement of Accounts 1874 Ref. PR2 Pamphlet Box: Societies
IV B2401
Bristol Pictorial Survey Ref. #737
Loxton Collection

Bristol Record Office

Avon County Council: Social Services: photographs of buildings and renovations
Photograph album Ref. 40945/1
Barton Regis Poor Law Union Annual Book 1897 Ref. 10900
Building plans and indices of the City Planning Officer
*Fishponds Road, Eastville - Workhouse, additions for - New Relief Depot and Casual
    Ward extension - J J Simpson for Guardians* Ref. Building plan/Volume 48/43a
Diocese of Bristol: Episcopal Records - Administrative records - Consecration papers
    Clifton Union Cemetery, Eastville Workhouse, Fishponds Road, Stapleton
        *Petition, act, sentence on consecration of land adjoining Comb Brook Lane,
        with plan* Ref. EP/A/22/CU/1a-c
        *Petition, act, sentence on consecration of additional land, with plan, and notice
        (formerly Stapleton parish, now St Mark Easton)* Ref. EP/A/22/CU/2a-b
        Petition and instrument of consecration of additional land, with plan Ref.
        EP/A/22/CU/3a-b
        *Correspondence and memorandum re part of land conveyed to Bishop, April
        1851, also re coalmines proposed under burial ground* Ref. EP/A/22/CU/4a-d
*Documents deposited by Veale, Benson & Co., Solicitors of Baldwin Street, Bristol
    (formerly Benson, Carpenter & Cross)*
        Clifton Poor Law Union - Statement of Accounts 1872-75 Ref. 22936/129
        Barton Regis Poor Law Union – Statements of Accounts 1881-1889 Ref. 22936/130
George Elliott Collection – Photographs – Albums – Photograph Album
        Photograph of Governors of 100 Fishponds Road Workhouse Ref. 42562/Ph/1/24/2
*Maps and plans, 1799-1947, deposited by J.P. Sturge and Sons, 24 Berkeley Square,
    Bristol, BS8 1HU, in Sep 1972.*
        Six manuscript plans of the Barton Regis Workhouse, Eastville Ref. 31965[STG]/99
*Papers from Meade King, solicitors - Deeds and documents relating to The East Bristol
    Collieries Limited*
        *Deeds and documents relating to mines and minerals under land in Fishponds,
        Bristol (Yalland)*
            Copy Release and Covenant Ref. 42228/1/1/1
            Agreement for sale and purchase Ref. 42228/1/1/2

Deeds and documents relating to mines and minerals lying under land in Eastville, Bristol
    Conveyance (copy) Ref. 42228/1/8/1
    Declaration (copy) Ref. 42228/1/8/2
    Declaration (copy) Ref. 42228/1/8/3
Plans of 100 Fishponds Road Ref. 40149/1-11
    Plans for various properties
    Bristol Workhouse, Eastville [100 Fishponds Road] Ref. 45110/1
    100 Fishponds Road Ref. 45110/2
Barton Regis Workhouse, Eastville - Ground floor plan Ref. 45110/3a
    Barton Regis Workhouse, Eastville - 1st and 2nd floor plans Ref. 45110/3b
Social Services Committee: Records of the Home for the Aged, Chronic Sick and Able
    bodied at 100 Fishponds Road (now closed), originally the workhouse of the Clifton
    Union at Eastville
    Registers of deaths
        1847 Sep 27-1868 Sep 22 Ref. 30105/3/1 [Microfiche Ref. FCEW/D/1/1-2]
        1868 Oct 5-1878 Mar 25 Ref. 30105/3/2 [Microfiche Ref. FCEW/D/2/1-2]
        1878 Apr 2-1888 Dec 29 Ref. 30105/3/3 [Microfiche Ref. FCEW/D/3/1-3]
        1889 Jan 4- 1898 Jun 15 Ref. 30105/3/4 [Microfiche Ref. FCEW/D/4/1-2]
Title deeds and other records relating to St Peter's Hospital and other poor law institutions
    in Bristol
    Abstracts of Title (Eastville) Ref. St PHosp/183
    Declaration (Eastville) Ref. St PHosp/184
    Conveyance of lands, Stapleton Ref. St PHosp/185
    Copy Conveyance of ground for Union Burial Ground (Eastville) Ref. St PHosp/190
    Documents and Judgement (Eastville) Ref. St PHosp/194
    Conveyance of Eastville Workhouse Ref. St PHosp/198

British Newspaper Archive (Findmypast Newspaper Archive Limited)

Diocese of Bristol
St Thomas the Apostle, Eastville, Faculty No. 1716, 10 March, 1972

Gloucestershire Archives
County Coroner: Lower Division (1855-1966)
    Inquests Ref. CO1/I
    Notices of Death Ref. CO1/N

The National Archive
Local Government Board and predecessors: Correspondence with Poor Law Unions and
    Other Local Authorities
    Clifton 143 Ref. MH 12/4001-4020 (1838-1877)
    Barton Regis 143 Ref. MH 12/4021-4045 (1877-1906)

Parliamentary Papers, Government Publications and Official Reports

Archer, I., Jordan, S., Ramsey, K., Wardley, P. and Woollard, M.
'Poor Law Statistics, 1835-1948' in Wardley P. (ed.) *Bristol Historical Resource* (Bristol: UWE, 2000)
'Health Statistics, 1838-1995' in Wardley P. (ed.) *Bristol Historical Resource* (Bristol: UWE, 2000)

Anon. *Reports from Commissioners: Poor Laws Vol XIX Eighth Annual Report of the Poor Law Commissioners Session 3rd February -18th August 1842* (London: HMSO, 1842)

Munro Smith, G. *Cholera epidemics in Bristol in the 19th Century British Medical Journal* July 10 1915

'Reports on the Nursing and Administration of Provincial Workhouses and Infirmaries, 1894-5 Barton Regis', *British Medical Journal*

'Return of paupers' (England), Parliamentary Paper, June 16 1884

Rowntree, J. *Poverty: a study of town life* (1901)

Tibbits et al. 'Report on workhouse infirmaries of Bristol, Clifton and Bedminster' *British Medical Journal* October 6 1867

Senior, N. W. and Chadwick, E. *Poor Law Commissioners' Report of 1834* (London: H.M. Stationery Office, 1905)

Symonds, J.A. 'Sanitary Statistics of Clifton' in Taylor, T.D. (ed.) *The British Association for the Advancement of Science*, Bath 1864: Authorised reprint of the reports in the special daily editions of the *Bath Chronicle* (London: Bath Chronicle, 1864)

Wilson, B. and Smallwood S., *Understanding recent trends in marriage* (Family Demography Unit, Office for National Statistics, 2007)

Newspapers and Periodicals

Bristol Mercury
Bristol Evening Post
Bristol Post
Bristol Times & Bath Advocate
Bristol Times & Felix Farley's Bristol Journal
Bristol Times & Mirror
British Medical Journal
The Clarion
The Independent
The Magpie
The Times
Western Daily Press

TV Programmes and Video

Cranitch, M. *Who Do You Think You Are?* BBC TV Series 11 Episode 2 of 10, broadcast 28 August 2014 http://www.bbc.co.uk/programmes/b04dw11r.

Pike, B., Kopacka, Z., Longhurst, R., Kirby, Z., Oshana, M. and Yankovsakya, V. *100 Fishponds Rd* (Bristol: UWE, 2015) http://www.brh.org.uk/site/articles/100-fishponds-road/

Sarkhel, S. *Clydebuilt: The Ships That Made The Commonwealth* BBC4 Documentary Episode 3 of 4: Robert E Lee broadcast 14 April 2014 http://www.bbc.co.uk/programmes/p01n8jf6

Walmsley, J. *Rosemary Green – Eastville Workhouse* BBC Inside Out West broadcast 19 January 2015 http://www.bbc.co.uk/programmes/b04ynq6r

Books, Journals and Pamphlets

Anon. *The Connoisseur: An illustrated magazine for collectors Vol. XXIX (January-April 1911)* Ed. Baily, J. T. H. (Forgotten Books, 2013)

Anon. *Old Ordnance Survey Maps: Bristol* (Ashley Down and Eastville) 1902 Gloucestershire Sheet 72.09 (Durham, Alan Godfrey Maps)

Arnold, N. *Disease, Class and Social Change: Tuberculosis in Folkestone and Sandgate, 1880-1930* (Cambridge: Cambridge Scholars Publishing, 2012)

Atterton, G. *Cotton Threads: The History of the Great Western Cotton Factory* (Bristol: Barton Hill History Group, 2015)

Ayers, G. M. *England's First State Hospitals* (Wellcome Institute of the History of Medicine, 1971)

Backwith, D., Ball R., Richardson M. and Hunt S. E. *Strikers, Hobblers, Conchies & Reds: A Radical History of Bristol, 1880-1939* (London: Breviary Stuff Publications, 2014)

Ball, R. *Tolpuddle And Swing: The Flea And The Elephant* Bristol Radical Pamphleteer #12 (Bristol: BRHG, 2012)

Baxter, G. R. Wythen (George Robert Wythen), *1815-1854. The book of the Bastiles; or, The history of the working of the new poor law* (London: J. Stephens, 1841)

Booth, C. *The life and labour of the people of London* (1889-1903)

Borrer, J. H. *Vagrancy: In Special Relation to the Berkshire System. A paper read at the West Midland Poor Law Conference* (London, Knight & Co, 1882)

Bristol Record Office
    Cemeteries and Burial Grounds (Bristol: BRO, 2009)
    The Poor Law in Bristol (Bristol: BRO, Dec 2013)

Bryher, S. *An Account of the Labour and Socialist Movement in Bristol.* (Bristol: Bristol Labour Weekly, 1929).

Caldicott, R. *Bedminster Union Workhouse and Victorian Social Attitudes on Epilepsy: A Case study of the Life and Death of Hannah Wiltshire* Bristol Radical Pamphleteer #35 (Bristol: BRHG, 2016)

Chesney, K. *The Victorian Underworld: A fascinating recreation* (Harmondsworth: Penguin, 1991)

Davis, M. Late *Victorian Holocausts: El Nino Famines and the Making of the Third World* (London: Verso, 2002)

Dickens, C. *Oliver Twist* (Oxford: Oxford University Press, 1994)

Erichsen, C. and Olusoga, D. *The Kaiser's Holocaust: Germany's Forgotten Genocide and the Colonial Roots of Nazism* (London, Faber & Faber 2011)

Fisher, J. et al *Bristol Then and Now*

Foucault, M. *Discipline and Punish: The Birth of the Prison* (Harmondsworth: Penguin Books, 1991)

Fowler, S. *Workhouse* (London: The National Archives, 2008)

Frost, G. S. *Victorian Childhoods* (London: Praeger, 2009)

Gardiner, J. and Wenborn, N. (Eds.) *The History Today Companion to British History* (London: TSP, 1995)

Hardiman, S. *The 1832 cholera epidemic and its impact on the city of Bristol* (Bristol: Bristol Historical Association, 2005).

Hardy, T. *Tess of the d'Urbervilles: A Pure Woman* (Bath: Folio Society, 1993)

Hawkings, D. T. *Pauper Ancestors: A Guide to the Records Created by the Poor Laws in England and Wales* (Stroud: The History Press, 2011)

Higginbotham, P.
> *The Workhouse Cookbook* (Stroud: The History Press, 2008)
> *The Workhouse Encyclopaedia* (Stroud: The History Press, 2012)
> *Grim Almanac of the Workhouse* (Stroud: The History Press, 2013)

Higgs, M.
> *The Tramp Ward* (1904)
> *Glimpses into the Abyss* (London: P.S. King & Son, 1906)

Holland, M. 'The Captain Swing Project' in Holland, M (Ed.) *Swing Unmasked: the agricultural riots of 1830 to 1832 and their wider implications* (Milton Keynes: FACHRS Publications, 2005)

Hurren, E. and King, S. "Begging for a Burial': Form, Function and Conflict in Nineteenth-century Pauper Burial' *Social History*, Vol. 30, No. 3 (Aug., 2005)

Hurren, E. T.
> *Protesting About Pauperism: Poverty, Politics and Poor Relief in Late Victorian England 1870-1900* (Suffolk: Royal Historical Society, 2015)
> 'Whose Body Is It Anyway? 'Trading the Dead Poor, Coroner's Disputes, and the Business of Anatomy at Oxford University, 1885–1929' *Bulletin of the History of Medicine*, Volume 82, Number 4, (2008)

Johnson, J. *Transactions of the Corporation of the Poor, in the City of Bristol, During a Period of 126 Years* (Bristol: P. Rose, 1826)

Jones, D. *Crime, Protest, Community, and Police in Nineteenth-Century Britain* (London: Routledge & Kegan Paul, 1982)

Kelly J. *The Graves Are Walking: The History of the Great Irish Famine* (London: Faber & Faber, 2013)

Kingsley, C. *The Water-Babies: a Fairy Tale for a Land-Baby* (Project Gutenberg E-book, August, 1997)

Kotouza, D. 'Lies and Mendacity' *Mute* Vol 2, No. 3 (2006)

Laqueur, T. 'Bodies, Death, and Pauper Funerals' in *Representations*, No. 1 (Feb., 1983)

Large, D.
  Bristol and the New Poor Law (Bristol: Historical Association, 1995)
  The Municipal Government of Bristol 1851-1901 (Bristol: Bristol Record Society, 1999)
Latimer, J. *The Annals of Bristol in the Nineteenth Century* (Bristol: W & F Morgan, 1887)
Linebaugh, P. 'The Tyburn riot against the surgeons' in *Albion's fatal tree: crime and society in eighteenth-century England* Ed. Hay, D. (London: Verso, 2011)
Longmate, N. *The Workhouse* (London: Pimlico, 2003)
Malpass, P. and Whitfield, M. *Public health in Victorian Bristol: the work of David Davies, Medical Officer of Health* ALHA Books No.19 (2015)
Martin, M.
  'Guardians of the Poor: A Philanthropic Female Elite in Bristol', *Regional Historian* Summer 2002, Iss. 9
  'Single Women and Philanthropy: A Case Study of Women's Associational Life in Bristol, 1880-1914', *Women's History Review*, 17, 3, 2008
Marx, K. *Capital Volume 1* (London: Penguin, 1990)
McNeil, J. *Ben Tillett* Bristol Radical Pamphleteer #20 (Bristol: BRHG, 2012)
Moore, G. *The Victorian Novel in Context* (London: Continuum, 2012)
Munson-Barkshire, A. *The Production and Reproduction of Scandals in Chronic Sector Hospitals* 1981 MSc. Dissertation in Sociology, Polytechnic of the South Bank 1981
Negrine, A. 'Practitioners and Paupers, Medicine at the Leicester Union Workhouse 1867- 1905' in *Medicine and the Workhouse* Reinarz, J. and Schwarz, L. (Eds.) (University of Rochester Press, 2013)
Noel, T. *The Pauper's Drive* (1842)
Parker, R. *Uprooted: The Shipment of Poor Children to Canada, 1867-1917* (Bristol: Policy Press, 2010)
Piketty, T. *Capital in the Twenty-First Century* (London: Harvard University Press, 2014)
Reed, M. and Wells, R. Class, *Conflict and Protest in the English Countryside 1700-1880* (London: Frank Cass, 1990)
Ribton-Turner, C. J. *A History of Vagrants and Vagrancy and Beggars and Begging* (London: Chapman and Hall, 1887)
Richardson, M.
  Bristol and the Labour Unrest of 1910-14 Bristol Radical Pamphleteer #27 (Bristol: BRHG, 2013)
  The Maltreated and the Malcontents: Working in the Great Western Cotton Works 1838-1914 Bristol Radical Pamphleteer #37 (Bristol: BRHG, 2016)
Rose, L. *'Rogues and Vagabonds': Vagrant Underworld in Britain 1815-1985* (London: Routledge, 2016)
Rose, M. 'The Allowance System under the New Poor' Law *Economic History Review*. New Series, Vol. 19 No. 3 (1966)
Rule, J. and Wells, R. *Crime Protest and Popular Politics in Southern England 1740-1850* (London: Hambledon Press, 1997)
Stack, D. *The first Darwinian Left: Socialism and Darwinism 1859-1914* (Cheltenham, New Clarion Press 2003)
Strange, J.M. Death, *Grief and Poverty in Britain, 1870-1914* [Cambridge Social and Cultural Histories] (Cambridge: Cambridge University Press, 2005)

Thompson, E. P.

The Making of the English Working Class (Harmondsworth: Penguin Books, 1986)
'The Moral Economy of the English Crowd in the 18th Century' *Past and Present* No. 50, 1971.
'Time, work-discipline and industrial capitalism' *Past and Present* No. 38(1), 56–97 (1967)

Tomlinson, R *Amazing Grace: The Man who was W.G.* (London: Little, Brown, 2015)

Vitucci, M.N. 'Emigration and the British Left, 1850-1870' in *Class, Culture and Community: New Perspectives in Nineteenth and Twentieth Century British Labour History* (Eds.) Baldwin, A., Ellis, C., Etheridge, S., Laybourn, K., and Pye, N. (Newcastle: Cambridge Scholars Publishing, 2012)

Wells, R. *Wretched Faces: Famine in Wartime England 1793-1801* (London: Breviary Stuff Publications, 2011)

Websites and Blogs

A vision of Britain through time http://www.visionofbritain.org.uk/
Bristol and Avon Family History Society http://www.bafhs.org.uk/
Bristol Home Children http://emigrated.bafhs.org.uk/
Bristol Radical History Group http://www.brh.org.uk
British Broadcasting Corporation http://www.bbc.co.uk/
British Home Child Group International http://britishhomechild.com/
Children's Homes http://www.childrenshomes.org.uk
Current Archaeology http://www.archaeology.co.uk/
David McFall R.A. (1919 - 1988) Sculptor http://www.davidmcfall.co.uk/
Epsom and Ewell History Explorer http://epsomandewellhistoryexplorer.org.uk
Exodus: Movement of the People http://www.exodus2013.co.uk
Flickr https://www.flickr.com/
GenGuide - UK and Irish Genealogy Sources, Aids and Contacts http://www.genguide.co.uk/
Guerilla Wire http://guerillawire.org/
Historic England https://www.historicengland.org.uk/
Know Your Place http://maps.bristol.gov.uk/knowyourplace/
Libcom https://libcom.org/
Measuring Worth https://www.measuringworth.com/
Mute http://www.metamute.org/
Old West Bromwich Photographs http://www.west-bromwich-photos.co.uk/
Socialist Health Association http://www.sochealth.co.uk/
The King's Norton Website http://www.kingsnorton.info/
The local history of Stoke-on-Trent, England http://www.thepotteries.org/
The Independent https://www.independent.co.uk
The Masked AMHP http://themaskedamhp.blogspot.co.uk
The Trussell Trust http://www.trusselltrust.org
The Workhouse http://www.workhouses.org.uk/
University of Waterloo (Canada) https://uwaterloo.ca/
Wikipedia: The Free Encyclopedia https://en.wikipedia.org

Acknowledgements

This book was a collective effort, not just for the authors who penned it (Roger Ball, Di Parkin and Steve Mills) from Bristol Radical History Group but for all those who took part in the research and activities of Eastville Workhouse Memorial Group.

Di Parkin deserves the most credit for picking up the research in 2012 after it had lain idle for several years. Di made the project a reality and drove it forward through her immense efforts in the Bristol Record Office, transcribing the details of the paupers who were buried in Rosemary Green. Di was assisted by Roger Ball, Steve Mills and Alan Brown from the Bristol Radical History Group. A team of researchers worked hard and fast in January 2015 to check and correct the burial data for publication online, these were Gloria and Mike Davey, Trish Mensah, Mike Richardson, Helen Wheeler and Peter Box. Richard Grove, Mike Baker, Mike Richardson, Moira Martin and Maureen Ball also made important contributions to the research at various stages. Jenny Walmsley and her colleagues from BBC TV's Inside Out West along with workhouse expert Peter Higginbotham, family historian Wendy Bull and members of BRHG produced a successful programme on the burial ground at Rosemary Green which helped give momentum to the project.

The research was greatly assisted (as always) by the efforts of Dawn Dyer and her colleagues at Bristol Central Reference Library who uncovered many useful sources for us. Julian Warren, Allie Dillon, Malcolm Boyns and David Emeney of the Bristol Record Office were very helpful, especially in collaborating with the BBC and providing us with photographic images of the Clifton/Barton Regis Union death registers. The history of Rosemary Green was enriched by the testimony of Jim McNeill, John Clevely, Victor Thame, Les Moore and Mike Baker; and without the help of Julian and his co-workers at Greenbank Cemetery, Vivien Curtis and Caroline at Canford Cemetery Office and Steve at Avonview Cemetery the final resting place of the pauper remains from Rosemary Green would have remained a mystery.

This book relied on a number of contributions which included photographs from Pauline Hendy, Stephen Dowle, Helen Wheeler and John Clevely and a number of maps and charts produced by Peter Box. The proof-readers included Lynda Mansell, Di Parkin, Trish Mensah, Gloria Davey and Jim McNeill. As ever, Richard Grove has done an excellent job in finding sources, designing the text and covers and obtaining permissions for the images.

Eastville Workhouse Memorial Group became a reality in 2014, achieved its aims to memorialise the burial ground at Rosemary Green in autumn 2015 and will be marking the location of Eastville Workhouse and the mass graves at

Avonview Cemetery in 2016. The project has been realized through the efforts of local residents, including Hazel Durn, Trish Mensah, Steve Mills, Gloria Davey, Mike Jempson, Roger Ball, Wendy Bull and Alan Brown. They were ably supported by Claire Tidman, Kate Din, Pauline Hendy, Shanthie Wild, Kieron Farrow, Peter Box, Samuel Kelly, Hugh Workman and Ruth Hecht. Matthew Billington, stone mason and sculptor produced a beautiful standing stone memorial, whilst Mike Baker, the plaque maker, has once again created a striking design for historical marker. These artists were aided by sign makers Ward & Co Ltd of Barton Hill who provided their skills and workshop space. Thanks go to the pupils of May Park Primary School for creating designs for the Rosemary Green memorial. Their efforts were coordinated and encouraged by teachers Paul Bull, Francis Fey and Matt Ford who were very helpful in engaging the school with the project. Students from UWE, Ben Pike, Zuzanna Kopacka, Ross Longhurst, Zee Kirby, Mark Oshana and Vikka Yankovsakya made an excellent and popular film about the project.

The John James Bristol Foundation, Greater Fishponds Neighbourhood Partnership and Living Easton helped fund the Rosemary Green memorial and garden, along with donations from the National Union of Journalists, Bristol Radical History Group and the relatives of the late Hannah Purbrick. The GMB Union, Rydon Construction, East Trees Health Centre and Bristol Radical History Group also made significant contributions to the cost of the history plaque at 100 Fishponds Rd.

Simon Peck and the 58th Bristol Scout Group deserve a special mention for allowing EWMG to use their facilities for their monthly meetings for free over 2014-15. Thanks also go to Bristol City Council officers Georgie Bryant, Abdulrazak Dahir, Richard Fletcher, Richard Stransom, Adrian Murdoch and Teija Ahjokoski for their help with funding applications, memorial and garden. The BCC Landscapes team, Mark, Paul and Terry also did an excellent job in installing the standing stone at short notice.

Tina Goede, Vicar of St Anne's Church and the congregation have been very supportive and a number of people from the diocese of Gloucester and Bristol have aided the project including Bishop Rachel Treweek, Diane Best, Bishop Mike Hill, Jules Barnes, Vanesther Rees and Ben Evans.

The authors would also like to thank their families and friends for having to put up with it all at one time or another.

This book is dedicated to all those who lived and died in Eastville Workhouse.

We never forget.

Bristol Radical History Group 2016

Name Index

Note: Indexed footnotes are shown in parentheses

General Index

Note: Indexed footnotes are shown in parentheses